Asian Regionalism

Asian Regionalism

Peter J. Katzenstein
Natasha Hamilton-Hart
Kozo Kato
Ming Yue

East Asia Program
Cornell University
Ithaca, New York 14853

The Cornell East Asia Series is published by the Cornell University East Asia Program and has no formal affiliation with Cornell University Press. We are a small, non-profit press, publishing reasonably-priced books on a variety of scholarly topics relating to East Asia as a service to the academic community and the general public. We accept standing orders which provide for automatic billing and shipping of each title in the series upon publication.

If after review by internal and external readers a manuscript is accepted for publication, it is published on the basis of camera-ready copy provided by the volume author. Each author is thus responsible for any necessary copy-editing and for manuscript formatting.

Submission inquiries should be addressed to Editorial Board, East Asia Program, Cornell University, Ithaca, New York 14853-7601.

Number 107 in the Cornell East Asia Series.
© 2000 by Peter J. Katzenstein. All rights reserved
ISSN 1050-2955
ISBN 1-885445-07-5 pb
Printed in the United States of America
14 13 12 11 10 09 08 07 06 05 04 03 02   9 8 7 6 5 4 3 2 1

COVER DESIGN BY KAREN K. SMITH

⊗The paper in this book meets the requirements for permanence of ISO 9706:1994.

Contents

Tables

Preface

This monograph assembles a set of papers that derive from dissertation and research projects completed at Cornell's Government Department in the late 1990s.

Asian regionalism is a subject of intrinsic interest for both Asian specialists and students of world politics. We hope that these essays add to our scant knowledge of a topic of far-reaching importance.

We would like to acknowledge the financial support of Reizo Utagawa of the Nippon Foundation who generously supported the research of Kozo Kato and Yue Ming and of the Abe Fellowship Program which has supported the work of Peter J. Katzenstein.

We would like to thank Cornell's East Asia Program for its willingness to include this monograph in Cornell's East Asia Series; two anonymous reviewers of the Cornell East Asia Series for their perceptive and timely criticisms, comments and suggestions; Sandra Kisner for her help in preparing the manuscript for publication with her customary efficiency; and Karen Smith for steering the manuscript through the production process.

Peter J. Katzenstein, Ming Yue   Ithaca
Natasha Hamilton-Hart   Canberra
Kozo Kato   Tokyo

Contributors

PETER J. KATZENSTEIN is the Walter S. Carpenter, Jr. Professor of International Studies at Cornell University. His current research focuses on regionalism in world politics.

NATASHA HAMILTON-HART is a postdoctoral fellow in the Department of International Relations, Research School of Pacific and Asian Studies, at the Australian National University. She completed a Ph.D. at Cornell University in 1999. Her current research looks at state systems in Southeast Asia, financial policy and capital mobility.

KOZO KATO is associate professor of political science at Sophia University, Tokyo. He received his Ph.D. from Cornell University in 1996. He is the author of *Development Cooperation Policy of "Trading States": Japanese and German International Positions and Domestic Structures* (1998 in Japanese). His current research focuses on the internationalization of the Japanese yen in the context of Asian regionalism.

MING YUE is a Ph.D candidate at Cornell University, and will complete his Ph.D. in the year 2000. He is currently doing research on overseas Chinese business networks and East Asia regionalism.

1
Varieties of Asian Regionalism

Peter J. Katzenstein

After the Cold War and in an era of globalization, regional order, not strategic bipolarity, is the central organizing principle in world politics. This is true of the Americas, where regional arrangements such as NAFTA and MERCOSUR are growing. It is true of Europe, where the EU is only the most prominent of an abundance of regional institutions. And it is true of Asia. In both security and economic affairs, global competition between two nuclear superpowers has been replaced by conflict and cooperation within distinctive regional orders.[1]

Asian regionalism is coming of age, and weak institutionalization makes it distinctive [Katzenstein 1997a]. 'Subregions' like Southeast Asia are expanding their membership while 'superregional' constructs, such as Asia-Pacific, are gaining wider currency. The intensity of the politics of naming these constructs, in terms of civilizational values, ethnicity, race, or geography illustrates how important regionalism has become in Asia. This introduction surveys some aspects of Asian regionalism that are treated in greater detail in the chapters written by Kozo Kato, Yue Ming and Natasha Hamilton-Hart dealing, respectively, with Japan and Asia (chapter 2), China and Asia (chapter 3), and financial regionalism in Asia (chapter 4).

Asian Regionalism in International Politics[2]
China and Japan are important centers of the new Asian regionalism, but in ways quite different from the regionalism of Japan's Co-Prosperity Sphere of the 1930s and 1940s or George Orwell's nightmarish projection of a tripolar world [Orwell 1949]. While the old regionalism emphasized autarchy and direct rule, the new one relies on interdependence and indirect rule.

Japan's growing role in the nine member states of The Association of Southeast Asian Nations (ASEAN) (Indonesia, Thailand, Malaysia, Philippines, Singapore, Brunei, Vietnam, Burma and Laos) can be traced easily in the areas of trade, aid, investment and technology transfer. In the two decades preceding the realignment of the major international currencies in the Plaza Accord of 1985, Japan accounted for close to half of the total aid and direct foreign investment in the region. The dramatic appreciation of the Yen after 1985 led to a veritable explosion in Japanese investment. Between 1985 and 1989 the total was twice as large as that between 1951 and 1984. The flow of aid also continued to increase as Japan recycled its trade surplus with the region. All governments in Southeast Asia became accustomed to bidding for Japanese investment capital, illustrated by the massive deregulation of their economies and the lucrative incentives that they were willing to grant to foreign investors. More importantly, Japan's "developmental state" became an object of emulation. The establishment of private trading companies and a general commitment by Southeast Asian governments to policies of vigorous export promotion give testimony to the wide-spread appeal of the Japanese model.

By the early 1990s the growth in Japanese influence in Asia had created widespread unease about the political consequences of intensifying economic relations with Japan. Japan's power was simply too large to be matched in the foreseeable future by any conceivable coalition of Asian states. With the total GNP of ASEAN amounting to no more than 15 percent of Japan's, any development of a world of self-contained regions in the Northern half of the globe would leave ASEAN's members at the mercy of a Japanese colossus. Most Asian states thus saw in China and the United States useful counter-weights to Japan's growing power.

Within a few years after Japan's financial bubble had burst, its anemic macro-economic performance and a deep crisis in its financial sector had transformed Asia's political landscape. Fear of too much Japanese power in organizing Asia's regional order was transformed into fear of too little Japanese power in dealing with its own economic and financial disorder. If Japan did not travel the road of macroeconomic growth and financial stability, how could the rest of Asia? The Asian financial crisis, which so dramatically affected Thailand, Indonesia and South Korea, suggested to many observers that financial stability and economic health could return to Asia only after Japan had made painful adjustments in some of its long-standing policies.

The rapid decline in fear of Japan was also a response to the rise of China in the 1990s. Deng's "southern trip" in 1992, a change in the statistical estimates of Chinese GDP by international financial institutions such as the IMF and the World Bank, sharp increases in the flow of direct foreign investment, extraordinarily high rates of economic growth, and the government's determined efforts to join GATT and the WTO all focused attention on China, rather than Japan, as a conceivable rival of the United States a decade or two into the next millennium.

China's reputation as a possible regional hegemon rests on its combination of control of access to the largest untapped market in the world, possession of nuclear weapons, and a permanent seat on the UN Security Council. This is not to deny the problems that China faces in its relations with Taiwan, Tibet, Japan, and the United States. Chinese foreign policy must reconcile a strong unilateralist stance on issues the government perceives to be of great national importance and a weaker multilateralist stance for ongoing diplomatic relations in, for example, the Asian Regional Forum (ARF). At the same time China is going through a wrenching process of adjustment in some of its major institutions, including inefficient state-owned enterprises, an oversized central bureaucracy, and financial institutions crippled by a mountain of bad debt. The uncertainties inherent in a dual-track foreign policy intersect with the uncertainties of large-scale domestic reform. They combine to make China's neighbors nervous about the regional role that the PRC will play in Asia.

The United States, finally, has been an Asian power with strong interests in and ties to the region throughout the 20th century. There is no evidence that the U.S. government will alter its traditional stance because of the end of the Cold War. With 100,000 ground troops stationed in East Asia, with the American navy firmly committed to a strong position in Asia, and with the consolidation of U.S.-Japanese security arrangements in the 1980s and 1990s, the United States is likely to remain a first-rate military power in Asia [Katzenstein and Okawara 1999]. Furthermore, since virtually all Asian countries run a substantial trade deficit with Japan and a large trade surplus with the United States, the United States is the economic anchor for national strategies of export-led growth and the integration of the regional economy of Asia-Pacific.

In the eyes of many Asian governments an Asia that includes the United States has several advantages. American involvement can diffuse economic and political dependencies on Japan and China with which the smaller Asian states would otherwise have to cope. It provides Japan with the degree of national security that reduces the pressure for a major arms-build up. And it offers China political opportunities for establishing itself as a recognized great power in Asia.

At the threshold of a new millennium, however, the domestic and foreign policies of Japan, China and the United States are also exposed to a number of significant uncertainties. "For the first time in two centuries Asian countries are in a position to shape their regional system and influence the character of the world system" writes Kenneth Pyle [1997, 6]. Currently,

Asian regionalism takes two different forms. If measured in terms of purchasing-power-parity GDP, the Japanese and the Chinese economies are of roughly equal size [Weidenbaum and Hughes 1996, 95-105, 116-17]. But each extends into Asia in different ways. Japanese capitalism is the result of indigenous economic developments and a conscious political strategy orchestrated jointly by government and business elites. Chinese capitalism lacks both an integrated, indigenous political economy and a coherent political strategy. "Unlike the Japanese" writes John Kao [1993, 24], "the Chinese commonwealth has, in computer terms, an 'open architecture.' It represents access to local resources like information, business connections, raw materials, low labor costs and different business practices . . . In contrast to the Japanese *keiretsu*, the emerging Chinese commonwealth is an interconnected yet potentially open system."

Asian regionalism is an idea whose time has come. Increasing regional cooperation is often invoked as a necessary response to regionalization elsewhere such as the European Union (EU) or NAFTA. Yet Asian regionalism has yet to be described adequately in terms of formal institutions. In the political norms that inform it and in the political capacity for collective action the Asian Regional Forum (ARF), for example, differs dramatically from its more interventionist European equivalents, the Organisation for Security and Cooperation in Europe (OSCE) and the North Atlantic Treaty Organization (NATO). And the shallow economic integration that is the aim of APEC is set it apart from the deep political integration that characterizes the European Union (EU). Lacking a functional base of binding commitments, ARF and APEC are primarily fora for the discussion of important policy issues and, thus, institutions useful for increasing trust. They are designed to strengthen regional economic cooperation only in the long-term.[3]

Japanese Regionalism

Japanese capitalism was the product of indigenous developments after the Meiji restoration that copied, adapted and improved Western technologies and principles of organization. Existing scholarship tells a familiar and compelling story of Japan's developmental state. The narrative focuses on the variable relations among important party politicians, business leaders and senior bureaucrats. In the latter part of the 19th century Japanese capitalism was propelled by the activities of interlocking government and business elites. Japanese businessmen realized quickly, however, that they could not easily displace the Chinese as Asia's dominant merchants. Hence Japan embarked on an ambitious policy of indigenous industrialization. Rapid industrialization under state auspices created in a very short time a hierarchy of economic organizations engaged in mass-production that were soon organized in conglomerate networks that often included a trading house to help penetrate foreign markets.

In contemporary Japan, there exist two kinds of conglomerates, inter-market groups and independent groups. As has been true in the past, they are social, not legal entities.[4] The six major inter-market firm groups consist of horizontal alliances among large firms that are leaders in different economic sectors such as steel, automobile, finance or trade. The presidents of these firms meet regularly to discuss the affairs of the whole group. The major member firms lead vertically organized networks of affiliates and subsidiaries, called *keiretsu*, that in turn are linked to a large number of often exclusive and long-term primary, secondary and tertiary subcontracting arrangements with medium-sized and small firms. Although such affiliated subcontractors are not formally part of the *keiretsu*, they tend to identify with it. These conglomerates compete with each other for shares in the national economy.

So-called independent groups are networks of vertically integrated firms in specific industrial sectors. They are structurally similar to the *keiretsu*, with very large parent companies linked to an intricate system of subordinate firms ranked by tiers. Subcontractors are often located in close proximity to the parent firm, as in the automobile industry, thus forming a geographic as well as an economic and social community. Despite their name, independent groups have links to other firms through mutual shareholding by financial institutions. Intra-group shareholding is extraordinarily high, ranging typically between 20 and 30 percent, and normally assures parent firms of a controlling interest in vertically affiliated firms. These financial ties are reinforced by other mechanisms, including interlocking directorates, the sharing of trademarks, programs to rotate managers and swap workers, bank loans, the activities of general trading companies, joint enterprises, joint membership in business associations, and joint participation in public relation campaigns. "Vertical control parallels a vertical integration of production . . . The main reason for constructing a solid vertical structure of subsidiary firms . . . is aimed at guaranteeing a mutually beneficial, self-sufficient industrial structure to leading firms and to affiliates . . . Self-containment of production and the group's ability to isolate itself from shifting market conditions" characterize the strategy of Japanese firm groups [Orrú, Hamilton and Suzuki 1997, 205, 207].

Japan's economic insularity is perhaps a function of the relatively small number of Japanese living in Asia. More than one million Overseas Chinese lived in Southeast Asia in the first half of the 19th century. Furthermore, the entire Chinese population in Southeast Asia doubled between 1900 and the early 1930s [Shiraishi and Shiraishi 1993, 7. Hui, 1995, 41, 143]. There were about 8-10 million ethnic Chinese in Southeast Asia in 1945, about 5-6 percent of the total population [Hui 1995, 143-44]. Corresponding figures for ethnic Japanese were much smaller. Throughout the 20th century Japan's population in the region has followed the network organization of state and business.[5] The spontaneous movement of marginal groups in Japanese society—prostitutes, pimps, and subsequently, shop owners, clerks, and plantations workers, among others—in the early decades of the twentieth century increased from only 2,800 in 1907 to 36,600 in 1936, and these populations were subsequently "recaptured" by the Japanese state. Local consulates, local bosses, local Japanese associations and, eventually, the spread of Japan's uniform education system beyond national borders, all served the purpose of the "re-Nipponization" of Japanese colonial communities throughout Southeast Asia. At the same time overseas Japanese relied on Chinese business networks to remain competitive especially in retail trade [Hui 1995, 175-76]. In 1945, the Japanese population in Southeast Asia dropped to the vanishing point. Thus, Japan's post-war relations with Asia were built on historical connections. As Robert Wade [1994, 68] notes, "the fact that Northeast Asian firms moving production offshore went to Southeast Asia rather than to Latin America or South Asia may be due to . . . regionally specific factors [including] overseas Chinese networks, similarities in business practices, and the advantages of geographical proximity."

Japan's economic influence began to spread once more in the late 1950s. Throughout the 1960s the Japanese government proposed a number of different schemes for the regional integration of Asia [Katzenstein 1997a, 16-18]. From the outset these attempts included the United States, Canada, Australia and New Zealand, presaging the broad conception of Asia-Pacific that was at the center of the diplomatic initiatives of the 1980s and 1990s. These efforts at integration were more successful than Japan's diplomatic initiatives to create regional organizations in the 1960s, which were stymied by the deep suspicions Asian states harbored of Japan and any attempts to build Asia under Japanese leadership.

In reaction to the failures of the 1960s, Japan moved subsequently, writes Edward Lincoln [1992, 13], toward an "informal and soft form of economic regionalization with other Asian countries." The Japanese government supported looser, non-governmental institutions that either diffused Japanese influence through broad memberships or operated without Japanese participation. The Pacific Basin Economic Council (PEBC) was the first such grouping. A nongovernmental organization, it was open initially (1968) to businessmen from the five Pacific Rim countries and subsequently included businessmen from many Asian states. In the 1990s more than 400 enterprises are members and attend annual meetings [Katzenstein 1997a, 17]. Other regional organizations followed. In contrast to the failed policy initiatives of the 1960s, all of these groups have been economic and nongovernmental and have emphasized personal networking and the exchange of information rather than political negotiations and binding decisions.[6]

The sharp appreciation of the Yen in 1985 began a surge of Japanese direct foreign investment and aid that set the stage for a dramatic regional extension of the *keiretsu* and related vertical networks of subcontractors and affiliated firms that characterize Japanese inter-market and independent groups. These groups moved quickly to recreate their accustomed supplier chains abroad, first in textiles and electronics, later in automobiles.[7] Such regional links have also developed in Asia's agricultural economy.[8] These chains link myriads of hierarchically organized subcontractors and producers of components in complex, multi-tiered arrangements. While such chains can be producer- or buyer-driven,[9] Japanese foreign investment creates production chains and methods of technology transfer that have a deep impact on the trajectory of economic sectors, individual countries and the entire Asian region.[10]

The massive inflow of Japanese investments created bottlenecks in the public sector infrastructures of countries like Indonesia and Thailand. And these bottlenecks were serious impediments for the future growth of Japanese investment. Roads and ports had to be expanded and modernized. The same was true of national systems of communications and public services more generally. The New AID Plan (New Asian Industries Development Plan) of 1987 signaled that Japan had serious, long-term interests in the region. The plan addressed the needs of the public sector as they related to Japanese industrial investments, and the regional restructuring of the Japanese economy more generally. Broadly speaking the program offered investment incentives for selected Japanese industries to relocate to ASEAN countries. From the vantage point of Japan, the evolving international division of labor in Asia was bound to be hierarchical.[11]

To some extent this was also Japan's view of its relations with the Newly Industrialized Countries (NICs) in Northeast Asia: South Korea, Taiwan, Hong Kong, and Singapore.[12] Their take-off into self-sustaining rapid growth occurred earlier than in Southeast Asia. In several of these countries Japanese trade, aid, investment and technology transfer were crucial to the rapid success that these countries have enjoyed in international markets. Japan even proved to be an important model for economic development strategies.

Japan's growing economic and political enmeshment in East and Southeast Asia thus has helped create an integrated Asian regional economy. It has also reinforced a triangular trade structure in which Japanese exports to and investments in Southeast Asia led to a rapid expansion of southeast Asian exports to Western markets, primarily the United States. Backed by a surge in foreign investment, trade, and the largest aid disbursements in the region, the Japanese government also sought to influence business and government abroad by exporting with minor modifications, more or less successfully, its prized system of administrative guidance. In the fall of 1990 MITI set up organizations in various Asian countries to facilitate periodic meetings between local businessmen, Japanese investors, government officials and MITI bureaucrats. These offices, it was hoped, would offer "local guidance" [Lincoln 1993, 125, 127-28, 145-46, 178, 192. Katzenstein 1997a, 37]. And Japanese aid programs exported to surrounding Asian countries the practice of bid rigging (*dango*) common in Japan's domestic public works. In the words of David Arase [1995, 161] Japan's request-based approach to foreign aid allows "for graft and corruption while giving the Japanese government deniability."

Walter Hatch and Kozo Yamamura [1996, 97-129] see a Japanese system of political and economic power that is especially adept at maximizing dynamic technological efficiencies and thus fortifying its economic and political leadership over an Asia that is developing in Japan's embrace. In their view, increasing technological disparities translate into economic and political domination. Asian regionalism is little else but an international extension of Japan's approach to economic development institutionalized since the mid-1980s in far-flung regional production networks and supported by a broad array of trade, aid, investment and cultural policies. This regional extension is remarkably coherent across different domains of policy, but not because it is guided by a secret master plan. Rather Japan's regionalization extends the useful life of domestic arrangements and practices that are simply taken for granted as Japanese elites seek to adapt to changing international conditions.[13]

Chinese Regionalism

For a thousand years, in Hill Gates' [1996] felicitous phrase, petty capitalism has been one of China's motors. This motor has both driven and undermined a state-managed tributary mode of economic production and exchange. The vast scale of Chinese commerce has been as notable as its persistence. Exploiting economic niches, petty capitalists have acted "with clever dishonesty. Their practices have been subversive, contorted, dangerous—and liberating" [Gates 1996, 43]. "If there is any 'cultural characteristic' that could generally describe the Chinese business diaspora," writes Po-Keung Hui [1995, 25; see also 287-88] "it is its 'unlimited flexibility' (to paraphrase Braudel), or pragmatism."

As the Chinese state crumbled in the 19th and 20th centuries, Chinese capitalism once again spread throughout Southeast Asia creating networks that overcame political divisions and state boundaries.[14] These networks covered finance, trade, and production. "With the decline, collapse, and disintegration of the Chinese political order," writes Gary Hamilton [1996, 336], "the real forces of Chinese capitalism moved to where money could be made—to safe havens on the coast such as Shanghai, Canton, and other treaty ports, as well as overseas to Southeast Asia, Hawaii, and the American West Coast."

Overseas Chinese are people of ethnic Chinese descent living outside Mainland China [Hui 1995, 18]. Before the 20th century, Overseas Chinese lacked a homogeneous identity: hometowns, dialects, blood relationships and guild associations were far stronger than the sense of being Chinese. Eventually a diaspora identity began to spread as a result of the revolutionary upheavals on the Mainland in the early 20th century. However, as a social category "Overseas Chinese" neglects or minimizes unduly the wide diversity of the Chinese experience in different parts of Southeast Asia.[15]

The Overseas Chinese economy is very large and ranks fourth in the world in terms of "economic size" [Kao 1993, 24]. In 1990, according to an estimate of the Economist, the GDP for the Overseas Chinese, apparently excluding those living outside of Southeast Asia, was $450 billion, 125 percent of the PRC's GDP at the time. Furthermore the liquid assets held by the Overseas Chinese ran between $1.5 and 2.0 trillion, excluding securities, about two-thirds of Japan's (which includes about twice as many people as the Overseas China) and larger than the PRC's [*Economist*, 1992, 21 quoted in Hui 1995, 16-17 and Brick 1992, 5. Katzenstein 1997a, 12-14]. Much of the Overseas Chinese assets are "new money" made after the Pacific War and especially since the early 1970s [Hui 1995, 183-87, 224]. While the capital of the Overseas Chinese is of vital importance in Southeast Asia, the Peoples Republic of China is much more interested in using their contacts and technology than in gaining access to their savings.

At home and abroad the carriers of Chinese capitalism are heads of households. In Taiwan, for example, whether they are large or small, organized in groups or independent, family firms, not large, vertically- or horizontally-integrated conglomerates, are the rule [Hamilton and Kao 1990, 142]. In these firms, in the words of one keen observer, "there is very little delegation of responsibility, even to the sons . . . if the old man says go right, you go right" [Ridding and Kynge 1997, 13] The business organization of the Overseas Chinese, in the view of entrepreneur Gordon Wu, is like a tray of sand. The grains are families, not individuals, held together by blood, trust and obligation, not law, government or national solidarity [Brick 1992, 5]. In a similar vein, family-centered enterprise groups, Gary Hamilton and Cheng-shu Kao insist, are not simply a matter of blood and marriage ties but rely on social norms that govern specific relationships marked by submission, trust, loyalty and predictability. Interpreted by the participants in both personal and instrumental terms, these social norms permeate the economic institutions of

Chinese society, embed economic activity, and produce distinctive forms of allocative efficiency [Hamilton and Kao 1990, 147-48].

John Kao's [1993] survey of more than 150 Chinese entrepreneurs confirmed that their way of thinking assumes that only family members can really be trusted. Keeping strict control within the family typically constrains size and growth, especially of high-tech firms. Because of the strength of kinship, wealthy businessmen often invest in extensive networks of small firms covering numerous economic sectors or sector segments. Hence economies of scale are achieved not from the acquisition of individual firms but from networks that connect small firms [Hamilton 1996, 334-35]. Statistically speaking, in terms of employment Taiwanese business groups, not firms, are five to six times smaller than Japanese business groups. They also hold a less central position in the national economy [Hamilton and Kao 1990, 140, 142]. In sharp contrast, Chinese tycoons dominate most of the economic life of Southeast Asia and of Hongkong. Chinese capitalism, Hamilton [1996, 335] argues, "is a nonpolitically based form of capitalism that is very flexible and readily adaptable to external economic opportunities."

The informality of China's business firms and the importance of personal trust facilitates regionalization processes.[16] "Throughout Southeast Asia, where many markets are underdeveloped and law is often unpredictable, informal networks have become the preferred vehicle for many complex transactions" [Weidenbaum and Hughes 1996, 52]. Local, regional and occupational groups and relational kinship systems, not the state, promoted the standardization and predictability that are necessary for the growth of economic transactions. For example, formal Overseas Chinese mutual aid associations are based on clan, province or dialect (including Cantonese, Hakka, Hokkien, or Chiu Chow). "These associations act like banks through which members can borrow money, trade information, recruit workers, and receive business introductions." Murray Weidenbaum and Samuel Hughes write that "they help enforce the 'handshake' deals on which much of Chinese business is based" [Weidenbaum and Hughes 1996, 51]. "Chinese firms, financial networks, and distribution systems are not merely economic enterprises. They are social systems as well," concurs Milton Esman [1986, 149].

These social systems have adapted to the vast changes that Asia has experienced since 1945, in particular the rise of developmental states and foreign multinationals. Chinese networks became important intermediaries connecting bureaucrats, the military and politicians on the one hand and foreign firms on the other, both in the phase of import-substitution during the 1950s and 1960s and in the phase of export-led industrialization since then. While the core of the business remained family-controlled, surrounding layers of equity holding and political control were taken over by members of the indigenous elite. In labor-intensive industries, such as textiles or cement, more than in capital-intensive sectors such as electronics or automobiles, Chinese firms became an important partner of and interlocutor between foreign business and national elites especially in Southeast Asia, where Chinese tycoons dominate economic life. "Family and networks were particularly crucial for Chinese business success in Asia" [Brown 1995b, 4].

In the past, state officials often were less supportive of than parasitic on business networks. But today "East Asia," writes Hill Gates, "is becoming Number One not because its social formations are becoming more capitalist but because of the dynamic of a tributary mode that has captured a petty-capitalist one is geared up yet further by the capture of capitalism" [Gates 1996, 276]. In a similar vein Gary Hamilton [1996, 331. See also Oxfeld 1993] argues that "the formation of Chinese capitalism cannot be understood apart from the dynamics of the global economy because . . . Chinese capitalism is *not* a domestic capitalism (i.e., the product of indigenous economic growth), but rather is integral to world capitalism itself." Po-Keung Hui [1995, 13-14, 219] argues that "it is difficult, if not impossible, to talk about one country's economic performance without paying attention to its economic connections with the rest of the region. Today as in the past, countries in the East Asian region cannot be treated as separated economic entities, but as part of a regional nexus . . . East Asia must be treated as a region which has been closely connected to the world economy . . . The rise of a Chinese 'capitalist layer' in East Asia in the postwar period is largely a result of a combination of the continuity of the historically strong overseas Chinese business networks and an upswing in the world economy."

This historical legacy left the government of the Peoples Republic of China with a difficult issue. The 1953 census listed the Overseas Chinese as part of China's population, and the 1954 Constitution of the PRC provided for representation of all of the Overseas Chinese in the National People's Congress. But soon thereafter the PRC government abandoned the doctrine of *ius sanguinis* and left the choice of national citizenship to the individual Overseas Chinese. A bitter conflict with Indonesia over the overtly discriminatory regulations with which it had targeted ethnic Chinese in the late 1950s eventually made the government of the PRC adopt a pragmatic policy, broken only during the early years of the Cultural Revolution, that sacrificed the interests of Overseas Chinese whenever important foreign policy interests of the PRC were at stake. The growing affluence of the Overseas Chinese and the policies of cultural indiginization and economic discrimination that Southeast Asian governments typically adopt have made the overwhelming majority of resident ethnic Chinese accept citizenship in their new homelands, claim equal rights, and hope for non-discriminatory policies.

Within the first two or three decades after the Communist take-over, more than 80 percent of the Overseas Chinese had adopted the nationality of their Southeast Asian host countries [Hui 1995, 191].[17] The connotations of the term "Chinese" became more cultural than political as "Overseas Chinese" now denotes ethnic Chinese of Southeast Asian birth and nationality [Hui 1995, 172, 191, 194]. Virtually all Overseas Chinese are firmly settled if not fully assimilated into the Southeast Asian polities; more than 95 percent of the Overseas Chinese were born in Southeast Asia [Hicks and Mackie 1994, 48].

With relations between the PRC and the Overseas Chinese clarified, since the 1980s the Chinese government has been very interested in strengthening economic relations with the Overseas Chinese through active encouragement of foreign investments, remittances and tourism. Government policy is now fully supportive of what Barry Naughton [1997] calls the China Circle that connects Hong Kong, Taiwan and the Overseas Chinese throughout Southeast Asia with the Chinese mainland.

The control which the Overseas Chinese enjoy over economic resources in each of the major Southeast Asian countries and throughout the whole region is impressively large. Ethnic Chinese control up to 80 percent of the corporate sector in Malaysia, Indonesia and Thailand and about 40 percent in the Philippines [Hui 1995, 254-58]. Since the mid-1980s about four-fifths of contracted and two-thirds of realized foreign investment in the PRC are estimated to come from regional business networks that link Hong Kong, Taiwan and Southeast Asia with the PRC.[18] In their substantive importance these networks greatly exceed formal institutions such as APEC.[19]

The special economic zones that the PRC has established to attract foreign investors are one important site in which these networks flourish. They are marked by a poor physical and legal infrastructure and a heavy political and bureaucratic presence. "To operate in such a realm," write Suzanne Berger and Richard Lester [1997, 132], "requires not only deep cultural and linguistic competence, but a network of relationships that substitute for the guarantees that rule of law, a secure system of property rights, and a neutral administration provide elsewhere but that are lacking here. The success of the Overseas Chinese networks in extending production systems into China derives precisely from their ability to provide alternative forms of social and material capital for building stable relationships in this legal no man's land."[20]

The nature of the economic institutions that the Overseas Chinese control resembles those of petty-capitalism on the mainland. The current retreat of the Chinese state from direct management of the economy elevates the importance of business networks as economic growth rates have soared and regionalization in China and across Asia accelerates.[21] Common culture, language, family ties and ancestral roots lower transaction costs and predispose ethnic Chinese to do business with one another across political borders.

A web of entrepreneurial relationships has reintegrated "Greater China" since the late 1980s.[22] Ethnic and familial ties help establish regional business networks that are "informal though pervasive, with local variations but essentially stateless, stitched together by capital flows, joint ventures, marriages, political expediency and common culture and business ethic" [Sender 1991, 29]. Through mutual shareholding and other mechanisms, Overseas Chinese firms have cooperated and thus strengthened each other. As in the past, these firms have been linked to small and medium-sized firms in retail and wholesale that have acted as intermediary agencies. At the same time the political connections of Chinese businesses in Southeast Asia have declined [Hui 1995, 198]. John Ridding and James Kynge [1997] go as far as to argue that after Asia's 1997 financial crisis closer tie-ups between Overseas Chinese and mainland Chinese will constitute the next phase in the spread of Asian business networks.

Sharp increases in trade and investment are not simply due to the reappearance of "natural" economic territories.[23] Rather they are a reaction to policies enacted by governments pursuing other objectives. Throughout the Third World export processing zones have become favored instruments of economic development. In 1970 there were 20 such zones in 10 countries; by 1986 those numbers had increased, respectively, to 175 and more than 50 [Yuan and Eden 1992, 1026]. The government of the PRC created special economic zones adjacent to Hong Kong and across the Straits from Taiwan not only as engines of economic growth and development, but also as instruments that might facilitate China's eventual political reunification [Harding 1993, 666-672. Shirk 1994. Weidenbaum and Hughes 1996, 85-89]. From those beginnings the boundaries of the transnational Chinese economy have expanded steadily to encompass virtually the entire Chinese coastline and Southeast Asia.

The informal character of the Overseas Chinese economic networks are widely viewed as their most defining characteristic. For a variety of reasons Chinese scholars and officials, for example, "advocate a more informal process of 'consultation' or 'co-ordination', in which governments will attempt to facilitate commercial relations rather than trying to negotiate formal trading blocs or common markets . . . increasingly, therefore, discussions of the transnational Chinese economy are featuring the significantly different concept of a network of overlapping and interlocking economic territories, some large and some small, rather than a single unified economic bloc" [Harding 1993, 669, 671].

In this multi-nodal constellation of Greater China, many of the economic circles or zones are not solely Chinese and spread beyond Southeast Asia,

Japan, and Russia to India and the United States. What John Kao [199, 24] calls the new Chinese "Commonwealth" thus is characterized by economic bargains rather than by formal state institutions or economic arrangements. Lacking a formal charter, headquarter, organization and summit meetings, that Commonwealth has nonetheless important political and economic effects.

The growing importance of "natural economic territories" (NET) is one of the defining characteristic of Asian regionalism. Driven by private investment, facilitated by common cultural practices, and supported by government policies that are removing barriers to preexisting complementarities, NETs are a patchwork of smaller subregional groupings involving the territories of several countries.[24] "NETs allow states to proceed along their own paths of economic growth and development without the need to agree on overarching regional goals" [Jordan and Khanna 1995, 435]. In Southeast Asia and South China the links between Singapore and Malaysia's Johor and Indonesia's Riau provinces and the special economic zones (SEZs) that China established initially in Guangdong and Fujian provinces and subsequently elsewhere all progressed through unilateral policies with which governments, sometimes fostering and sometimes responding to grass roots economic relations, have sought to advance their economic and political interests. In the words of Michael Borrus we are witnessing "the apparent emergence of coherent sub-regional trade and investment patterns that lie 'below' the aggregate regional picture but 'above' the interaction between states—a kind of parallel in the productive sphere to the region's noted 'investment corridors'" [Borrus 1994, 5].

In Northeast Asia similar subregional developments are occurring, for example, in the Yellow Sea Rim which connects Kyushu with Korea's west coast and China's northern coastline. But progress is hindered by unresolved security issues. Economic relations remain primarily bilateral in nature and government cooperation is modest.[25] The ambitious Tumen River project has been all but abandoned.[26]

Compared to Northeast Asia and Greater China, Southeast Asian subregional cooperation has received much more government assistance. The growth triangle connecting Indonesia, Malaysia and Singapore, for example, is the region's oldest and brings together the complementary resources of the Riau Islands, the neighboring peninsula of Johor, and Singapore. In the words of Shannon Smith [1997, 382] it is slightly misleading to call the triangle a market-driven process since "governments often intervene to shape comparative, and competitive, advantage and market forces . . . [it] is essentially no more than a pragmatic context for bilateral cooperation." Indonesia and Malaysia also form a growth triangle with Thailand building on existing cross-border trade links that governments are interested in strengthening.

This is true also of the "Golden Quadrangle" that connects northern Thailand, China's Yunnan province, northern Burma and Laos [Jordan and Khanna 1995, 450-60].

Asian subregionalism affords states an instrument for economic development that is not constraining. Market-driven and state-assisted, these proliferating subregional arrangements are informal and marked by little institutionalization. "This subregionalism," writes James Mittelman [1998, 29] "is more spontaneous, springing from within and below." Subregions are an essential ingredient for the spread of production chains across Asian borders. They are a vital complement to family and ethnic networks criss-crossing the Asian region.

In its Chinese variant Asian regionalism can be thought of in a variety of different territorial domains. In one view it consists of three different zones: a northern zone consisting of Japan, Korea, and Northeast China; a southern zone covering Indonesia, Malaysia and Singapore; and a central zone around China's southern coast including Hong Kong, Shanghai and Taiwan [Weidenfeld and Hughes 1996, 47]. An alternative conception views Asian regionalism as a set of concentric circles radiating out from Hong Kong: Greater Hong Kong (Hong Kong, Macao and Guangdong); Greater South China (Greater Hong Kong plus Taiwan and the southeastern coast of the PRC up to Shanghai); Greater *Nanyang* (Greater South China plus Singapore and Overseas Chinese in the rest of Southeast Asia); and All China (Greater *Nanyang*, the PRC, and Overseas Chinese worldwide) [Harding 1993, 666-67]. Finally, Chinese regionalism might eventually take the form of "a more Sinocentric continental arrangement" thus deviating from the "Mediterranean" pattern [Rohlen 1995, 29] that has been the primary focus of this introduction. Whatever the specific image we choose, the existence of the Chinese networks and their importance for the informal organization of Asia's regional political economy is beyond doubt.

Japanese and Chinese Regionalism Compared

Both the Japanese and Chinese variants of Asian regionalism are essentially defined in market terms [Katzenstein 1997a, 14], but the historical sources and characters of those markets differ greatly. Japanese capitalism flowered between 1870 and 1930 in an era of state-building, Chinese capitalism, developing at the same time, bears the marks of state-collapse [Hamilton 1996, 332-33, 336]. The population of overseas Japanese has been dwarfed by the Chinese diaspora since the mid-19th century, and Chinese business networks are more extensive and have deeper historical roots than their Japanese counterparts. Japanese officials have built up Japanese networks in full awareness of the severe limitations that Japanese firms face in confronting Chinese merchants in Asia.[27] Different historical origins thus have shaped the characters of China's and Japan's economic extensions into Asia. In the words of Joel Kotkin, "in contrast to the exceedingly close ties between the Japanese *salarimen* abroad and their home islands, the Chinese global network posses no fixed national point of origin, no central 'brain'" [Kotkin 1993, 167].

This general pattern is evident in specific industrial sectors, such as electronics.[28] Japanese networks of firms rely substantially on known Japanese suppliers with comparable technical capacities. Overseas Chinese firms work through networks that draw on the increasingly high technical specialization of small and medium-sized firms scattered throughout Asia. Japanese networks are closed, Japan-centered, and long-term. Chinese networks are open, flexible and disposable [Borrus 1994, 3].

The contrast between Japanese and Chinese business networks is evident in the case of Thailand. Using careful field research, Mitchell Sedgwick [1994, 8], for one, concluded that "Japanese multinationals in Thailand have reproduced an atomization of labor and strong centralization of decision-making authority—the 'Fordism'—that they managed to avoid in post-war Japan . . . Beyond internal plant dynamics, however, the strict centralization is also reflected in the position of subsidiaries vis-à-vis headquarters. Subsidiaries in Thailand are part of a tightly controlled and rigorously hierarchical organizational structure extending down from Japan." Thailand's Chinese-dominated business community has taken different forms over time, but in the last three decades the younger Chinese entrepreneurs have responded to the internationalization of the Thai economy by running their businesses along traditional Chinese lines and maintaining close contacts with the Chinese business communities in Hong Kong, Singapore, Taiwan and China. Rapid corporate growth resulted from the horizontal and open networks of the Overseas Chinese, rather than vertical and closed ones, which are typical of Japan [Hamilton and Walters 1995, 94, 99-100].

Thus, Asian regionalism is built on organizational characteristics that differ greatly along dimensions that set vertical Japanese firm networks apart from horizontal Chinese ones [Hamilton, Orrú and Biggart 1987, 100. Hamilton and Feenstra 1997, 67-73]. In vertical organizations groups are controlled through ownership shareholding, while horizontal networks favor family ownership and partnership. Within a group, vertical networks control through cross-shareholding and mutual domination; horizontal ones through multiple positions held by core personnel. Vertical systems organize between group networks with cross-shareholding; horizontal ones favor loans and joint ventures by individuals and firms. In the former, subcontract relations are structured or semiformal; in the latter, they are informal and highly flexible. And growth patterns are differentiated by bank-financing in vertical systems and informal financing and reinvestment in horizontal ones [Orrù, Biggart and Hamilton 1997, 183].

The Japanese and Chinese regionalisms are, in some ways, complementary. Chinese and Japanese businesses are often locked in competition with one another, but the new crop of Chinese tycoons in Southeast Asia has colluded with Japanese business in, for example, the Siam Motor Group in Thailand, the Astra Company and Rodamas Group in Indonesia, the Yuchenco Group in the Philippines, and the Kuok Brothers in Malaysia [Hui 1995, 189]. In fact, Japanese firms find it very difficult to work without Chinese middle men. For instance in 1974 of 138 joint ventures between Japanese and Indonesian firms, 70 percent of the Indonesian partners were local Chinese [Hui 1995, 189. Brick 1992, 3-4].

In the view of Walter Hatch and Kozo Yamamura the benefits of cultural affinities and old familial and business ties in overcoming problems of trust and reliability offer only fleeting advantage to a mode of organizing that is inherently inferior to Japanese production alliances. In their view Chinese entrepreneurs adhere to a "strategy of turning quick profits, rather than investing for the long run" [Hatch and Yamamura 1996, 96]. Chinese networks cultivate rent-seeking, Japanese ones dynamic technological efficiency. The architecture of the Japan-centered Asian regionalism is hierarchical. Japan controls the flow of aid and technologies and provides producers in other countries with capital and intermediate inputs. South Korea and Taiwan, though closing the development gap quickly, specialize in somewhat less sophisticated goods and remain dependent on Japanese imports of key technologies and intermediate products. Thus, they have taken their place between Japan and the NIE's in Southeast Asia, which currently provide raw materials and markets and are upgrading industrial platforms for assembly and increasingly indigenous production [Hui 1995, 207].

Thus while Asian regionalism is defined in market terms, Asian markets are not consist of a series of unconnected and atomized individual transactions. They give expression instead to institutionalize relationships that deeply implicate both business and government. Following the growth of Japanese direct foreign investment, especially after 1985, multinational corporations control an unprecedented share of foreign trade in Asia. Japan intracompany trade accounts for about 80 percent of total Japanese exports and half of Japanese imports [Encarnation 1994, 2], and foreign investment has spurred the growth of vertical *keiretsu* structures from Japan throughout Asia as Japanese producers have extended their domestic subcontracting arrangements on a regional scale.

Both types of business network avoid formal institutionalization,[29] and Asian regionalism is defined primarily by those institutions operating in markets. Japanese *keiretsu* structures and Chinese family firms bring about economic integration without explicit institutional links. In the 1990s, this Asian regionalism is open to developments in the global economy, its economic form is network-like, and its political shape is multicephalic while its political definition remains contested.

Financial Globalization and an Asia in Crisis

Like the opening of the Berlin Wall, the end of the Cold War and the peaceful disintegration of the Soviet Union, Asia's financial crisis came unannounced and was largely unanticipated by pundits and politicians, specialists in finance, and scholars of Asia.[30] A conference sponsored by the Bank of Indonesia and the IMF concluded in November 1996 that "ASEAN's economic success remains alive and well . . . the region is poised to extend its success into the twenty-first century" [IMF 1996, 378]. In a April 25, 1997 press conference, IMF Managing Director Camdessus remarked that the global economic outlook warranted "rational exuberance"; and at the spring 1997 meeting, the Interim Committee of the IMF approved a plan to amend the Articles of Agreement to extend the IMF's jurisdiction to cover the movement of capital, thus completing the "unwritten Chapter" of Bretton Woods, according to Camdessus [IMF 1997, 129].

IMF policies proved to be inadequate even before the financial crisis hit Asia. Bulgaria's financial meltdown was a dress-rehearsal for what was happening in Asia only a few months later in the latter half of 1997. After years of half-hearted policy reforms by different governments and the IMF, international speculation against the lev forced Bulgaria to surrender its economic sovereignty and accept a currency board as the only plausible avenue in a disastrous situation.[31] Yet as late as the spring of 1997 IMF officials were celebrating the advantages of policies of liberalization without realizing the potentially disastrous effects of that policy for Bulgaria and other economies lacking the institutional preconditions for financial and economic liberalization.

Just as the end of the Cold War gave a healthy shock to students of national security and spurred a debate that touched on all of the premises of analysis, so debate has begun among students of political economy in the wake of the Asian financial crisis. Before the summer of 1997, even critics of the Asian developmental state model agreed that cozy relations between business and government were important in lowering transaction costs and, thus, helping bring about national growth rates in Asia that were four times higher than the OECD average. But by the end of 1997 economic and business analysts had convinced each other with surprising ease that Asian markets had lacked sophistication and that banks had lent and business had invested in violation of established prudential principles. Far from lowering transaction costs, lack of transparency and systemic corruption were now judged to be the main impediments to a resumption of economic growth in Asia. This drastic and implausible shift in assessing economic policy led to a very public split between the IMF and the World Bank as well among specialists in international economics.

The consensus policy, embraced more widely by economists inside than outside of the IMF, held to traditional policy prescriptions in the face of new conditions. Economic contagion became the 1990s' analogue to the 1960s' geo-strategic domino theory. International financial markets can easily lose confidence in the value of national currencies, especially in emerging markets that are exposed to the volatile flows of very liquid capital. When such capital flows out, the ensuing credit crunch can undermine even the trade credits of large corporations and set in motion a downward spiral that chokes off most business activities.

The economic crises in Thailand, Indonesia and South Korea were of a very different character. In each, volatile global financial markets intersected with distinctly local political crises. Thailand's was a macro-economic and a financial crisis. The deficit in its current account stood at 7 percent of GDP in 1997. Despite repeated off-the-record warnings by the IMF and highly public discussions in business journals, the Thai government did not change course. Extremely rapid credit growth, even in the non-tradable sector, and high levels of credit denominated in foreign currencies triggered the run on the baht. And after the onset of the crisis the economy was immobilized by a political crisis that lasted for four months until a new cabinet finally took over.

In Indonesia the enormous wealth of the Suharto clan had created widespread suspicion and opposition. In contrast to Thailand, a looming succession crisis in the government seemed to threaten the stability of the regime. Chinese businessmen began to lose confidence in the regime and the rupiah as early as 1996, and, according to well-informed sources in Japan's Ministry of Finance, withdrew about $100 billion from Indonesia between 1995 and 1997.

American and IMF officials viewed the situation largely in economic categories and insisted on American-style economic reforms. Growing volatility in global capital markets had brought to the surface far-spread corruption and a lack of regulatory oversight that, in the interest of investor confidence, needed to be redressed through fundamental institutional reforms and a drastic dose of deflation. Eager to protect the ill-gotten and far-flung assets of his six children and acutely aware of the dangers for the legitimacy of his regime and Indonesia's stability that the crisis had brought about, General Suharto dragged his feet in implementing the reforms the IMF insisted on. A leading scholar of Indonesia, Clifford Geertz, worried at the time that Western financial institutions were so fundamentally misreading Javanese culture that they turned a desperate situation into a dangerous one. IMF economists were not aware of cultural expectations that define the goodness of the father by the extent of protection that he provides for his spoiled children and that makes insisting on public acknowledgement of mistakes an act of supreme rudeness in a society that prides itself on its civility. Had the IMF behaved differently, Geertz argues, it "might have gotten what it wanted from the start. But I guess you don't expect that from economists" [Shenon 1998, A17]. The IMF's approach helped push General Suharto to tap into a deep strain of Javanese nationalism. The result were deadly anti-Chinese pogroms and the downfall of the regime.

In 1997 Korea was also undergoing far-reaching institutional and policy changes in a volatile geo-strategic situation on the Korean peninsula. The crisis exploded into the open in the last weeks before the presidential election of December 1997.[32] Rival candidates disavowed the IMF package, which had been put together in record time in November 1997. This undermined further the confidence of international financial markets in Seoul's political capacity for reform.

In the face of sharp increases in dollar-denominated debt burdens, illiquidity and bankruptcy, all three governments guaranteed the assets of creditors and defended national currencies until they had used up virtually all of their reserves. This forced the IMF to put together three bail-out packages, for a total of $120 billion. This stretched the financial and political limits of the Fund without contributing to stabilization of economic conditions in other emerging markets stretching from Russia to Brazil. In addition, the bail-outs undermined the Fund's eroding political support in the U.S. Congress.

The IMF's reform packages differed somewhat in each of the three countries, but at bottom, the IMF sought to affect far-reaching economic and political change in the interest of international liberalization. This required a substantial reorganization of financial markets and ways of doing business as much as the acceptance of foreign partners and the introduction of new accounting rules. Whether and how this imposition of American institutional practices will work remains to be seen. In its first comprehensive assessment of the crisis the World Bank was harshly critical of the high-interest policies that both the IMF and the US government imposed once international investors began to withdraw their liquid assets from national economies that had been all too eager to absorb easily available and inexpensive international credits. With estimated levels of bankruptcy in Indonesia as high as 75 percent, the Bank's chief economist, Joseph Stiglitz, argued that "you cannot have a country perform with 75 percent of its firms in bankruptcy" [Sanger 1998, A20]. Compared to Indonesia the chances of success are much greater in South Korea, where President Kim dae Jung is seeking to exploit IMF pressure to further his own agenda of reforming state and society.

Variable national conditions in Thailand, Indonesia and South Korea are not the only factors shaping Asia's financial future. Much will depend on the future course of the financial reform policies adopted by China, Japan and international financial institutions. China's financial system is in a very precarious situation due to a volume of bad debts estimated in excess of 25 percent of GDP. Financial consolidation is an extremely difficult task at a time in which major institutional changes are transforming radically many sectors of Chinese economy and society.

After years of delay, the Japanese government has moved in 1998-99 to a massive rescue effort of its financial sector. The lack of transparency and "crony capitalism," often cited as the main root of the crisis, extends beyond Japan. International banks, such as Credit Suisse, have made substantial profits in the 1990s in assisting Japanese banks in window-dressing their balance sheets and thus concealing from regulatory agencies the true depth of their problems [Tett 1999].

Inside the US Treasury, the IMF, and the World Bank discussions continue on whether and how to modify the Washington consensus and reform the international financial system. These discussions include issues such as imposing some restraints on capital flows, modifying the lending practices of the Fund and the Bank, reevaluating the role of regional monetary funds, and reconsidering the suitability of exchange rate regimes, currency boards, and policies of "dollarization" for small open economies.[33]

The full implications of the financial crisis for Asian regionalism are complicated and far from clear. Japanese efforts to offer in August 1997 a regional approach to crisis management were half-hearted, given the weakness of the Japanese economy and prematurely brushed aside as IMF and US Treasury officials later acknowledged [Kristof 1998, A6]. Because of its enormous costs, especially for the lower-middle class and the poor, resentments linger. In Malaysia, for example, the government has managed to stay in power with its legitimacy impaired by the deep split between Prime Minister Mahathir Mohamad and his deputy and heir-apparent Anwar Ibrahim and the latter's trial and conviction on what to many Malaysians look like trumped-up charges. The Malaysian policy of restricting the inflow of short-term capital, an anathema to the Washington consensus, appears to have worked remarkably well. In the wake of the financial crisis there are strong political suspicions in Southeast Asia and South Korea that the Washington consensus is little more than an ideological smoke-screen for the determined efforts of US business to go on a shopping spree for Asian financial and industrial assets, at bargain basement prices.

The openness of Asian regionalism has two different, closely inter-twined sources that are clearly illustrated by Japan: dyadic and systemic vulnerability. First, Japan is embedded in a relationship of dyadic dependence on the United States that creates extraordinary military and economic vulnerabilities. Japan depends on the US navy to patrol the sealanes through which its imported raw materials and exports flow. Even after diversifying away from the United States for the last two decades, 30 percent of Japanese exports are still destined for US markets. Military, economic and political dependence thus constrains any Japanese inclination to build an inward-looking Asia. More generally, dyadic and systemic vulnerability affect most other Asian states as much, or more, than Japan.

Secondly, the combination of Japan's relations of vulnerability and interdependence imposes, as Kozo Kato argues in chapter 2, severe constraints on an inward-looking Asian bloc. Along numerous dimensions of trade, aid, investment and technology transfer, among others, Japan has a more broadly diversified set of economic and political links to both rich and poor countries, than does, for example, Germany which lives internationally inside a European cocoon [Lincoln 1993, 135. Wan 1995, 98]. The Asian financial crisis illustrates Japan's strong commitment to contribute to the continued functioning of the international system on which its economic prosperity depends so heavily. By September 1998 Japan's level of contribution to the solution of the Asian financial crisis amounted to about one-third of the total of $127 billion, compared to $12 billion for the United States and $7 billion for European states, even though the exposure of European banks was comparable to those of Japanese banks [Kristol 1998, A6]. About half of the Japanese credit was committed to bilateral credit lines to be disbursed under IMF bail-out plans.

The Asian financial crisis illustrates that Asian regionalism was not strong enough to prevent the establishment of beachheads in markets that used to be closed to foreign investors. An IMF-centered, global approach to the regional financial crisis rather than reliance on an Asian-centered, Japanese-led effort revealed the weakness of an exclusive and cohesive East Asian regionalism without US involvement. In the immediate aftermath of the crisis the links between Asian regionalism and global financial markets have grown stronger.

On this score the contrast with the European Monetary Union (EMU) is striking. The EMU is driven by political considerations and is on schedule for full operation by the year 2002, when it will contribute to the creation of a regional actor and a regional political economy that is likely to raise the profile of the EU without displacing the role of the dollar as lead currency. In contrast, the Asian financial crisis illuminates, and is likely to advance, a process of regional economic opening rather than political or policy closure.

An open Asian regionalism will encompass politically and economically the United States. In contrast to the 1930s, the political and economic coalitions prevailing in the United States have no interest in abdicating their influence in various regions. Yet, despite its preponderant international position the United States lacks the resources to be the cornerstone in all of the world's major regions. Instead, the United States acts as a pivot in a number of important regions.

In Asia, this pivot rests on a combination of U.S. military power, economic presence, and social appeal that reflects diverse interests and ideologies in the United States and is relevant to important political elites, economic sectors and social strata in Asia. With the end of the Cold War and the withdrawal of most U. S. ground forces from Europe, a 100,000 ground troops in East Asia are the main reason why the United States has not returned to its traditional role as a naval power. Compared to Europe and Asia the position of the U.S. territorial economy has probably declined somewhat during the last 30 years. But the competitive position of U.S. corporations in international markets has increased substantially, especially in the last decade. American multinational corporations perform strongly and are often at the cutting edge in the development of new technologies and products. Their full presence in global markets gives American policy makers a strong incentive to maintain a liberal international economy. Finally, with English as the only universal language, American mass culture has a natural advantage over all of its competitors in disseminating its products on a global scale.

A pivot, however, is not the same as a cornerstone for Asia's regional order. The 21st century will be nobody's century: not America's, not Asia's, and not Europe's. In an economically more open Asia, American-Asian relations are likely to illustrate instead the politics of open regionalism in a more plural world.

NOTES

1. Lake and Morgan 1997. Fawcett and Hurrell 1995. Mansfield and Milner 1997. Frankel 1997.

2. Material in this section draws in part on Katzenstein 1993 and Katzenstein and Shiraishi 1997. For other writings on Asian regionalism see also Aggarwal 1993. Aggarwal and Morrison 1997. Bergsten 1997. Brown, Lynn-Jones and Miller 1996. Chen and Kwan 1997. Chu 1995. Deng 1997a, 1997b. Doherty 1994. Frankel and Kahler 1993. Funabashi 1995. Gallant and Stubbs 1997. Gipouloux 1994. Hatch and Yamamura 1996. Hellmann and Pyle 1997. Higgott 1994. Higgott, Cooper and Bonnor 1990. Taylor 1996. Higgott, Leaver and Ravenhill

1993. Higgott and Stubbs 1995. Ikenberry 1998. Iriye 1992. Iwasaki 1995. Kahler 1997. Katzenstein and Shiraishi 1997. Korhonen 1994, 102-107. Lim 1995. Mack and Ravenhill 1995. Peng 1995. Ravenhill 1995. Rohlen 1995. Root 1996. Ross 1995. So and Chiu 1995. Stubbs 1994, 1998. Whitley 1996. Yamazawa 1992. Zhao 1998. Zhao 1997.

3. Acharya 1997.

4. Orrú, Hamilton and Suzuki 1997. Gerlach 1992.

5. Katzenstein 1997a, 35-37.

6. Yamamoto and Kikuchi 1998. Watanabe and Kikuchi 1997. Rix 1993.

7. Doner 1993, 1997. Dobson and Yue 1997.

8. McMichael and Kim 1994.

9. Cheng and Gereffi 1994. Gereffi 1996. Gereffi and Korzeniewicz 1994. Gereffi and Wyman 1990.

10. Tokunaga 1992. Chen 1994. Korkonen 1994. Bernard and Ravenhill 1995.

11. Katzenstein 1997b. Katzenstein and Rouse 1993.

12. Cumings 1987.

13. Hatch, forthcoming.

14. Hodder 1996. Seagrave 1997. Gungwu 1991. Brown 1995a.

15. Suriyadinata 1989. Brown 1995a.

16. Lim 1994.

17. *Far Eastern Economic Review* 1978. Esman 1986.

18. Katzenstein 1997a, 38. Berger and Lester 1997, 5. Esman 1986, 150-53. McVey 1992. Mackie 1992a, 1992b. Hui 1995, 259-68. Lampton et al. 1992.

19. Zhang 1998, 1997. Moore and Yang 1998. Chen and Kwan 1997. Brown 1995a. Peng 1995, 1998.

20. See also Luo and Howe 1993; Hsing 1996.

21. Goodman and Segal 1994. Kleinman, n.d. Womack and Zhao 1994.

22. Harding 1993. East Asia Analytical Unit 1995. Katzenstein 1997a, 37-39.

23. Weidenbaum and Hughes 1996, 101-05. Lardy 1994. Naughton 1997. Jones, King, and Klein 1993.

24. Thant, Tang, and Kakazu 1994. Mittelman 1998. Katzenstein 1997a, 14.

25. Jordan and Khanna 1995, 444-50. Burns 1995.

26. Burns 1994. Kouriatchev 1993.

27. Hamashita 1988, 1997. Curtin 1984, 90-178. Skinner 1979.

28. Katzenstein 1997a, 39-40; 1998.

29. Katzenstein 1997a, 40-41. Deng 1997a.

30. Acharya 1999. Biers 1998. Goldstein 1998. Institute of Social Science 1998. Johnson 1998. Laurence 1999. McLeod and Garnaut 1998. Moon 1998. Pempel 1999. Wade 1998, 1999.

31. Minassian 1999.

32. Moon 1998.

33. Eichengreen 1999. Rajan 1999.

REFERENCES

Acharya, Amitav. 1997. "Ideas, Identity, and Institution-Building: From the 'ASEAN Way' to the 'Asia-Pacific Way'?" *Pacific Review* 10, 3: 319-46.
———. 1999. "Realism, Institutionalism, and the Asian Economic Crisis," *Contemporary Southeast Asia*, 21, 1 (April): 1-29.
Aggarwal, Vinod. K. 1993. "Building International Institutions in Asia-Pacific," *Asian Survey* 32, 11 (November): 1029-1042.
Aggarwal, Vinod K. and Charles E. Morrison. 1998, eds. *Asia-Pacific Crossroads: Regime Creation and the Future of APEC*. New York: St. Martin's Press.
Arase, David. 1995. *Buying Power: The Political Economy of Japan's Foreign Aid*. Boulder, Co.: Lynne Rienner.
Berger, Suzanne and Richard K. Lester, eds. 1997. *Made by Hong Kong*. Hong Kong: Oxford University Press.
Bergsten, C. Fred, ed. 1997. *Wither APEC? The Progress to Date and Agenda for the Future*. Washington: Institute for International Economics.
Bernard, Mitchell and John Ravenhill. 1995. "Beyond Product Cycles and Flying Geese: Regionalization, Hierarchy, and the Industrialization of East Asia," *World Politics* 47 (January): 171-209.
Biers, Dan, ed. 1998. *Crash of '97*. Hong Kong: Review Publishing Co.
Borrus, Michael. 1994. "MNC Production Networks and East Asian Integration: A Research Note," Berkeley Roundtable on the International Economy, University of California, Berkeley.
Brick, Andrew B. 1992. "The Emergence of Greater China: The Diaspora Ascendant," *Heritage Lectures* No. 411. Washington, DC: Heritage Foundation.
Brown, Michael E., Sean M. Lynn-Jones, and Steven E. Miller, eds. 1996. *East Asian Security: An International Security Reader*. Cambridge: MIT Press.
Brown, Rajeswary Ampalavanar, ed. 1995a. *Chinese Business Enterprise in Asia*. London: Routledge.
———. 1995b. "Introduction: Chinese Business in an Institutional and Historical Perspective," in Rajeswary Ampalavanar Brown, ed., *Chinese Business Enterprise in Asia*, pp. 1-26. London: Routledge.
Burns, Katherine G. 1995. "Subnational Autonomy and Regional Integration: The Case of Northeast Asia." Unpublished paper, MIT.
———. 1994. "Subnational Power and Regional Integration: The Case of Tumen River Development," MIT Japan Program, Center for International Studies, MIT, MITJP 94-10.
Chen, Edward K.Y. "Intraregional Investment and Technology Transfer in the Asian-Pacific Region: An Overview," in Asian Production Organization, ed., *Intra-Regional Investment and Technology Transfer in Asia: A Symposium Report*, pp. 11-40. Tokyo: Asian Production Organization.

Chen, Edward K.Y. and C.H. Kwan, eds. 1997. *Asia's Borderless Economy: The Emergence of Subregional Economic Zones.* St. Leonards NSW: Allen and Unwin.

Cheng, Lu-Lin and Gary Gereffi. 1994. "The Informal Economy in East Asian Development," *International Journal of Urban and Regional Research* 18, 2 (June): 194-219.

Chu, Yun-han. 1975. "The East Asian NICs: A State-Led Path to the Developed World," in Barbara Stallings, ed., *Global Change, Regional Response: The New International Context of Development*, pp. 199-237. New York: Cambridge University Press.

Cumings, Bruce. 1987. "The Origins and Development of the Northeast Asian Political Economy: Industrial Sectors, Product Cycles, and Political Consequences," in Frederic C. Deyo, ed., *The Political Economy of the New Asian Industrialism*, pp.44-83. Ithaca: Cornell University Press.

Curtin, Philip D. 1984. *Cross-Cultural Trade in World History.* New York: Cambridge University Press.

Deng, Yong. 1997a. *Promoting Asia-Pacific Cooperation.* New York: St. Martin's.

————. 1997b. "Chinese Relations with Japan: Implications for Asia-Pacific Regionalism," *Pacific Affairs* 70, 3 (Fall): 373-91.

Dobson, Wendy and Chia Siow Yue, eds. 1997. *Multinationals and East Asian Integration.* Ottawa and Singapore: International Development Research Centre and Institute of Southeast Asian Studies.

Doherty, Eileen M., ed. 1994. *Japanese Investment in Asia: International Production Strategies in a Rapidly Changing World.* Berkeley: The Asia Foundation's Center for Asian Pacific Affairs and the Berkeley Roundtable on the International Economy (BRIE).

Doner, Richard F. 1993. "Japanese Foreign Investment and the Creation of a Pacific Asian Region," in Jeffrey A. Frankel and Miles Kahler, eds., *Regionalism and Rivalry: Japan and the United States in Pacific Asia*, pp. 159-216. Chicago: University of Chicago Press.

————. 1997. "Japan in East Asia: Institutions and Regional Leadership," in Peter J. Katzenstein and Takashi Shiraishi, eds., *Network Power: Japan and Asia*, pp. 197-233. Ithaca: Cornell University Press.

East Asia Analytical Unit. 1995. *Overseas Chinese Business Networks in Asia.* Department of Foreign Affairs and Trade, Commonwealth of Australia.

The Economist. 1992. "A Driving Force," (July 18): 21.

Eichengreen, Barry. 1999. *Toward a New International Financial Architecture: A Practical Post-Asia Agenda.* Washington, DC: Institute for International Economics.

Encarnation, Dennis J. 1994. "The Regional Evolution of Japanese Multinationals in East Asia: A Comparative Study," MIT Japan Program and Pacific Basin Research Program, Kennedy School of Government, Harvard University (November 1).

Esman, Milton. 1986. "The Chinese Diaspora in Southeast Asia," in Gabriel Sheffer, ed., *Modern Diasporas in International Politics*, pp. 130-63. New York: St. Martin's.

Far Eastern Economic Review, "The Overseas Chinese," (June 16): 17-24.

Fawcett, Louise and Andrew Hurrell, eds. 1995. *Regionalism in World Politics: Regional Organization and International Order*. Oxford: Oxford University Press.

Frankel, Jeffrey A. 1997. *Regional Trade Blocs in the World Economic System*. Washington, DC: Institute for International Economics.

Frankel, Jeffrey A. and Miles Kahler, eds. 1993. *Regionalism and Rivalry: Japan and the United States in Pacific Asia*. Chicago: University of Chicago Press.

Funabashi, Yoichi. 1995. *Asia Pacific Fusion: Japan's Role in APEC*. Washington, DC: Institute for International Economics.

Gallant, Nicole and Richard Stubbs. 1997. "APEC's Dilemmas: Institution-Building around the Pacific Rim," *Pacific Affairs* 70, 2 (Summer): 203-18.

Gates, Hill. 1996. *China's Motor: A Thousand Years of Petty Capitalism*. Ithaca: Cornell University Press.

Gereffi, Gary. 1996. "Commodity Chains and Regional Divisions of Labor in East Asia," *Journal of Asian Business* 12, 1: 75-113.

Gereffi, Gary and Miguel Korzeniewicz, eds. 1994. *Commodity Chains and Global Capitalism*. Westport, CT: Greenwood Press.

Gereffi, Gary and Donald L. Wyman. 1990. *Manufacturing Miracles: Paths of Industrialization in Latin America and East Asia*. Princeton: Princeton University Press.

Gerlach, Michael L. 1992. *Alliance Capitalism: The Social Organization of Japanese Business*. Berkeley: University of California Press.

Gipouloux, François, ed. 1994. *Regional Economic Strategies in East Asia: A Comparative Perspective*. Tokyo: Maison Franco-Japonaise.

Goldstein, Morris. 1998. *The Asian Financial Crisis: Causes, Cures, and Systemic Implications*. Washington, DC: Institute for International Economics.

Goodman, David S.G. and Segal, Gerald. 1994. *China Deconstructs: Politics, Trade and Regionalism*. London: Routledge.

Hamashita, Takeshi. 1988."The Tribute Trade System and Modern Asia," *Memoirs of the Research Department at the Toyo Bunko*, No. 46: 1-25.

———. 1997. "The Intra-Regional System in East Asia in Modern Times," in Peter J. Katzenstein and Takashi Shiraishi, eds., *Network Power: Japan and Asia*, pp. 113-35. Ithaca: Cornell University Press.

Hamilton, Gary G. 1996. "Overseas Chinese Capitalism," in Tu Wei-ming, ed., *Confucian Traditions in East Asian Modernity: Moral Education and Economic Culture in Japan and the Four Mini-Dragons*, pp. 328-42. Cambridge: Harvard University Press.

Hamilton Gary G. and Robert C. Feenstra. 1997. "Varieties of Hierarchies and Markets: An Introduction," in Marco Orrú, Nicole Woolsey Biggart and

Gary G. Hamilton, *The Economic Organization of East Asian Capitalism*, pp. 55-94. Thousand Oaks, CA: Sage.

Hamilton Gary G. and Cheng-Su Kao. 1990. "The Institutional Foundations of Chinese Business," *Comparative Social Research* 12: 135-51.

Hamilton, Gary G., Marco Orrú, and Nicole Woolsey Biggart. 1987. "Enterprise Groups in East Asia: An Organizational Analysis," *Shoken Keizai* 161 (September): 78-106.

Hamilton Gary G. and Tony Walters. 1995. "Chinese Capitalism in Thailand: Embedded Networks and Industrial Structure," in Edward K.Y. Chen and Peter Drysdale, eds., *Corporate Links and foreign Direct Investment in Asia and the Pacific*, pp. 87-111. New York: Harper Educational in association with The Pacific Trade and Development Conference Secretariat, the Australian National University, Canberra and the Centre of Asian Studies, University of Hong Kong, Hong Kong.

Harding, Harry. 1993. "The Concept of 'Greater China': Themes, Variations and Reservations," *China Quarterly* 136 (December): 660-86.

Hatch, Walter. Forthcoming. "Rearguard Regionalization: Preserving Core Coalitions in the Japanese Political Economy," Ph.D. dissertation, Political Science, University of Washington, Seattle.

Hatch, Walter and Kozo Yamamura. 1996. *Asia in Japan's Embrace*. Cambridge: Cambridge University Press.

Hellmann, Donald C. and Kenneth B. Pyle, eds. 1997. *From APEC to Xanadu: Creating a Viable Community in the Post-Cold War Pacific*. Armonk, NY: M.E. Sharpe.

Hicks, George and J.A.C. Mackie. 1994. "Overseas Chinese: A Question of Identity," *Far Eastern Economic Review* (July 14): 46-48.

Higgott, Richard, ed. 1994. *Ideas, Policy Networks and International Policy Coordination in the Asia-Pacific*, special issue of *Pacific Review* 7, 4.

Higgott, Richard, Andrew Fenton Cooper, and Jenelle Bonnor. 1990. "Asia-Pacific Economic Cooperation: An Evolving Case-Study in Leadership and Co-operation Building," *International Journal* XLV, 4 (Autumn): 823-66.

Higgott, Richard, Richard Leaver, and John Ravenhill, eds., 1993. *Pacific Economic Relations in the 1990s: Cooperation or Conflict?* Boulder: Lynne Rienner.

Higgott, Richard and Richard Stubbs. 1995. "Competing Conceptions of Economic Regionalism: APEC versus EAEC in the Asia Pacific," *Review of International Political Economy* 2, 3 (Summer): 516-35.

Hodder, Rupert. 1996. *Merchant Princes of the East: Cultural Delusions, Economic Success and the Overseas Chinese in Southeast Asia*. New York: John Wiley.

Hsing, Y. 1996. "Blood, Thicker than Water: Interpersonal Relations and Taiwanese Investment in Southern China," *Environment and Planning* 28: 2241-61.

Hui, Po-Keung. 1995. "Overseas Chinese Business Networks: East Asian Economic Development in Historical Perspective," Ph.D. Dissertation, Sociology, State University of New York, Binghamton.

Ikenberry, G. John. 1998. "Globalization and the Emerging Asia-Pacific Region," *Ritsumeikan Journal of International Relations and Area Studies* 13 (March): 115-40.

Institute of Social Science, 1999. *Social Science Japan: The Financial Crisis in Asia*, 13 (August). Tokyo, University of Tokyo.

International Monetary Fund (IMF), 1996. "ASEAN's Sound Fundamentals Bode Well for Sustained Growth," *IMF Survey* (November 25): 377-78.

————, 1997. "IMF Wins Mandate to Cover Capital Accounts, Debt Initiative Put in Motion," *IMF Survey* (May 12): 129-33.

Iriye, Akira. 1992. *China and Japan in the Global Setting*. Cambridge: Harvard University Press.

Iwasaki, Mikiko, ed. 1995. *Varieties of Regional Integration*. Muenster: LIT.

Johnson, Chalmers. 1998. "Economic Crisis in East Asia: The Clash of Capitalisms," *Cambridge Journal of Economics*, 22: 1-9.

Jones, Randall S., Robert E. King, and Michael Klein. 1993. "Economic Integration between Hong Kong, Taiwan and the Coastal Provinces of China," *OECD Economic Studies* 20 (Spring): 115-44.

Jordan, Amos A. and Jane Khanna. 1995. "Economic Interdependence and Challenges to the Nation-State: The Emergence of Natural Economic Territories in the Asia-Pacific," *Journal of International Affairs* 48, 2 (Winter): 433-62.

Kahler, Miles. 1997. "Does Legalization Have Regional Limits? The Asia-Pacific Case," paper prepared for the Annual Meeting of the American Political Science Association, Washington, DC, 28 August.

Kao, John. 1993. "The Worldwide Web of Chinese Business," *Harvard Business Review* 71 (March-April): 24-36.

Katzenstein, Peter J. 1993. "Regions in Competition: Comparative Advantages of America, Europe, and Asia," in Helga Haftendorn and Christian Tuschhoff, eds., *America and Europe in an Era of Change*, pp. 105-26. Boulder: Westview Press.

————. 1997a. "Introduction: Asian Regionalism in Comparative Perspective," in Peter J. Katzenstein and Takashi Shiraishi, eds., *Network Power: Japan and Asia*, pp. 1-44. Ithaca: Cornell University Press.

————. 1997b. "Regional Orders: Technology in Asia and Europe." Unpublished paper.

————. 1998. "Regional Orders: Technology in Asia and Europe." Unpublished manuscript.

Katzenstein, Peter J. and Martin Rouse. 1993. "Japan as a Regional Power in Asia," in Jeffrey A. Frankel and Miles Kahler, eds., *Regionalism and Rivalry: Japan and the United States in Pacific Asia*, pp. 217-44. Chicago: University of Chicago Press.

Katzenstein, Peter J. and Takashi Shiraishi. 1997. "Conclusion: Regions in World Politics, Japan and Asia—Germany in Europe," in Peter J. Katzenstein and Takashi Shiraishi, eds., *Network Power: Japan and Asia*, pp. 341-81.

Kleinman, Anne Simone. n.d. "Across China: Regional Pluralism and Developmental Imbalance." Unpublished paper.

Korhonen, Pekka. 1994. "The Theory of the Flying Geese Pattern of Development and Its Interpretation," *Journal of Peace Research*, 31, 1: 93-108.

Kotkin, Joel. 1993. *Tribes: How Race, Religion and Identity Determine Success in the New Global Economy*. New York: Random House.

Kouriatchev, Mikhail. 1993. "Economic Cooperation in the Asia-Pacific Region: The Tumen River Area Development Project," The Program on U.S.-Japan Relations, Harvard University, Center for International Affairs and the Reischauer Institute of Japanese Studies.

Kristof, Nicholas D. 1998. "Japan Sees Itself as a Scapegoat of Washington in the Asia Crisis," *New York Times* (September 21): A1, A6.

Lake, David A. and Patrick M. Morgan, eds. 1997. *Regional Orders: Building Security in a New World*. University Park: Pennsylvania State University Press.

Lampton, David M. et al. 1992. *The Emergence of 'Greater China': Implications for the United States*. New York: National Committee on United States-China Relations.

Lardy, Nicholas R. 1994. *China in the World Economy*. Washington, DC: Institute for International Economics.

Laurence, Henry. 1999. "Financial System Reform and the Currency Crisis in East Asia," *Asian Survey* 39, 2 (March/April): 348-73.

Lim, Linda Y.C. 1994. "The Role of the Private Sector in ASEAN Regional Economic Cooperation," in Lynn K. Mytelka, ed., *South-South Cooperation in a Global Perspective*, pp. 125-68. Paris: OECD Development Centre.

———. 1995. "Southeast Asia: Success through International Openness," in Barbara Stallings, ed., *Global Change, Regional Response: The New International Context of Development*, pp. 238-71. New York: Cambridge University Press.

Lincoln, Edward J. 1992. "Japan's Rapidly Emerging Strategy toward Asia." Paris: OECD, Research Program on Globalisation and Regionalization.

———. 1993. *Japan's New Global Role* (Washington, DC: Brookings Institution).

Mack, Andrew and John Ravenhill. 1995. *Pacific Cooperation: Building Economic and Security Regimes in the Asia-Pacific Region*. Boulder: Westview.

Mackie, Jamie. 1992a. "Changing Patterns of Chinese Big Business in Southeast Asia," in Ruth McVey, ed., *Southeast Asian Capitalists*, pp. 161-90. Ithaca: Cornell University, Southeast Asia Program.

———. 1992b. "Overseas Chinese Entrepreneurship," *Asia-Pacific Economic Literature* 6, 1 (May): 41-64.

Mansfield, Edward D. and Helen V. Milner, eds. *The Political Economy of Regionalism*. New York: Columbia University Press.

McLeod, Ross H. and Ross Garnaut, eds. 1998. *East Asia in Crisis: From Being a Miracle to Needing One?* London: Routledge.

McMichael, Philip and Chul-Kyoo Kim. 1994. "Japanese and South Korean Agricultural Restructuring in Comparative and Global Perspective," in Philip McMichael, ed., *The Global Restructuring of Agro-Food Systems*, pp. 21-52. Ithaca: Cornell University Press.

McVey, Ruth. 1992, "The Materialization of the Southeast Asian Entrepreneur," in Ruth McVey, ed., *Southeast Asian Capitalists*, pp. 7-34. Ithaca: Cornell University, Cornell Southeast Asia Program.

Minassian, Garabed. 1999. "Bulgaria and the International Monetary Fund," unpublished paper, Institute of Economics, Bulgarian Academy of Sciences, Sofia.

Mittelman, James H. 1998. "Rethinking the 'New Regionalism' in the Context of Globalization," in Björn Hettne, András Inotai, and Osvaldo Sunkel, eds., *The New Regionalism and the Future of Security and Development*, pp. 25-53. London: Macmillan.

Moon, Chung-in. 1998. "In the Shadow of Broken Cheers: The Dynamics of Globalization in South Korea," paper prepared for delivery at a conference on "Coping with Globalization," sponsored by the Center for the Study of Global Change of Indiana University, Alexandria, Virginia (July 31-August 1).

Moore, Thomas G. and Dixia Yang. 1998. "China, APEC, and Economic Regionalism in the Asia Pacific," paper prepared for presentation at the 94th Annual Meeting of the American Political Science Association, Boston, MA, 3-6 September.

Naughton, Barry, ed. 1997. *The China Circle: Economics and Technology in the PRC, Taiwan, and Hong Kong*. Washington, DC: Brookings Institution.

Orrú, Marco, Gary G. Hamilton, and Mariko Suzuki. 1997. "Patterns of Interfirm Control in Japanese Business," in Marco Orrú, Nicole Woolsey Biggart and Gary G. Hamilton, *The Economic Organization of East Asian Capitalism*, pp. 188-214. Thousand Oaks, CA: Sage.

Orwell, George. 1949. *Nineteen Eighty-Four: A Novel*. New York: Harcourt, Brace and World.

Oxfeld Ellen. 1993. *Blood, Sweat, and Mahjong: Family and Enterprise in an Overseas Chinese Community*. Ithaca: Cornell University Press.

Pempel, T.J., ed. 1999. *The Politics of the Asian Economic Crisis*. Ithaca: Cornell University Press.

Peng, Dajin. 1995. "The Rise of a Pacific Community? Evolution and Trends of Asia Pacific Economic Cooperation," Ph.D. dissertation, Princeton University, Woodrow Wilson School of Public and International Affairs.

————. 1998. "Ethnic Chinese Business Networks and the Asia Pacific Community," paper prepared for delivery at the 1998 Annual Meeting of the American Political Science Association, Boston, MA.

Pyle, Kenneth B. 1997. "Old New Orders and the Future of Japan and the United States in Asia." The 1997 Edwin O. Reischauer Memorial Lecture, International House of Japan (June 12).

Qi, Luo and Christopher Howe. 1993. "Direct Investment and Economic Integration in the Asia Pacific: The Case of Taiwanese Investment in Xiamen," *China Quarterly* 136 (December): 746-69.

Rajan, Ramkishen. 1999. "The Brazil and Other Currency Crises of the 1990s," *Claremont Policy Briefs*, Issue 99-02.

Ravenhill, John. 1995. "Economic Cooperation in Southeast Asia," *Pacific Affairs*, 35, 9 (September): 850-66.

Ridding, John and Kynge, James. 1997. "Empires Can Strike Back," *Financial Times* (November 5): 13.

Rix, Alan. 1993. "Japan and the Region," in Richard Higgott, Richard Leaver and John Ravenhill, eds., *Pacific Economic Relations in the 1990s: Cooperation or Conflict?*, pp. 62-82. Boulder: Lynne Rienner.

Rohlen, Thomas P. 1995. "A 'Mediterranean' Model for Asian Regionalism: Cosmopolitan Cities and Nation-States in Asia," Asia/Pacific Center, Stanford University, Stanford, CA.

Ross, Robert S., ed. 1995. *East Asia in Transition: Toward a New Regional Order.* Armonk, NY: M.E. Sharpe.

Root, Hilton L. 1996. *Small Countries, Big Lessons: Governance and the Rise of East Asia.* New York: Oxford University Press for the Asian Development Bank.

Sanger, David E. 1998. "U.S. and I.M.F. Made Asia Crisis Worse, World Bank Finds," *New York Times* (December 3): A1, A20.

Seagrave, Sterling. 1997. *Lord of the Rim.* London: Corgi Press.

Sedgwick, Mitchell W. 1994. "Does the Japanese Management Miracle Travel in Asia? Managerial Technology Transfer at Japanese Multinationals in Thailand," paper presented at the Workshop on Multinationals and East Asian Integration, MIT Japan Program, Cambridge, MA (November 18-19).

Sender, Henny. 1991. "Inside the Overseas Chinese Networks," *Institutional Investor* (August): 29-43.

Shenon, Philip. 1998. "Of the Turmoil in Indonesia and its Roots," *New York Times* (May 9): A15, A17.

Shiraishi, Saya and Takashi Shiraishi. 1993. "The Japanese in Colonial Southeast Asia: An Overview," in Shiraishi and Shiraishi, *The Japanese in Colonial Southeast Asia*, pp. 5-20. Ithaca: Cornell University, Southeast Asia Program.

Shirk, Susan L. 1994. *How China Opened Its Door: The Political Success of the PRC's Foreign Trade and Investment Reforms.* Washington, DC: Brookings Institution.

Skinner, G. William, ed. 1979. *The Study of Chinese Society: Essays by Maurice Freedman.* Stanford: Stanford University Press.

Smith, Shannon L.D. 1997. "The Indonesia-Malaysia-Singapore Growth Triangle: A Political and Economic Equation," *Australian Journal of International Affairs* 51, 3 (1997): 369-82.

So, Alvin Y. and Stephen W.K. Chiu. 1995. *East Asia and the World Economy.* Thousand Oaks: Sage Publications.

Stubbs, Richard. 1994. "The Political Economy of the Asia-Pacific Region," in Richard Stubbs and Geoffrey R.D. Underhill, eds., *Political Economy and the Changing Global Order*, pp. 366-77. New York: St Martin's.

————. 1998. "Asia-Pacific Regionalism versus Globalization: Competing Forms of Capitalism," in William D. Coleman and Geoffrey Underhill, eds., *Regionalism and Global Economic Integration: Europe, Asia and the Americas*, pp. 68-80. London: Routledge.

Suriyadinata, Leo, ed. 1989. *The Ethnic Chinese in the ASEAN States: Bibliographic Essays.* Singapore: Institute for Southeast Asian Studies.

Taylor, Robert. 1996. *Greater China and Japan: Prospects for an Economic Partnership in East Asia.* London: Routledge.

Tett, Gillian. 1999. "Special Report: The Hidden Truth behind the Mask," *Financial Times* (June 18): 10.

Thant, Myo, Min Tang, and Hiroshi Kakazu, eds. 1994. *Growth Triangles in Asia: A New Approach to Regional Economic Cooperation.* New York: Oxford University Press for the Asian Development Bank.

Tokunaga, Shojiro, ed. 1992. *Japan's Foreign Investment and Asian Economic Interdependence: Production, Trade, and Financial Systems.* Tokyo: University of Tokyo Press.

Wade, Robert. 1994. "Selective Industrial Policies in East Asia: Is *The East Asian Miracle* Right?" in A. Fishlow et al., eds., *Miracle or Design? Lessons from the East Asian Experience.* Washington, DC: Overseas Development Council.

————. 1998. "From 'Miracle' to 'Cronyism': Explaining the Great Asian Slump," *Cambridge Journal of Economics*, 22: 693-706.

————. 1999. "Lessons from the Asian Crisis," paper prepared for the Asian Development Bank annual meeting (April 30).

Wan, Ming. 1995. "Spending Strategies in World Politics: How Japan has Used its Economic Power in the Past Decade," *International Studies Quarterly* 39, 1 (March): 85-108.

Wang, Gungwu. 1991. *China and the Chinese Overseas.* Singapore: Times Academic Press.

Watanabe, Akio and Tsutomu Kikuchi. 1997. "Japan's Perspectives on APEC: Community or Association?" in Donald Hellmann and Kenneth Pyle, eds., *From APEC to Xanadu: Creating a Viable Community in the Post-Cold War Pacific*, pp. 126-47. Armonk, NY: M.E. Sharpe.

Weidenbaum, Murray and Samuel Hughes. 1996. *The Bamboo Network: How Expatriate Chinese Entrepreneurs are Creating a New Economic Superpower in Asia*. New York: The Free Press.

Whitley, Richard. 1992. *Business Systems in East Asia: Firms, Markets and Societies*. Newbury Park: Sage.

Womack, Brantley and Guangzhi Zhao. 1994. "The Many Worlds of China's Provinces: Foreign Trade and Diversification," in David S.G. Goodman and Gerald Segal, eds., *China Deconstructs*, pp. 131-76.

Yamamoto, Yoshinobu and Tsutomo Kikuchi. 1998. "Japan's Approach to APEC and Regime Creation in the Asia-Pacific," in Vinod K. Aggarwal and Charles E Morrison, eds., *Asia-Pacific Crossroads: Regime Creation and the Future of APEC*, pp. 191-213. New York: St. Martin's Press.

Yamazawa, Ippei. 1992. "On Pacific Economic Integration," *Economic Journal* 102 (November): 1519-29.

Yuan, Jing-dong and Lorraine Eden. 1992. "Export Processing Zones in Asia: A Comparative Study," *Asian Survey* 32 (November): 1026-45.

Zhang, Yunling. 1997. "China and APEC: Interests, Opportunities and Challenges," in Donald C. Hellmann and Kenneth Pyle, eds., *From APEC to Xanadu: Creating a Viable Community in the Post-Cold War Pacific*, pp. 213-11. Armonk, NY: M.E. Sharpe.

Zhang, Yunling. 1998. "China and APEC," in Vinod K. Aggarwal and Charles E. Morrison, eds., *Asia-Pacific Crossroads: Regime Creation and the Future of APEC*, pp. 213-32. New York: St. Martin's Press.

Zhao, Suisheng. 1997. *Power Competition in East Asia*. New York: St. Martin's.

———. 1998. "Soft versus Structured Regionalism: Organizational Forms of Cooperation in Asia-Pacific," *Journal of East Asian Affairs* 12, 1 (Winter): 96-134.

2

Open Regionalism and
Japan's Systemic Vulnerability

Kozo Kato

The Japanese policy of open regionalism in Asia has been stable and persistent, regardless of structural or environmental changes in the region. Japan's responses to the Asian economic crisis after the summer of 1997 confirmed the point yet again and demonstrated how difficult it is for the Japanese government to adopt a policy of Japan-centered, exclusive regionalism. The failure of the government attempt to establish the Asian Monetary Fund as a regional institution for Asians is a case in point. The fund was to have been a formal institution that served as a lender of last resort, without deference to Americans and Europeans, using the yen as a vehicle currency for intervention and trade settlements [*Nihon Keizai Shimbun* 29 September 1997, 13th ed., 9; 5 November 1997, 13th ed., 7]. In the end, the Japanese government advocated consolidating existing international regimes, and integrated the regional plan into the International Monetary Fund (IMF) and the Asian Development Bank (ADB), in the expectation that they would prescribe measures to restart the Asian economies and to keep the regional order stable and open. Japan planned to contribute an estimated $80 billion to the effort, close to two thirds of the $127 billion (Y16,650 billion) in unprecedented expansionary budget measures that the government proudly announced, in April 1998, would stimulate the domestic economy and avert a world depression. Out of the $80 billion, $19 billion was committed to bilateral credit lines to be disbursed under IMF bailout plans. This contribution accounted for 36 percent of total bilateral commitments ($52.5 billion) from all industrialized countries [Gaimusho 1997; IMF, 1997].[1] American influence was critical in deflecting Japan's attempt to assume regional leadership. However, it was not clear why Tokyo, despite Japan's economic, technological, and financial dominance in Asia, gave in so easily and chose to stick to open measures.

This chapter systematically explains Japan's policy of open regionalism by examining both the hierarchical economic structure between Japan and Asia, and the complex interdependencies among Asian countries that are linked through Japanese production networks. By coupling the former, realist, perspective and the latter, liberal, one, it becomes clear that Japan's open regionalism derives from a political compromise between dependency and interdependency, in which national economic security and competitiveness within the dynamically changing international division of labor is produced by networking functionally different states and firms on a global scope.

The existing literature tends to focus on the structural asymmetry found in the economic interdependence between Japan and other Asian economies and, then, to depict emerging production networks as precursors of a Japan-centered regional bloc. Particularly noteworthy is Walter Hatch and Kozo Yamamura's work on Asian production networks that synthesizes Japanese domestic developmentalism and the hierarchical inter-firm alliances developing in Asia [1996]. However, such structural analysis cannot easily explain why, despite the hierarchical relationships between Japanese and Asian companies, the Japanese state and Japanese firms have institutionalized open regionalism, and seem to have avoided hierarchical integration designed to exclude westerners and draw Asians under the unrestricted control of a Tokyo headquarters? An eclectic approach that combines hierarchical structure and complex interdependence offers a solution to the questions surrounding open regionalism in general, and Asian inter-firm networks in particular. In short, Japan's odd combination of openness and national power shows us a way of conceptualizing regionalism that differs from that which was useful in the 1930s.

Hierarchical Structure and Open Regionalism
Hierarchical Structure in Asia

For the last decade, structural analyses of Asian regionalism have generally predicted that Japan should become interested in building an Asian economic bloc that would be dominated by Japanese financial and technological power. For example, Stephen Krasner claims that Japan's relations with East Asia in aid, investment, and trade are completely consistent with an effort to create a set of economic links that engender asymmetrical opportunity costs of change and thereby enhance Japanese power [1993, 373]. James Fallows concurs, noting that there is a political version of the phototropism that keeps growing plants directed toward the sun most countries on the East Asian arc are redirecting their plans toward a future in which Japan is the center of technology, money, and ideas about how to succeed [1994, 249].

Although the Asian financial turmoil of 1997 threw these scenarios into doubt, their arguments are empirically grounded. Structural evidence of a political dynamic toward Japan-centered, closed regionalism abounds. An examination of the three nodes of regional interdependence in Asia—Japan-Asia relations, Asia-U.S. (U.S.-Japan) relations, and intra-regional relations—suggests a Japanese preference for deep integration, rather than open and wide regionalism. First, the Japan-Asia relationship, unlike intra-European relations, is characterized by an extreme, structural gap in income distribution.

For example, in 1990 Japan's GDP accounted for three quarter of the combined GDP of the so called East Asian Economic Caucus (EAEC) countries, that is, the Association for South-East Asian Nations (ASEAN) and East Asia, while, for example, Germany contributed only one quarter of the EC's GDP. The gap has been increasing in Asia, while it has shrunk in Europe. Japan's share of the EAEC's GDP increased from 57 to 73 percent between 1970 and 1990, while Germany's percentage of the EC's GDP declined from 27 to 25 percent during the same period [Katzenstein and Shiraishi 1997, 365]. Although China's GDP, if measured by purchasing power parity, may moderate Japan's dominance, per capita disparities in Asia highlight the structural gap. Japan's per capita income in 1991, $27,000, was more than double Hong Kong's, the second richest country in East Asia, and almost 90 times China's [World Bank 1992]. Reliance on Tokyo was also increased by the substantial economic aid Japan provided Asian nations. Japan accounted for 69 percent of total foreign aid received by Thailand in 1989, 62 percent of Indonesia's receipts, 57 percent of Malaysia's, 48 percent of the Philippines' and 39 percent of China's and Myanmar's [Rix 1993, 143; *The Economist*, 12 November 1994, 4 (survey)].

Secondly, the decreasing dependence of Asian countries on the American market and their shift to intra-regional economic transactions should have induced Japan to favor some sort of exclusive regionalism. In the past, Asia dependence on the American market has been extremely high, as countries pursued export-oriented strategies, while intra-regional trade and dependence on Japan was relatively small since, at least until the late 1980s, that market was almost closed to Asian manufactured products.[2] Between 1980 and 1984 the United States imported an estimated 70 percent of the growth in manufactured exports from East and Southeast Asia and the Pacific, while Japan absorbed only 9 percent [Borthwick 1992, 509]. In the 1980s, almost a quarter of the exports of Asian developing countries, mostly labor-intensive goods manufactured in East Asia, ASEAN, and South Asia, was absorbed by the U.S. market, while Japan imported only 15 to 20 percent, and other intra-regional countries purchased another quarter [Watanabe 1991, 290]. Even now, Japan has not concluded any regional or bilateral agreements on preferential trade with Asian countries.[3] This trade structure partly explains why virtually all Asian countries run a trade deficit with Japan and a trade surplus with the United States. Thus it is not surprising that the international, especially American, political backlash that Japan experienced in the 1980s has turned on Asian developing countries in the 1990s. In this vein, Joseph Grieco attributes the weak institutionalization of Asian integration, compared to Europe, to Asia's higher dependence on the American market [1995].

However, this centrifugal force, running from Asia to the United States, has weakened, and centripetal tendencies, toward East Asia and ASEAN, have increased since the late-1980s. Structural change has been especially evident in the fields of trade and foreign direct investment (FDI). Systematic exploitation of differences in factor costs of production has increased trade and investment opportunities among East Asian newly industrializing economies (NIEs), ASEAN countries, China, and Vietnam. Not only did these countries' total foreign trade, both imports and exports, surpass that of Japan in 1987, but in the same year, Hong Kong outranked Japan as China's largest trade partner for the first time since 1965. In 1991, China, ASEAN, and other Asian NIEs combined to account for 14 percent of world trade, exceeding the share of the United States. When U.S. protectionism mounted, and the Congress decided to discontinue General Special Preference (GSP) status for some ASEAN countries in 1991, East Asian NIEs started to provide markets to absorb the products of other East Asian and ASEAN countries. Since 1988, Asian NIEs have absorbed most of the growth of East Asian (except Japanese) and ASEAN exports and surpassed Japan and the United States as export markets. The intra-regional share of exports from Asian countries (including Japan) increased from 31 percent in 1986 to 43 percent in 1992, while dependence on the American market shrank from 34 percent to 24 percent [Kan 1994, 5]. Japan's reliance on the U.S. market has also been declining. Japan's trade, both imports and exports, with the rest of Asia surpassed that with the United State in 1989, and Japan's trade surpluses with Asia exceeded that with the United States in 1993 [*Nihon Keizai Shimbun* 23 February 1994, 13th ed., 5; 19 April 1994, 13th ed., 1].

The Asian NIEs have also led in FDI in Asia. Since 1988, East Asian NIEs' direct investment in Malaysia, Indonesia, and the Philippines has surpassed that of any other country. In the late 1980s, Japan's FDI exceeded that of the NIEs' only in Thailand, and even that lead has been narrowed. In 1994, Asian NIEs' intra-regional FDI in NIEs, ASEAN, and China amounted $41.4 billion, compared to Japan's $8.6 billion and America's $8.2 billion [Japan External Trade Organization 1996, 19]. In short, intra-Asia economic integration has been steadily advancing without Japan.[4]

As Asian economies consolidate regional integration, the Japanese production networks known as *keiretsu* have been expanding all over the region.[5] A Japanese *keiretsu* is a vertical alignment of small and medium enterprises (SMEs) under inter-market firm groups (*kigyo shudan*), which consist of horizontal alliances among various economic sectors such as finance, trade, chemical, or steel. Each *keiretsu* in a specific sector establishes exclusive networks that connect thousands of SMEs on a long-term but non-legal basis.[6] In the wake of massive foreign direct investment in the late 1980s and early 90s, the organizational arrangements of domestic *keiretsu* networks were regionalized throughout Asia, bandwagonning on the regional drive toward deepening economic integration. The structural analyses of *keiretsu* seek to understand the efficiency of Japanese industrial organizations by focusing on dependency in the Japanese *keiretsu*, where hierarchical layers of subcontractors get clustered under a core multinational. Thus, analysts, especially during the 1950s, described the hierarchical relations between a core firm and its *keiretsu* subsidiaries as a "dual structure," under which the core firm exploited SMEs to buffer the shock of cyclical downturns and guaranteed itself higher profitability than its subordinates.[7] The domestic, dual structure, it is often argued, is now being transplanted to Asia through Japanese FDI.

The continuing structural gap between Japan and other Asian countries, decreasing dependence on the American market, and increasing intra-regional economic integration in Asia under the hierarchical *keiretsu*, all suggest widening political opportunities for the Japanese state to advance regional policies independent of Western countries. However, Japanese regional policies have not matched expectations derived from structural analyses. For example, in the field of aid policy, the most effective way for the Japanese state to exploit vertical inter-firm relations and enhance Japanese competitiveness would be to link official aid to Japanese private exports or foreign investment. In fact, Japan's development cooperation policy has been liberalized since the late 1970s, decreasing tied aid, diversifying aid recipients on a global scale, and emphasizing social and humanitarian aid, rather than economic infrastructure [Kato 1996, chapter 2]. More curiously, those Asian countries that have sought the consolidation of a relatively closed regional integration have been the structurally less powerful, like Malaysia, which advocated the creation of the EAEC in the early 1990s, or Thailand, which sought to establish the Asian Monetary Fund during the 1997 financial crisis. With the structural gap between Japan and these Asian countries widening, those less powerful states should have opposed institutionalization of the regional economic order under the rising, Japanese hegemon [Grieco 1997].

Japan's Choice of Open Regionalism

Japan developed the idea of open regionalism in Asia in the mid-1960s, when the state began to regain self-esteem as an economic power in the world economy. Since then the government has called the region the Asia-Pacific. In 1967, then foreign minister and later prime minister (1974-76), Takeo Miki stated:

> Recently, interest in Asia has been increasing remarkably not only in Australia and New Zealand but also in Pacific countries such as the United States and Canada . . . Therefore, we now need to think of Asian matters within a framework of Asia-Pacific. I am fully aware that this way of thinking is irreversible when I consider contemporary trends and historical developments [Gaimusho 1967b (supplement), 5].

Miki defined Japan's position as a tangent point (*setten*) between Asia and the Pacific countries [Gaimusho 1968b, 6-7]. In the same context, as early as the mid-1960s, Masayoshi Ohira, future prime minister (1978-80), then a member of the Diplomacy Committee of the Policy Affairs Research Council of the Liberal Democratic Party (LDP), observed at an LDP private study group that Japan-U.S. or Japan-European diplomacy is not independent of Japan-Asia diplomacy. Japan should be a pipe that extracts nutrition from the former and enriches the latter [Ohira Masayoshi Kaisoroku Kankokai 1982, 181]. Fifteen years later, he, then prime minister, realized this policy with slogans such as loose joint (*yuruyakana rentai*), and open joint (*hirakareta rentai*). Ohira reasoned that the institutionalization of regional cooperation in Asia, following the European example, was not realistic, since Asia was composed of countries at different stages of development [Nagatomi 1984, vol. 2, 57]. The Pacific Basin Cooperation Study Group, Ohira's private study group, which was chaired by Saburo Okita, foreign minister in his cabinet, and included liberal intellectuals, such as Kiyoshi Kojima (an economist of international trade and investment), who had, since the 1960s, collaborated closely with Australia and other OECD members in establishing regional institutions, published several policy recommendations to implement Ohira's idea [Okita 1980]. In the 1970s and 1980s, increasing economic interdependence with both the United States and the Asian Pacific countries cemented the Asia Pacific framework. In 1982, prime minister Zenko Suzuki announced Japan's basic principles for promoting Pacific cooperation by describing the Pacific Ocean as the sea of peace, the sea of freedom, the sea of diversity, the sea of reciprocity, and the sea of openness [Gaimusho 1983b, 407-08].

Under open regionalism, most plans for institutionalizing Asian economic cooperation, although short lived, were inclusive and attempted to contain geographically diverse countries.[8] Thus, the Pacific Free Trade Area

(PAFTA), one of the earliest, included five industrialized countries, the United States, Japan, Australia, Canada, and New Zealand, and no Asian developing countries. In 1968, the idea of PAFTA developed into the Organization for Pacific Trade and Development (OPTAD), which was to be a sister organization to the Organization for Economic Cooperation and Development (OECD). That same year regional academic groups established the Pacific Trade and Development Conference (PAFTAD), which included the United States and Canada as well as Asian countries. Asian businessmen also attempted to organize the Pacific Basin Economic Council (PBEC), which admitted such Latin American countries as Mexico, Peru, and Chile. In 1980, after these initiatives had failed, the Pacific Economic Cooperation Conference (PECC), the most geographically comprehensive organization so far, was created to provide a focal point for regional economic integration, included members of both PAFTAD and PBEC.

The most recent effort to advance regional institutionalization, Asia Pacific Economic Cooperation (APEC), is no more regionally comprehensive than the previous attempts. When it was established, Foreign Minister Taro Nakayama explained Japan's view of APEC to his Asian colleagues by noting that what the Asia-Pacific region need to do is to secure long-term stability in the region by making the best use of existing mechanisms or places to promote dialogue for international cooperation in a comprehensive and multifarious manner [Gaimusho 1991b, 427-28]. Following this line, the Foreign Ministry officially noted:

> Japan has been asserting that regional integration and cooperation must proceed in a manner consistent with the GATT, and without creating discriminatory effects against extra-regional countries, and thereby contribute to world prosperity . . . This is based upon recognition that in the Asia-Pacific region, where economic systems, development stages and cultural and religious backgrounds are of such diversity, the multilateral free trading system is the way to maintain and strengthen existing regional economic vitality, thereby contributing to the growth and development of the world economy [Ministry of Foreign Affairs 1994, 79].

Japan's approach to regional cooperation transcends ministerial differences.[9] One MITI official endorsed the policy, saying, "We have a regional policy for Asia, but not a policy on regionalism" [*Far Eastern Economic Review* 18 June 1992, 46]. MITI also hopes that the APEC will become a model case of open regional cooperation. In this context, the government has been willing not only to be a bridge between the United States and Asian countries but also to invite EU members as observers to APEC [*Asahi Shimbun* 1 January 1994, 12th ed. (satellite), 2]. It was within this policy line that *Japan's Official Development Assistance Charter*, known as the constitution of Japanese foreign aid, adopted by the Cabinet in 1992, juxtaposed non-Asian countries to Asia.

To summarize, structural explanations, whether focusing on the regional economic structure in Asia or emphasizing the regional extension of Japanese domestic *keiretsu*, do not effectively account for Japan's consistent pursuit of open regionalism. Japan's emergence as a leading supplier of aid, capital and technology through the regional extension of the *keiretsu* and the increasing ability of Asian countries to absorb their products, both have substantially reduced dependence on American economic hegemony in the region and have widened political opportunities, especially for Japan, to build an exclusive economic bloc in Asia and to abandon open regionalism. As the rest of this paper will show, structuralism's loss of empirical validity follows from its neglect of the international and domestic contexts in which Japan and, in particular, the Japanese industrial production system have been embedded.

International and Domestic Contexts
Scope of Interdependence
The Japanese state and Japanese firms have been discouraged from exploiting the structural power derived from asymmetrical interdependence between Japan and Asia by a political constraint we term systemic vulnerability. Albert Hirschman's concept of vulnerability, which might be called dyadic vulnerability, is the product of an asymmetrical structure of costs of change in bilateral, interdependent relations [1980]. James Caporaso succinctly explains dyadic vulnerability by identifying two kinds of capabilities that constitute national power:

> Power for Hirschman is not an attribute or distributional parameter. It is more tied to network and exchange theory than to attribute theory. The threat of using power is a threat to withdraw something rather than to deliver something. Understanding international influence networks is an important project that will help to round out the realist conception of power [1993, 463].

In this line, the Japanese state in Asia can be characterized as possessing substantial exchange capabilities derived from the asymmetrical structure of interdependence. That structural power may even be huge enough to compensate for the attribute weakness of a state that lacks cultivable land and natural resources. Such an exchange, or network, power state should see that the threat to withdraw economic cooperation would be made more effective if the dependent countries were integrated into a closed regional system that made it difficult to find alternative partners for economic exchange. But Japan has avoided threatening to take advantage of the asymmetrical opportunity costs of changing partners because, we maintain, the network that creates Japan's structural power simultaneously imposes a kind of vulnerability on the Japanese state.

Systemic vulnerability refers to political constraints that prevent the stronger state from manipulating the asymmetrical interdependence.[10] Such constraints are not a necessary concomitant of interdependence. Systemic vulnerability emerges and influences structural power, if, and only if, the state has to depend on a wide variety of *unlike units* in interdependence. In this line, Kenneth Waltz's definition of interdependence: "high inequality among like units *is* low interdependence" [1970, 207] does not capture the vulnerabilities of Japanese interdependence. For Japan, while the units are unequal and their economic relations tend to be hierarchical in the world economy, interdependence forces the stronger power to contribute to the complexity of international production. That is, inequality among unlike units can produce high interdependence.

A structural analysis treats dyadic vulnerabilities in Japan's international political relations as if they constitute discrete bilateral relations among like units. The indicators of Japan's dyadic vulnerability are well known: 30 percent of exports go to a single country, the United States, and members of the Organization of Petroleum Exporting Countries (OPEC) provide more than 80 percent of Japan's imported oil, while OPEC's reliance on Japanese capital and technology is very marginal. By these standards, however, Japan is much less vulnerable than, for example, Canada, which depends on the American market for 80 percent of its total exports, while the United States sends only 20 percent of its total exports to the Canadian market. But, what matters in gauging Japanese vulnerability is the economy's *scope of interdependence* with unlike units, which the Japanese state cannot manage bilaterally or regionally. The scope of interdependence is not the same as its size.[11] Scope measures unlikeness of interdependent counterparts. In the current discussions, the level of interdependence is usually calculated using measures of export dependence, multinationality of foreign investment or volume of international capital mobility. Empirical analyses based upon such size measurements tend to conclude that increased interdependence promotes liberalization of trade policy and leads to smooth coordination of monetary and fiscal policies among industrialized countries.[12] According to such yardsticks, Japan should be less concerned about international cooperation and not so supportive of a policy of open regionalism. The Japanese economy's dependence on international trade has been stable since the 1960s, with imports plus exports holding at 25 percent of GNP, while, for example, Germany's trade dependence doubled from 25 percent to 50 percent over the last four decades [Komiya 1990, 77]. In terms of scope, however, the Japanese state is embedded in a system that is made up of functionally different economies, and Japanese multilateral enterprises operate in a broadly interdependent market in which unlike firms are linked through complex, hierarchically and horizontally, networks.

In this liberal world, Japan is vulnerable, rather than collectively secured, because its competitiveness in world markets is threatened by malfunctions of interdependent processes. For the Japanese state, exchanges within the whole need to be complete in order to realize national power and competitiveness, and enhancing interdependence and networking joins national competitiveness as a state policy goal in its own right. This odd coupling of complex interdependence and national power, or cooperative networks and asymmetrical interdependence, is particular characteristic of Japan. Japanese national security and economic gains can be achieved only through dense networks that include a variety of states and firms that supply functions that Japan lacks. Interrupting the interdependence linkage, even if the opportunity costs of doing so are lower for Japan than for targeted countries, could lead to a collective collapse threatening the entire economy. Michael Mandelbaum succinctly pointed out:

> Japan's reliance on an open international economic order, in sum, was greater than that of any other country, because it could not do without foreign raw materials and overseas markets, because the economic network on which Japan depended was unusually broad, stretching to the Persian Gulf, the source of its oil, and to North America as well as to countries closer to the Japanese archipelago, and because the cultural and political distance between the Japanese and those with whom they had to do business to sustain their standard of living was unusually pronounced. For Japan, more than for any other country, therefore, the problem of ensuring economic well-being was like the problem of providing collective arrangements for security [1988, 338-39].

The circumstance that requires Japan to maintain collective arrangements and construct global networks in order to realize national objectives is what we mean by systemic vulnerability. As has been often pointed out by students of American foreign policy, there is no doubt that the collective arrangements that made Japan's global-scope of interdependence possible have been provided and guaranteed by the United States throughout the post-war period. However, this fact does not explain Japan's persistent support of the existing, American-led regimes even in the face of obvious political opportunities to exit and build its own regional sphere. Thus, the question is not one of structure, but of the context of interdependence. Japan's vulnerability is not a function of an American power structure, but of the scope of the interdependent networks within which Japan's economic welfare is realized.

The more networking Japanese interdependence becomes, the more the state becomes vulnerable to a collapse of the international system.

Domestic Production Networking

A similar discussion of systemic vulnerability can be applied to domestic contexts. Very roughly, there are two strands to the discussions of Japanese economic efficiency. One is structural, and the other is contextual. The former emphasizes structural hierarchies that reduce transaction costs associated with intra-organizational exchanges. Oliver Williamson's microeconomics theory suggests that one way to escape the uncertainties and asymmetrical information structures associated with inter-organizational transactions, is to internalize the transactions through hierarchical integration [1975, 1985].[13] Supporters of this position often cite the Japanese production network referred to as a *keiretsu*. Comparative works emphasize the *keiretsu* as uniquely Japanese and identify institutional differences in production systems not only between Asian and European and American countries, but also among East Asian countries (Japan, Taiwan, South Korea). The regional extension of the *keiretsu* to embrace local firms under Japanese multinationals naturally suggests a vision of the emerging regional order as Japan-centered, integrated, and structured to enhance Japanese national competitiveness.[14]

Hirschman's concept of asymmetrical interdependence is often used to illuminate exploitative relations between stronger, multilateral firms and weaker, domestic ones. The power relations of such unequal exchanges are explained mainly by noting the asymmetrical opportunity costs of "exit" from the existing exchanges. Oliver Williamson's notion of "*asset specificity*" is useful in measuring such inequality. An asset's specificity is defined as the "degree to which an asset can be redeployed to alternative uses and by alternative users without sacrifice of productive value" [Williamson 1975, 12]. More concretely, the more parts a firm produces that are suitable only for a single or a limited number of assemblers, the harder it is for the firm to exit the transactions or find alternative buyers when orders are reduced or suspended. Within the discussion of Asian regionalism, it is often asserted that, because asset specificity of Asian parts suppliers is high and their products are geared only to Japanese parents companies, those parent companies maintain bargaining power in deciding quantities and prices for the products they purchase.[15]

This emphasis on asymmetry in *keiretsu* totally neglects the social processes that characterize relations among functionally different firms. As with Japan's international interdependence, the domestic networks consist of broad scope interdependence among a large number of small and medium enterprises (SMEs) under a small number of core firms; consolidating social interdependency, not hierarchical integration, has been the normative way to achieve national competitiveness. This conflation of sociological liberalism and political realism is possible, because deepening social interdependence increases economic efficiency and competitiveness. For Japanese firms, high asset specificity in exchanges among SMEs is not a means of exploitation, but a way to increase their own international competitiveness.

Eshun Hamaguchi calls this approach contextualism and contrasts it to individualism and groupism [1985]. Reversing the structural logic that connects hierarchical institutions with economic efficiency and competitiveness, he treats interdependence among actors of differing qualifications as a natural circumstance of economic exchanges. Interdependence can be an end in itself, rather than a means to realize economic efficiency. The sociologically liberal approach describes Japanese social contexts as fields of a learning process in which mutually dependent actors exchange uncodified, relational skills and information on a non-contractual basis.[16]

Unlike a hierarchical structure that controls partners with legally binding contracts, horizontal networks have to rely on social values of trust, morality, or loyalty. Following Douglass North and his collaborators in their recognition of the importance of ideology and culture in the measurement and enforcement of contracts, the sociologically liberal approach favors an argument that Japanese cultural and social norms favor obligational, informal relations to arm's-length, contractual agreements. Japanese norms are based upon goodwill, and they set the social contexts in which Japanese big enterprises choose stable, long-term relations with subcontractors and maintain outsourcing strategies, rather than following the lead of western conglomerates and internalizing all functions.[17]

Industry and organization economists interested in Japanese firms resonate to this sociological analysis and emphasize the importance of information sharing and long-term, non-binding contractual relations between core firms and subcontractors, attributing the efficiency of Japanese supplier systems to their organizational arrangement.[18] In market terms, big buyers can also suffer from opportunism derived from high transaction costs associated with high asset specificity. The small and medium sized enterprise (SMEs) with which they contract are usually deficient in capital. If such an SME is economically rational, as is assumed in the hierarchy argument, it will find little incentive to make large investments in production lines that manufacture products marketable only to a limited number of buyers. Therefore, its parent firm may have to arrange finances and shoulder the risk of establishing a specified production line. Should the SMEs' business fail, the parent company's investment could be unrecoverable. Furthermore, uniqueness of assets could allow SMEs to realize quasi-rents in the process of contracting with big firms. Thus the Japanese practice of networking to buy from a large number of SMEs on a long-term basis may not be a matter of using production relations for exploitation. Instead, such relations may be a core firm strategy to avoid the market failures of opportunism and, thus, to realize its own economic efficiency.[19]

The industrial, organizational, and sociological approaches converge and become mutually complementary in explaining economic efficiency. As Williamson suggests, following Kenneth Arrow's argument about the economics of information, even intra-organizational transactions can be dependent on a larger context in which cultures affect the integrity of trading parties who share information. The governance structure, which is defined by Williamson as consisting of frequency of transactions, uncertainty, and asset specificity, can be a dependent variable that is explained by societal context [1985, 9 and 405-6]. Thus, whether a firm establishes a hierarchical integration of suppliers or builds horizontal networks depends on specific social contexts shaped by culture or history.[20]

We contend that what distinguishes Japanese networking is that Japanese social networks, relying on such social norms as homogeneity, harmony, mutual trust, consensus, etc., are synchronized with a state strategy designed to extract higher gains from world markets than than those obtained by other countries, especially when they present Japan with dyadic vulnerabilities. Walter Powell elaborates the concept of networks in a liberal context by stating:

> Networks can be complex: they involve neither the explicit criteria of the market, nor the familiar paternalism of the hierarchy. A basic assumption of network relationships is that one party is dependent on resources controlled by another, and that there are gains to be had by the pooling of resources. *In essence, the parties to a network agree to forego the right to pursue their own interests at the expense of others* [1990, 303] (italics added).

Far from seeking the social welfare of all involved, Japan has firmly embedded these complex networks in a context of international, realist competition. Japan's natural resources diplomacy is most illustrative on this point. International vulnerability to an unsecured oil supply makes domestic politics uneconomical; consumer welfare, which could have been realized by acquiring cheaper raw materials through markets, has been sacrificed to the goal of maintaining the stability of the entire economy [Samuels 1989]. A sense of vulnerable community between business and government made it possible for the state to diversify supply sources, making long-term supply deals with resource-rich countries all over the world, while promoting energy-efficient, technological development [Katzenstein and Okawara 1993, 141-48].

In more general terms, one key to understanding Japanese liberalism lies in institutions that display dual characters. On the one hand, such institutions presume functional differentiation among individuals controlled by central authority (structural hierarchy); on the other hand, diverse individuals act as if they were a homogeneous group when engaged in collective action (social harmony) [Murakami, Kumon, and Sato 1979, 223-53]. This eclectic institutional arrangements are behind terms such as networks, contexts, and fields, which are used to delimit highly dense interactions between labor and management, government and business, and state and society. In Japan, neither state nor society is independent of, or parasitic on, the other. They are relational, constantly adjusting the political distance between them to respond to policy issues, economic environments, or international competition.[21]

The Japanese economy has been dependent on interdependence in both internationally and domestically. Internationally, interdependence with Asian countries has been the sine qua non of competition and survival in the hierarchical, international division of labor that includes both inter- and intra-industry trade with, and investment in, industrialized and industrializing economies. Domestically, production networks inside Japan, although they are hierarchically organized under parent firms, are based on an affirmed social principle of outsourcing from thousands of suppliers. To distinguish such relations from liberal complex interdependence, which aims at collective welfare, I will call production processes in which functionally different units are interdependent for a shared goal of efficiency and competitiveness "networking." The regional and international extension of Japanese liberal networks in coordination with realist objectives results in a political order that is outside the conventions of mainstream international relations theories. That is, international cooperation (openness) and state interests (competitiveness) are in a loop of mutual dependence in which national gains from interdependence are recycled to the international economy to sustain a liberal order and openness.[22] This is also true to of the regional order in Asia. The rest of the chapter will explain specifically how Japan's extension of liberal production networks to Asia produces national gains, while maintaining openness in the regional order. A conceptual summary of the preceding theoretical discussion is provided in Table 2.1.

Japan's Global-Scope Interdependency
Japan's international position is distinguished from that of other major industrialized countries by its combination of global scope and hierarchical structure. For the entire post-war period, interdependence has entailed both developing and industrialized countries, inter-industry and intra-industry trade, and mass production and flexible specialization. The trajectory of post-war

Table 2.1. Lines of Argument

	Hierarchical integration	Networking	Complex interdependence
Efficiency rationale	Reducing transactions costs	Converting social contexts into economic exchanges	Consolidating social trust through long-term and recurrent exchanges
Political consequences	Asymmetric interdependence	Dependence on interdependent processes	Symmetrical interdependence
Regional order	Regional bloc	Open regionalism	Internationalization/ globalization

Japanese industry has been to advance the sophistication of its own industrial structures within a global, hierarchical international division of labor.

In Asia, the Japanese state has attempted to foster the region as a partner in a dynamic duo competing in the changing global division of labor. Put differently, Japan's regional strategy has been to put the right countries (including itself) into the right places in the hierarchical international division of labor in order for both Asian countries and Japan to survive global competition. Structural changes in Japanese industries have coordinated the timing, speed, and order of development for their regional followers. Under this dynamic division of labor, little distinction can be made between exports, foreign direct investment, license contracting, and local production. All are aggregated through complex, inter-firm networking.

Thus, the Asian trajectory has been described as flying-geese economic development (*Ganko Hikogata Keizai Hatten*), multiple-layered catch-up (*Jusoteki Tsuiseki*), or chained structural transformation (*kozo tenkan rensa*).[23] The dynamic nature of regional development is, thus, a part of Japan's global-scope interdependency. Japanese global production networks alternate dependency and interdependency, or hierarchical and horizontal inter-firm relations, according to an individual country's relative position within the dynamic international division of labor. Therefore, the evolution of economic interdependence within Asia has been far from single-track, ordinal, or regular, as the product-cycle theory predicts [Bernard and Ravenhill 1995]. In Japanese terms, Asian economic integration will be deepened, if at all, less by throwing Asian countries into liberal competition in world markets than as a natural outcome of Japan's strategic placement of Asian economies, including itself, within global interdependence.

In short, to Japan, Asia has been a subsystem of Japan's global interdependence ever since the war, and much has remained constant since the late 1940s. Originally, Japan's interdependence and Asia's place in it was made possible under the American-led liberal economic order. However, it must be emphasized that the hierarchical structure incorporating the United States, Japan, and Asia set up a social context of open regionalism that has survived the demise of American dominance in Asia.

Origin of Japanese Production Networks in Asia

Japan's global interdependence began with the triangular integration of Japan, the United States, and East (South Korea and Taiwan) and Southeast Asian countries during the 1940s and 50s. Originally, the triangle was American-led and hierarchical, with the United States at the apex, Japan beneath the United States, and Southeast Asia at the bottom. American policy-makers expected economic integration to boost Southeast Asian industrialism and accelerate Japan's economic recovery, producing favorable spillover effects on regional security in Asia. Promoting Japan's economic recovery and the expected spill-over into Southeast Asian countries was simply a part of an American grand-strategy, which included reducing Great Britain's dollar debt and relieving French burdens in Indo-China. Japan was expected to be the workshop of Asia, like Germany in Europe, in the post-war, new world order.[24] It was as the factory of Asia that Japan was able to export capital goods to Southeast Asia in the name of "economic cooperation (*keizai kyoryoku*)" and receive needed raw materials in return. Simultaneously, the United States opened its markets to Japanese semi-finished goods and provided financial and humanitarian aid to devastated economies in Asia. Japan's freedom to make foreign economic policy was quite limited, and initiatives that ran contrary to the American strategy were out of the question. It is said that Prime Minister Shigeru Yoshida (1946-47, 48-54) once stated that history provides examples of winning by diplomacy after losing a war and that Japan should trade with rich men, not beggars, to make the state prosperous.[25] However, economic interdependence with poor Asian countries under American leadership was a precondition for Japan's entry into its new international position.

Interdependence began as hierarchical integration, managed under American hegemony. By the beginning of 1949, American policy had moved beyond passive containment to the positive rollback of communist encroachments in northeast Asia. The policy revision culminated in National Security Council document number 48, so called NSC 48, in which a hierarchical structure was laid out for the regional economies, with America at the core, Japan in the semi-periphery, and South Korea, Taiwan, Southeast Asia, and others on the periphery. Bruce Cumings explains:

A draft (of the document) referred to certain advantages in production costs of various commodities in the United States, Japan, and Southeast Asia, which suggest the mutually beneficial character of trade of a triangular character between these three areas. In other words, this theory of comparative advantage and the product cycle elaborated a tripartite hierarchy of American core heavy industries, Japanese light industries and heavy industries revived to acceptable ceilings, and peripheral raw materials and markets [Cumings 1993, 45].

The Eisenhower administration abjured the rollback strategy following the Korean War. Instead, it opted to open American markets to Japan, in order to secure Japan's political stability and pro-Western orientation. This was the historical origin of the heavy dependence of Asian economies on American markets, which continued at least until the late 1980s. In the early 1950s, trade between Japan and China was stagnant, despite relaxed export controls, and the Southeast Asian countries lacked the purchasing power needed to be reliable markets for Japanese goods [Shimizu 1991]. Outside Asia, almost half of the GATT's members invoked safeguard provisions against Japanese exports. Even after Japan's admission to GATT as a contracting party, in 1955, 14 countries, including the United Kingdom, France, the Netherlands, Belgium, Australia, India, and New Zealand, which together accounted for about 40 percent of Japan's exports to GATT members, invoked Article 35 and refused to have GATT relations with Japan. Later, even though they joined after Japan, many former colonies of the United Kingdom and France used the same option. While Canada, West Germany, Italy and the Scandinavian countries gave Japan most-favored-nation (MFN) treatment, the U.S. had the only market reliable enough to support the revival of the Japanese economy after the end of the special procurements of the Korean War.[26]

The settlement of Japanese war reparations to Southeast Asian countries strongly reflected the U.S. strategy of integrating the country into a cross-Pacific hierarchical interdependence.[27] Fortunately for Japan, the American-led regional strategy allowed a shift of Japanese economic cooperation away from China, its pre-war focus, to Southeast Asia, and legitimized the expansion of economic cooperation and the restoration of economic ties between Japanese firms and recipient governments.[28] As early as December 1945, the Truman administration was planning to move Japan's surplus production capacity to Southeast Asian countries as war reparations. Thus raising Asian industrial standards without depressing Japan's. By the end of 1950, the transfer of surplus capital to China, the Philippines, England, and Holland was valued at $45 million [Fielder 1969, 83]. As the Cold War in East Asia developed in the early 1950s, the settlement of reparation issues and normalization of diplomatic relations with Asian countries were of serious concern to the United States. Washington believed that satisfactory settlement of reparation issues constituted a key to the development of a stable Japan-Southeast Asia economic zone. By 1953 when the talks between Hayato Ikeda, chairman of the Liberal Party's Policy Committee and Walter Robertson, Assistant Secretary of State for Far Eastern Affairs, confirmed Japan's deep economic, rather than military, involvement in Southeast Asia, no single South, Southeast, or East Asian country had signed a reparations treaty. The Japanese government wanted American mediation, and hoped that the United States would not only guarantee reparations payments but link American aid to Southeast Asian countries to their acceptance of Japanese reparations. The outcome was that Japan decreased its total burden and was able to use reparations to subsidize exports to Southeast Asian countries.[29]

Japanese attempts during the 1950s to institutionalize economic cooperation with Southeast Asian countries outside the triangle drew American protests, and eventually failed. Prime Minister Nobusuke Kishi (1957-60) advocated an Asia policy independent of U.S. influence, and attempted to use bilateral security treaties to strengthen Japan's political leadership in Asia.[30] As one-time chief of Manchurian industrialization and as Hideki Tojo's minister of commerce and industry, Kishi believed strongly in the need for an immediate economic recovery and reconstructed economic integration with Asian nations. While he favored a state-led industrial policy, in opposition to Yoshida's market liberalism, Washington did not object. However, when he launched political initiatives to create the Southeast Asian Development Fund, Washington interfered. In 1960, the fund finally materialized as a domestic aid institution, named the Overseas Economic Cooperation Fund (OECF), that provided developing countries in general with low-interest yen loans [Takagi 1995, 22]. Consequently, Kishi's desire to return to Asia had to be adapted to the American idea of international liberalism. It was the Kishi administration that officially established a compromise between Japan *and* Asia, on the one hand, and Japan *in* the American led, international society, on the other. The so-called three pillars of post-war Japanese diplomacy, which consisted of bilateral cooperation with the United States, internationalism under the United Nations, and regional cooperation with Asian countries, survived for the entire post-war period. In 1958, under the comprehensive framework for Japanese foreign policies, MITI devoted its first white papers to defining Japanese economic cooperation as a new form of international economic relations that would produce mutual benefits for industrialized and developing countries [Tsusho Sangyosho 1958a, preface (no page number)].

Japan's economic interdependence with China was limited, at least until the Japan-China Friendship treaty, signed in 1978, marked the resumption of official economic cooperation. Communist China was situated outside the context of the triangle of integration between America, Japan, and Southeast Asia. Any hopes of expanding trade with China vanished in the face of opposition from the United States and the U.S.-led, anti-communist international regime called the China Committee (ChinCom) [Mastanduno 1992, 80, 98-100]. Japan's desire to revive economic relations with mainland China was strong in the early 1950s. Prime Minister Yoshida stated in 1949, "I don't care whether China is red or green. China is a natural market and it has become necessary for Japan to think about markets" [Nester 1991, 143]. Yoshida reiterated his commercial interest in mainland China in an article that appeared in *Foreign Affairs*:

> In some quarter a fear is entertained that a separate peace might permanently sever Japan's trade with Red China. Red or white, China remains our next-door neighbor. Geography and economic laws will, I believe, prevail in the long run over any ideological differences and artificial trade barriers [Yoshida 1951, 179].

However, Japan could not return to mainland China, unless, as Dulles warned Yoshida, it was ready to give up the San Francisco Peace Conference of 1951 and, consequently, membership in the international community. Obviously, the Japanese government had to choose the San Francisco option, and the signing of a peace treaty with Taiwan in 1952 followed automatically [Tanaka 1991, 33-42]. Subsequently, Japan's trade with China was marginal. Although Japan became China's largest trading partner in 1965, China accounted for only two to three percent of Japan's total trade into the late 1970s.

The effects of international constraints were most evident in Japan's constriction of domestic credits for export to China. In spite of strong pressures from the China lobby within Japanese business, the Export Import (Exim) Bank of Japan suspended export credits for Japanese suppliers to China, and that restriction was the crucial impediment to economic relations between the two countries. When Prime Minister Hayato Ikeda (1960-64) proposed, in 1963-64, using official credits for Kurashiki Rayon and Nichibo's exports of vinylon plants, Taiwan was outraged, and a settlement required intervention by the retired Yoshida. He wrote a letter in mid-1964 to Generalissimo Chiang Kai-Shek promising that Exim funds would not be used again in trade with China. Ikeda eventually withdrew the proposal, and the government suspended official credits to China until 1971.[31]

Neither Nixon's surprising announcement that he planned to visit China in 1971 nor the friendship treaty Japan signed with China in 1978 substantially changed the international context that shaped bilateral relations with China. While Japan resumed intensive economic cooperation with China after 1978, it restricted ODA to China, to mitigate the impact of a resumption on the international and regional order. Particular attention was paid to relations with the United States and Southeast Asian countries. In 1979, the government announced basic conditions for future economic cooperation with China: consultation with Western allies before committing aid to China; attention to the balance of ODA between China and ASEAN countries; and restriction of Chinese use of Japanese ODA to non-military purposes. Chalmers Johnson once argued that Japan's policy toward China was an example of one of the most skillfully executed foreign policies pursued by Japan in the postwar era; clever, covert adaptation by Japan to the Cold War and a good example of Japan's essentially neo-mercantilist foreign policy [Johnson 1986, 405]. In fact, Japan's international position did not allow the state to engage in mercantilist cooperation with China. Even in the mid-1990s, China's share of Japan's total exports was only about five percent, almost equivalent to that of Singapore. Without international constraints, Japanese firms could have expanded their production networks into China much earlier than the 1990s.

In addition to creating the triangular interdependence, American-led international regimes contributed to broadening the scope of Japanese interdependence beyond the triangle. Japan's participation in international institutions and the financial resources disbursed through them expanded the outer boundary of Japanese economic transactions. Japan joined the World Bank in 1952, four years before becoming a member of the United Nations.[32] Membership enabled Japan to obtain concessional loans from the Bank to rebuild its industrial infrastructure and reconstruct its economy. Also in 1954, Japan, with the help of the United States, became a donor member of the Colombo Plan for Co-operative Economic Development in South and Southeast Asia, which had been set up in 1950 to coordinate economic assistance activities in the Commonwealth countries [Hatano 1994, 228-31. Takagi, 1995, 12-13]. Japan's first bilateral official aid loan, to India, was made in a multilateral context in 1958, when a U.S.-led group of Western donor countries established the first World Bank consultative consortium for that country. Similarly, the major recipients of the Export-Import Bank of Japan's loans in the late 1950s and early 1960s were India and Pakistan [Takagi 1995, 11, 14]. Accordingly, Japanese business sought opportunities to acquire reliable sources for natural resources and to export its products not only in Southeast Asia, but on a global scale, including South Asia and North and South America. Big projects bloomed all over the world: pulp in Alaska (1953), iron ore in Brazil (1957) and oil in Saudi Arabia and Indonesia (1958, 1960 respectively) [Komiya 1988, 230-31; Harrell 1973, 38-39].

Japan was also pushed into the Development Cooperation Group (DAG) (which was later renamed the Development Cooperation Committee, or DAC) of the OECD in 1961, before it was admitted into the OECD in 1964. The United States used the DAG to put pressure on Japan to expand economic cooperation in Asia. For example, in 1965 the DAG and the United States urged Japan to increase aid to Taiwan and South Korea.

In sum, a pattern of Japanese interdependence was built from the 1940s through the 1960s within an intersection of vertical but geographically diversified interdependence between Japan, the United States, Southeast Asian countries and other natural resource-rich countries. The Japanese state's desire to climb the hierarchical ladder had to be coordinated with efforts to maintain global-scope interdependence: dependence on the American market; deepening economic cooperation with Southeast Asian countries, while avoiding close economic relations with China; and cooperation with the American-led multilateral financial regimes. The paradoxical task of conflating economic advances and international cooperation existed as a historical and exogenous fact from the beginning of the post-war period. Asia constituted a part of a global interdependence that has remained in force to today.

Trade, Investment, and Technology
The global-scope of Japanese interdependence persisted even after the 1960s, when Japan's rising economic power was drastically altering the international structure. As detailed below, Japanese patterns of international trade, foreign direct investment (FDI), and technology transfers are managed through systems that distinguish industrialized from developing countries, flexible from mass production, and Western from Asian countries.

Trade. In terms of extension and diversity, Japan's trade has been demonstrably more internationalized than that of other industrialized countries. As Table 2.2 shows, Japanese trade, since the 1960s, has been almost perfectly balanced between OECD and developing, non-OECD, countries and has reached regions irrespective of distance. North America, particularly the United States, and Asia have been consistently major markets. In this vein, although it is too early to extrapolate, the current resurgence of Asia as Japan's biggest export market can be read as a part of a long-term pattern in which Asia and North America have alternated in that position: Asia led in 1960, 75, 80, 95 and North America in 65, 70, 85, 90. Outside Asia, Europe has increased in importance as economic integration has advanced, and Japan still relies heavily on the Middle East for crude oil imports. In short, little change has occurred in the structure of Japanese international trade over the post-war period.

Table 2.2
Japanese Trade by Region
% and (rank)

	1960		1965		1970		1975	
	Imp	Exp	Imp	Exp	Imp	Exp	Imp	Exp
OECD	50.2	40.8	49.8	49.3	53.6	52.6	39.8	40.6
North America	40.7 (1)	28.1 (2)	33.3 (1)	32.2 (1)	34.4 (1)	34.0 (1)	24.4 (2)	22.2 (2)
Oceania	--	--	7.5 (6)	4.4 (6)	8.8 (5)	3.6 (6)	7.8 (4)	3.8 (8)
Europe	9.6 (3)	12.7 (3)	8.9 (4)	12.6 (3)	10.4 (4)	14.9 (3)	7.6 (5)	14.5 (3)
Non-OECD	49.8	59.2	50.2	50.7	46.4	47.4	60.2	59.4
Europe	3.0 (6)	2.1 (6)	3.4 (8)	3.0 (8)	3.2 (8)	2.6 (8)	2.4 (8)	4.2 (7)
Africa	3.3 (5)	9.0 (4)	4.3 (7)	9.6 (4)	5.8 (7)	7.3 (4)	4.0 (7)	9.8 (4)
Latin America	8.3 (4)	8.0 (5)	8.7 (5)	5.4 (4)	7.3 (6)	5.8 (5)	4.3 (6)	8.4 (6)
Middle East	--	--	13.1 (3)	3.3 (7)	11.9 (3)	2.8 (8)	27.9 (1)	9.8 (4)
Asia & Oceania	35.3(2)	40.3 (2)	19.2 (2)	26.9 (2)	17.0 (2)	26.5 (2)	21.1 (3)	26.9 (1)

Sources: OECD, *Stratistics of Foreign Trade* (Series A), February 1962, pp. 54, 56; August 1964, pp. 66, 68 for 1960 figures; OECD, *Historical Statistics of Foreign Trade*, pp. 46-47, 60-61 for figures during 1965-85; *Monthly Statistics of Foreign Trade* (Series A), January 1987, pp. 52-53, 66-67 for 1985 figures; January 1990, pp. 52-53, 68-69 for 1990 figures; June 1997, pp. 60-61, 78-79 for 1995. In 1995 figures, North America includes Mexico; Oceania and Japan includes Korea.

Foreign Direct Investment (FDI). The strategic character of Japanese FDI is reflected in its close association with structural changes in domestic industries, from heavy machines and manufacturing to high-tech services. Like international trade, Japanese FDI reflects the state's reliance on global-scope interdependence. Thus, Japanese FDI has been aimed at industries in which the host country has a comparative advantage, and the sectors and countries to which Japanese FDI flows have shifted on a global scope in accord with the "sophistication of industrial structures (*sangyo kozo no kodoka*)" within Japan.[33]

Table 2.2 (continued)
Japanese Trade by Region
% and (rank)

	1980		1985		1990		1995	
	Imp	Exp	Imp	Exp	Imp	Exp	Imp	Exp
OECD	33.7	46.1	39.7	58.1	50.2	58.9	52.8	55.9
North America	20.8 (3)	26.4 (2)	23.5 (2)	40.1 (1)	26.0 (2)	34.0 (1)	26/3 (2)	29.7 (2)
Oceania	5.5 (5)	3.1 (7)	6.4 (5)	3.7 (6)	6.0 (5)	2.8 (6)	10.2 (4)	9.3 (4)
Europe	7.4 (4)	16.6 (3)	9.5 (4)	14.4 (3)	18.2 (3)	22.1 (3)	16.3 (3)	17.0 (3)
Non-OECD	66.3	53.9	60.3	41.9	49.8	41.1	47.2	44.1
Europe	1.5 (8)	3.0 (8)	1.4 (8)	2.0 (8)	1.7 (7)	1.4 (8)	1.6 (7)	0.4 (8)
Africa	3.2 (7)	5.9 (6)	2.7 (7)	2.6 (7)	1.6 (8)	1.9 (7)	1.4 (8)	1.7 (7)
Latin America	4.0 (6)	6.5 (5)	4.7 (6)	4.4 (5)	4.1 (6)	3.9 (4)	2.9 (6)	3.2 (5)
Middle East	31.3 (1)	10.0 (4)	22.6 (3)	6.2 (4)	13.3 (4)	3.0 (5)	9.4 (5)	2.0 (5)
Asia & Oceania	25.8 (2)	28.1 (1)	28.8 (1)	26.6 (2)	29.1 (1)	31.4 (2)	31.9 (1)	36.7 (1)

Table 2.3 describes how the regional distribution of Japanese FDI has shifted from developing to industrialized countries. From 1960 into the early 1970s, overseas FDI was concentrated on extracting raw materials in developing countries, including oil in North Sumatra, iron ore in Malaysia, the Philippines, and India, copper ore in the Philippines, and natural gas in Brunei. During the 1960s, mining and related manufacturing took 30 percent and 25 percent, respectively, of total investment, and 65 percent of Japanese FDI in ASEAN countries between 1951 and 1984 went to Indonesia's oil industries [Morrison 1988, 436; Komiya and Wakasugi 1991, 51; Krasner 1993, 374]. Japan's concentration in developing countries was remarkably divergent from the international pattern of that time. For example, in 1971, German firms had only 40 percent of their foreign manufacturing in less developed countries, while over 90 percent of overseas Japanese manufacturers were located in developing countries [Franko 1978, 109]. FDI for non-extractive industries was, however, out of the question. Before 1970, Japan

Table 2.3
Japanese foreign direct investment (FDI) by region
% and (rank)

	North America	Europe	Oceania	Developing Countries	Latin America	Asia	Middle East	Africa
1960	31.0 (1)	1.0 (5)	0.7 (6)	67.3	29.9 (2)	17.3 (4)	19.7 (3)	0.4 (7)
1965	27.7 (2)	3.1 (5)	0.0 (7)	69.2	39.0 (1)	22.0 (3)	6.9 (4)	1.3 (6)
1970	21.2 (2)	37.1 (1)	13.6 (4)	28.1	5.1 (5)	18.5 (3)	3.1 (6)	1.5 (7)
1975	27.6 (2)	10.2 (4)	5.5 (6)	56.7	11.3 (3)	33.6 (1)	6.0 (5)	5.5 (6)
1980	34.0 (1)	12.3 (4)	9.5 (5)	44.2	12.5 (3)	25.3 (2)	3.4 (6)	3.0 (7)
1985	45.0 (1)	15.8 (3)	4.3 (5)	34.9	21.4 (2)	11.7 (4)	0.4 (7)	1.4 (6)
1990	47.8 (1)	25.1 (2)	7.3 (4)	19.8	6.4 (5)	12.4 (3)	0.0 (7)	1.0 (6)
1995	45.2 (1)	16.7 (3)	5.5 (5)	32.5	7.5 (4)	24.0 (2)	0.3 (7)	0.7 (6)

Note: Figures are based on new investment in the year.

Sources: Ryutaro Komiya, *The Japanese Economy: Trade, Industry, and Government* (Tokyo: University of Tokyo Press, 1993), p. 123 for 1960 figures (total of 51-61); Kotaro Horisaka, "Japan's Economic Relations with Latin America," in Barbara Stallings and Gabriel Székely (eds.), *Japan, the United States, and Latin America: Toward a Trilateral Relationship in the Western Hemisphere* (Baltimore: Johns Hopkins University Press, 1993), p. 55 for figures during 1965-90; The Ministry of Finance, Japan, http://www.mof.go.jp/fdi/1c000a2.htm, for 1995 figures.

regarded other developing countries as competitors whose catch-up industries might threaten Japan. MITI regarded the appearance of catch-ups as the "dilemma of foreign aid" and proposed providing government support to domestic sectors, such as infant industries, SME companies and agriculture, which were challenged by competition from developing countries.[34]

As Japan became capital rich, FDI flowed toward industrialized countries in both North America and Europe. The Foreign Exchange and Control Law of 1949 was substantially relaxed in 1972, leaving Japan's capital outflows almost unrestricted. With official backing from Foreign Investment Insurance since 1970, revision of tax provisions for investment losses, and the Export-Import Bank's financial support, total overseas investment during the four years of 1973-76 was nearly double that of the preceding twenty years.[35] After the 1970s, MITI no longer regarded economic cooperation as threatening, but accepted it as a means of encouraging domestic industrial structures to pursue higher positions in the international division of labor.[36] The attitude change was further confirmed during the era of oil crises. A MITI official noted that "[The basic idea] behind our resource diplomacy is to meet people and make thing work. . . [Japan] has the technology, the capital and human resources to make us increasingly indispensable to developing countries who need our help" [*Far Eastern Economic Review* 28 September 1979, 64]. As Japan's industrial structure became sophisticated, the volume of FDI in technologically advanced, industrialized countries rocketed to around $50 billion in the late 1980s. In contrast, the share of developing countries shrank from 53 percent to 24 percent between 1980 and 1991. Together the United States and Europe claimed 61 percent of cumulative Japanese FDI during the four decades between 1951 and 1991 [*Intereconomics* May/June 1993, 124; Abegglen 1994, 212].

While the United States has consistently dominated Japanese FDI, European countries, especially Germany, have become increasingly important. Until the early 1970s, Japanese FDI in Europe was concentrated in efforts to raise funds in the less regulated Euro-dollar markets and increase exports from Japan into the region. Beginning in the 1970s, and especially after the yen's climb in the 1980s, Europe's relatively low wage rates and rapidly integrating market attracted Japanese investment in manufacturing, especially in England. Since the late 1980s, Germany has become a major recipient of Japanese investment, after England and the Netherlands. During 1988-90, investment in Germany tripled, from $400 million to $1,200 million. The joint venture agreement between Mitsubishi group and Daimler Benz in 1990 symbolized the increasing importance of Germany to Japanese business in the post-Cold War era. In the 1990s, Japanese firms concentrated their investment in Germany in high-tech research and development.[37]

Sectorally, Japanese FDI in services, such as banking, flags of convenience, commerce, real estate, and research and development (R&D), has grown 28 percent between 1976 and 1990, much faster than investment in the primary sector, 10 percent, or the secondary sector, 21 percent. In 1991, the service sector accounted for 67 percent of Japan's FDI, while services made up 59 percent of Germany's FDI and 47 percent of the United States'. The high-tech and information sectors have become primary targets of Japanese FDI in industrialized countries [UNCTC 1985, 76, 83; UNCTC 1987, 26; UNCTAD 1992, 18; Doner 1993, 169].

In Asia, Japanese FDI has been redirected toward manufacturing. This intra-regional FDI has further adjusted to ongoing global restructuring by shifting production sites in accordance with variations in relative degree of industrial advancement. Manufacturing FDI concentrated in NIEs during 1985-87, moved to ASEAN countries after 1988, and in 1995, China became the largest Asian recipient [JETRO 1997, 26-27]. Japanese FDI in ASEAN manufacturing sectors skyrocketed in the late 1980s, and investment between 1985 and 1989 was reported to be more than twice the total invested from 1951 to 1985 [*Far Eastern Economic Review* 20 December 1990, 48-49].

The sectoral shift of investment corresponded to the geographical transition. Since the 1970s, Japanese investment in manufacturing machine tools in Asian NIEs has increased continuously, while funds to labor-intensive industrial sectors, like textiles, have been moving from NIEs to ASEAN and to China. In the mid-1980s, in Taiwan and Singapore, machine manufacturing absorbed about 50 percent of Japanese FDI, almost parallel to the pattern in the United States [Kojima 1989, 33-35]. Since the 1990s, labor-intensive manufacturing has started to shift to China, with massive FDI by Japanese SMEs. Japanese SMEs first focused their investment in Asia on machinery but in the 1990s they moved to textiles, especially in China, which claimed about half of their total investment [Maruyama and Narita 1995, 140-43]. Japanese businesspeople moved to Asia with their capital. In 1990, 50,000 Japanese were long term residents in Asia, while 95,000 lived in North America, and 55,000, in Western Europe. Six years later, the Asian figure had doubled, to 100,000, approaching the 110,000 in North America, and far surpassing Europe's 55,000 [Gaimusho 1991a, 14; 1997a, 14]. However, it should be noted that Japanese FDI in Asian manufacturing constitutes only a small part of Japan's global investment. For example, even the big push of Japanese FDI to ASEAN countries in the late 1980s accounted for less than 10 percent of total FDI, and China, Asian NIEs, and ASEAN together claimed only one-third of Japanese manufacturing FDI in the early 1990s [Kan 1994, 29].

The pattern of the balance of payments also traces the trajectory of the Japanese global-scope FDI. From the mid-1960s to the early 1980s, Japan ran a surplus with the United States and Europe in both trade and long-term capital accounts, and it recycled the surplus to developing counties as capital exports. In 1983, Japan started recycling the trade surplus as long-term capital to the United States and Europe as well as to developing countries. From 1986, Japan started to record trade surpluses with developing countries, and, as a result, Japan's long-term capital outflows expanded. During the decade after 1980, when capital outflows were completely liberalized, the cumulative deficit of the basic account (current account plus long-term capital flows) amounted to $220 billion. Japan's role as an international financial mediator that recycles current account surpluses as long-term capital outflows to the world has remained unchanged since even after the domestic economy began to stagnate in the 1990s [Tanaka 1989, 132; Nihon Ginko 1996, 15].

Fragmented anecdotal evidence and interview data suggest that the global and dynamic orientation of Japanese interdependence has solidified in the 1990s. For example, Mitsubishi Corporation, one of the largest Japanese trading firms, transferred staff from London and New York to regional departments in charge of China and other areas in Asia in order to design business strategies "on a globe." In the mid-1990s, almost all the presidents of major Japanese trading companies had served as presidents of their American subsidiaries [*Asahi Shimbun* 15 February 1995, satellite 13th ed., 12; *Nihon Keizai Shimbun* 20 May 1998, evening 3rd ed, 5]. The Japan International Development Organization (JAIDO), a semi-public FDI project company funded by *Keidanren* (industry trade groups) initiatives in 1989, has carefully avoided any concentration of projects in Asia. As of May 1993, there were only 8 projects in Asia, 13 in Central and South Africa, 10 in the Middle East and Africa, and 12 in Europe [JAIDO, *Projects under Consideration, May 1993.* Interviews, Nos. 9, 12, 24, Tokyo, 24 June 1993, 12, 29 March 1994]. In the wake of the regional financial crisis of 1997, Japanese multinational manufactures, especially auto makers, have started to shift their strategies in a more global direction to capitalize on the devaluation of currencies. Honda's President said, "We're in the process of looking for new markets for our Asian-made cars all over the world." Toyota is also preparing to export its Thai-made cars to markets such as Australia and New Zealand (which used to buy directly from Japan), Africa, South America, the Middle East, and the Indian subcontinent [Shuchman 1998, 1, 24].

It has been commonly argued that the Japanese economy entered the age of FDI after the Plaza Accord of 1985, and that the massive FDI in manufacturing in Asia, which was pushed by the high-powered Japanese yen during the late 1980s and early 1990s, is now creating a Japan-centered production alliance in Asia. However, Japanese FDI has been globally trade-oriented since the 1950s, and has changed in response to changes in Japan's own industrial structure.

Technology. Japan's hesitation to transfer technology to Asian countries has often been interpreted as a reflection of the state's pursuit of technological autonomy and national security.[38] In the context of global-scope interdependence, however, technological autonomy connotes something other than autarky. Technology autonomy, in the Japanese sense, involves finding the "right" partners and buying, selling, or transferring "appropriate" technologies, depending on the partner country's industrial sophistication. Hence, Japanese technology trade has been extremely malleable. As U.S. technology exports to Japan have turned technology dependence into interdependence, Asian countries have also become less dependent in the wake of increasing technology exports from Japan to Asia.

As Table 2.4 shows, the scope of Japan's technology interdependence has been global. Thus, while Japan's exports to Asia have grown rapidly, Japan's long-term reliance on the United States seems unready to disappear. Royalty payments for American licensed technology were three times receipts in 1987. The technology trade deficit with the United States stood at about $1 billion even in the 1990s. This is why, while Japan has sold more technology than it imported since the early 1970s, the overall balance of technology-related payments did not run in the black until 1993. Of total Japanese R&D expenditures, 55 percent was spent in the United States in 1990, 21 percent in Europe, and 9 percent in Asia. In contrast, Japanese technology exports to Asian countries have been growing, claiming almost half of Japan's total technology exports. Technology exports to developing countries are characteristic of Japanese trade. Developing countries paid around 60 percent of Japan's royalties in 1980, while, Germany received less than 10 percent of royalties from that source, and the United States, about 20 percent [UNCTC 1988, 177; OECD 1989, 9, 11; Borthwick 1992, 515; *The Economist* 22 May 1993, 91; Odagiri and Goto 1996, 105; Kagaku Gijyutsucho 1997, 466-67].

In short, in the field of technology, Japanese dependence on America and Asian dependence on Japan have been interwoven in a complex way so that the dyadic vulnerabilities that stem from technology dependence become less effective, and dependence is transformed into interdependence. This political mechanism becomes clearer, when we examine the international extension of Japanese domestic processes of industrial production.

Inter-Firm Complex Networks in Japan and Asia

Just as the institutional structure of states and economies affect long-term macro-economic performance, the organizational performances of firms are strongly influenced by their social and historical contexts.[39] Japanese social contexts have set fundamental rules for industrial production that nurture flexibility in adjusting to external changes. The domestic contexts in which production networks are embedded look little different from the pattern of international interdependence. The scope of interdependence among firms with different functions is enormous, and in most cases there exists no centralized authority to organize the processes of industrial production. Decentralization, complexity, and broad interdependence have been accepted as socio-economic norms needed to make the economy competitive, and in particular, to make industrial production more efficient.

Inter-Firm Networks in Japan

Japanese production networks involve inter-organizational arrangements that govern relational processes in which firms compete and cooperate.[40] This conception of domestic production networks as conveyers of social exchanges, rather than market-based, individual exchanges, makes production networks look much less like hierarchies. Yasusuke Murakami and Thomas Rohlen's analysis of Japanese *keiretsu* networks emphasizes reciprocity and mutual benefit by noting that "subcontractors and parent firms share the burden of risk in three key areas—employment, financing, and the development of new technology indifferent proportions. This is clearly an exchange of unspecifiables, or a social exchange by our definition" [1992, 98].

The structural gap between big and small firms in terms of profitability, productivity, and wages, narrowed after the 1950s.[41] More importantly, the proportion of suppliers dependent on a sole customer has declined, especially since the early 1970s. As of 1987, only 17 percent of SME subcontractors sold exclusively to one buyer, while 26 percent traded with three to five firms, and 22 percent, more than ten firms [Sako 1991, 459].[42] If Japanese parent firms wanted to exploit *keiretsu* relations, they should have internalized the subcontracting firms, instead they have allowed them to expand their business outside the *keiretsu* circle.

The contextual, social processes of interdependence are most distinctive in modes of production where variable parts made by a large number of SMEs are integrated by a core firm through complex inter-firm networks that extend only within a specific industry. Functional specialization by big Japanese firms is distinctive, but often overlooked. As Fruin explains:

> In contrast to comparable Western companies, Japanese firms are not widely diversified and corporate conglomerates are a rarity . . . Only 35-40 percent of Japan's largest industrial firms (far fewer in the pre-war period) produce in two or more distinct market segments, and half of

Table 2.4
Japanese Technology Trade
% and (Y billion)

Export	1960	1965	1970	1975	1980	1985	1990	1995
Asia			26	39.2 (54)	34.0 (54)	37.4 (86)	45.2 (153)	50.0 (281)
Korea				7.1	3.3	7.8	13.7	11.5
Taiwan				4.4	6.2	3.4	4.6	7.9
Singapore					5.1	2.6	5.5	5.1
Thailand					2.6	2.7	7.3	8.2
Indonesia				7.2	4.8	4.0	5.8	3.8
China					12.2	14.6	2.0	3.2
North America			23	21.4 (14)	18.5 (30)	25.1 (59)	31.9 (108)	30.8 (173)
Europe			30	21.1 (14)	18.2 (29)	19.4 (45)	18.1 (61)	16.9 (94)
Others			21	18.3	29.4	18.1	4.9	2.5
Total			100	100 (67)	100 (106)	100 (234)	100 (339)	100 (562)

Table 2.4 (continued)
Japanese Technology Trade
% and (Y billion)

Import	1960	1965	1970	1975	1980	1985	1990	1995
North America	61.2	56.2	56	63.6 (108)	65.5 (157)	71.7 (210)	69.3 (258)	71.3 (279)
Europe	29	37.6	35	35.4 (60)	34.3 (82)	27.8 (82)	30.3 (113)	28.0 (110)
Others	9.8	6.2	9	1	0.2	0.5	0.3	0.68
Total	100	100	100	100 (170)	100 (240)	100 (293)	100 (372)	100 (392)

Notes: The figures between 1960 and 70 are calculated based upon number of cases; others, upon payment related to technology trade.

Sources: Kagaku Gijyutsucho (Science and Technology Agency), Kagaku Gijyutsu Hakusho [White Paper on Science and Technology] (Tokyo: Okurasho Insatsukyoku), 1980, pp.165, 175; 1974, p.287; 1977, pp.310-311; 1988, pp.454-55; 1997, pp.466-67.

this diversification effort is full-line diversification as opposed to new-product diversification. This is at least 50 percent lower than leading American and European industrials [1992, 22].[43]

Within a specialized industrial segment, inter-firm networks among SMEs integrate thousands of parts. SMEs are unusually dominant in Japan. Self-employed workers and unpaid family workers (in such industries as manufacturing, agriculture, and retailing) constitute a far larger proportion of the labor force in Japan (29 percent) than in Germany (14 percent) or the United States (9 percent). In Japanese manufacturing almost half of the labor force works for firms with fewer than 50 employees. Hence the number of Japanese manufacturing firms, which was about 600,000 in the late 1980s, far exceeded that of Germany, 340,000, or the United States, 290,000. More importantly, 80 percent of Japanese subcontractors have no equity participation from their parent companies [Patrick and Rohlen 1987, 335-36; Kiyonari, Tanaka, and Minato 1996, 32-33, 52-53].

Japanese automobile industries, for example, procure about 70-80 percent of all components from subcontracting production networks, while their American counterparts internalize parts production under in-house operations, and make 50 to 60 percent of necessary parts [Aoki and Okuno-Fujiwara 1996, 156]. The processes of procurement involve complex strategies that include both direct and recurrent dealings with a few largest suppliers and indirect and distant procurement from thousands of SMEs [Fruin 1992, 268-73]. Large Japanese firms view direct dealings with a relatively small number of firms as a means of improving the quality of parts. The suppliers that belong to this higher tier in the subcontracting hierarchy are expected to compete more vigorously than they would in a free market. Limiting the number of such firms makes it possible for rival companies to have face-to-face contacts with each other and with the core firm, and to increase information-sharing about new technologies and innovations developed by competitors or required by the core firm. Peer pressure and incentives from the parent firm encourage companies to catch up with the leaders and strive to maintain long-term, stable contracts with the parent firm. Also the small number transaction enables the core firm to monitor contract execution. Such competition within a small group of major contractors is termed "visible-hand competition (*mieru te no kyoso*)" [Itami 1988] or "face-to-face competition (*kao no mieru kyoso*)" [Ito 1989]. To win the quality race, suppliers are required to accumulate what Banri Asanuma calls the "relation-specific skills" to respond efficiently to the specific needs of the core firm through repeated transactions [1989]. Learning through long-term, social interactions is the norm in the Japanese production system. Fruin succinctly summarizes:

Japanese industrial companies are inclined to have a focused set of core technologies while less closely related technologies are delegated to outside, affiliated firms (interfirm networks). To the extent that firms maintain this focus, the need for elaborate portfolio and strategic planning exercises diminishes. Instead of trying to allocate capital efficiently among scores and perhaps hundreds of different divisions (the American multi-divisional model), Japanese companies concern themselves with several to perhaps a half-dozen core business [Fruin 1992, 201].

For the thousands of small suppliers and affiliates engaged in indirect and distant dealings with the core assemblers, membership in a *keiretsu* provides a chance to acquire knowledge and expertise from high-ranked companies in the *keiretsu* as well as from the core firm. Since supplier networks are so wide and complex, quality control hardly reaches the bottom-end small suppliers, of which, for example, there are more than 40,000 under the Toyota Corporation. In order for all these SMEs to supply reliable parts with marginal defect rates, the leading companies of each hierarchy and the core firms must transfer skills and technologies to the SMEs. This technology transfer produces know-whys, rather than know-hows, and makes each supplier understand how serious the consequences can be if even a small defect remains unsolved.[44] Hence, during the post-war period, many suppliers once dependent on a parent firm have succeeded in nurturing domestic technology and became interdependent. Or many formerly independent firms have joined the supplier association of a *keiretsu* and become interdependent [Fruin 1992, 277-88].

In sum, the final assembler, though it stands at the apex of the Japanese supplier system, has little direct control over huge numbers of its suppliers; companies at each tier of the structure are responsible for transferring the contextual skills to subordinate members of the association group. Flexible adjustments by Japanese manufactures to changing external environments, therefore, are a function of a balanced combination of a large firm's authority and centralized control with the autonomy and decentralized coordination of many small firms.[45]

Before we move to the overseas extension of *keiretsu*, it should be noted that Japan's networking production system seems not so much a product of strategic planning by the state or big firms as an legacy of the postwar Japanese economy.[46] The outsourcing strategies of Japanese firms emerged in the 1930s, when *zaibatsu* enterprises had to rely on SMEs to satisfy the burgeoning national demand for military supplies. The subcontracting relations revived in the early 1950s, when the so-called Special Procurement from the American army during the Korean War required Japanese industrial expansion and re-launched outsourcing. After occupation policy dissolved the *zaibatsu*, Japanese firms lacked the financial resources to internalize factories that supplied parts and machinery. Instead, the domestic labor market and industrial relations through the late 1940s to the 1950s provided favorable conditions for the big firms to impose low-wage and long-overtime work on small subcontractors. While unemployment increased, unionized labor in big firms responded to the new wave of democracy by becoming militant and hostile and opposing management attempts to expand production lines. The SMEs absorbed the unemployed and started to make parts for big assemblers. Under these circumstances, technology transfer from the big firms to capital-poor but labor-rich subcontractors constituted a fundamental condition for realizing the high quality manufacturing needed to produce goods marketable to American buyers.

Inter-Firm Networks Overseas

When the Japanese invest directly abroad, their interdependent, inter-firm production networks also cross the sea. In order to spread economic and political risks to local partners and Japanese subsidiaries, Japanese investors favor joint ventures and minority affiliates, rather than majority or wholly owned subsidiaries.[47]

While Japanese manufacturers investing in America and Europe are inclined to transplant an entire level of the division of labor, they still leave the process open to local firms and consolidate interdependent partnerships with them as well as with Japanese suppliers. For example in the United States, more than 300 Japanese or Japanese-U.S. joint automotive parts suppliers were established to support large assemblers, such as Toyota, Honda, Nissan. Like a *keiretsu* in Japan, Toyota, for example, created a Japanese-style supplier federation (*kyoryokukai*) called the Bluegrass Automotive Manufacturers Association. Far from excluding American suppliers, Toyota has worked to include them. Seventy-five percent of the 174 domestic suppliers to Toyota's Georgetown, Kentucky, plant are long-standing U.S. companies. Honda also has extensive programs to develop its U.S. supplier base. A guest engineer program sends engineers from American suppliers to Japan, and a loaned executive program puts Honda executives in American companies to help overcome difficulties and integrate the suppliers into the Honda system. Consequently, some American parts suppliers have started complementing Japanese manufacturing processes by conducting their own product development and R&D [Kenney and Florida 1993, 126-54].[48] Although the evidence is still quite limited, interdependency among functionally different firms seems to be creating a social context overseas.

Following their experiences in America and Europe, Japanese production networks have been expanding in Asia since the mid-1980s. It is true that the Japanese transplants in Asia import vast amount of parts and capital goods from Japan, contributing to the chronic bilateral trade imbalance between Japan and Asia.[49] However, as occurred in the United States, Japanese transplants in Asia have been increasing procurement from local small firms as well as from Western multinationals and overseas Chinese businesses since the late 1980s.[50] Despite less restrictive local content rules in Asia than in America and Europe, the share of total procurement by Japanese firms supplied by local manufactures in Asia rose from 23 percent in 1988 to 33 percent in 1993, while the equivalent figures were 18 and 27 percent in North America, and 12 and 38 percent in Europe. Japanese automobile companies in ASEAN procured about 30 to 40 percent of all necessary parts from local, ASEAN suppliers, more than the 20 to 35 percent purchased from transplanted Japanese subsidiaries [Koshiba 1997, 97-98, 106-8]. An equivalent level of purchasing from local-in-origin companies (about 40 percent), was realized in the Japanese electronics industries in Asia [Takada 1994, 29-31].

Technology transfer from Japanese firms to local Asian firms has been selective, depending on the degree of industrial sophistication of each country. Japanese FDI in Asia started among the NIEs, and involved transplanting both Japanese suppliers and assemblers. Then, as Japanese investment shifted to the ASEAN countries, so did the pattern of production. The big firms expected their subsidiaries to nurture local supporting industries and establish a technological base for future spin-offs.[51] The productivity differentials between Japanese and ASEAN suppliers were conspicuous (by a factor of three to four), although both used the same Japanese-made machinery. Technology transfers were unavoidable, if the Japanese were to continue to invest in the ASEAN countries. Detailed on-site research showed that the difference lay in worker flexibility (*jukuren*), which enabled employees to be rotated across positions, in response to accidents or changes in demand [Koike and Inoki 1987]. Thus, MITI stated, in an official publication concerning economic cooperation between Japan and ASEAN, "To summarize the current technological level of the ASEAN countries, although mass production technology is being absorbed and assimilated, sufficient quality levels have not been achieved. In the areas of technology improvement, design and product development, progress has only just begun" [Tsusho Sangyosho 1993a, 112].

To transfer necessary skills and technologies to Asia, Japanese companies tend to use R&D funds to build facilities in support of local production and dispatch Japanese experts to local firms. Although such expenditures were a minimal part of R&D, the number of such facilities in Asia was huge. There were as many as 81 in 1990, close to the 95 in the United States but far exceeding the 25 in Europe [Odagiri and Goto 1996, 105-6]. Such transfers of know-why and relational skills from Japanese experts seems to compensate for the fact that Japanese R&D expenditures in Asia so much lower than those in industrialized countries. Japanese companies have sent a remarkable number of Japanese employees to such support facilities, especially in ASEAN countries: Thailand hosted 2,263 in 1994, and Malaysia, 1,765, more than Singapore, with 1,220, or Korea, with 365 [Chin and Hayashi 1995, 67]. Government aid has also encouraged private technology transfer. So-called "two-step loans" are provided to ASEAN public financial institutions, which then re-lend to promising local companies. This is similar to the mechanism inside Japan in which the Japan Development Bank and other semi-governmental financial organizations borrow funds from the government and inject the money into Japanese SMEs. The government, especially MITI, has urged increased flexibility in lending to small Asian firms that demonstrate a high potential for technological innovation.[52]

Since the late 1980s, technological advances in Asian NIEs have been remarkable, but much of their progress is attributable to the strategies of East Asian countries themselves. They upgraded their technologies first by receiving technical assistance from foreign multinationals, then by establishing joint ventures with them and becoming original equipment manufacture (OEM) suppliers, and now in the 1990s by creating own-design manufacture (ODM) and own-brand manufacture (OBM) skills [Hobday 1995]. They are no longer as dependent on Japanese technologies as they were in the 1970s. From 1980 to 1993, the number of industrial patent acquisitions registered in the United States by Taiwanese companies increased from 61 to 1189, which exceeded the 1126 registered by the Swiss in the same year. Similarly, registrations by Korean companies rose from 8 to 779, which was close to the Netherlands' 801 [Chin and Hayashi 1995, 2].

In sum, the international efficiency and competitiveness of Japanese firms cannot be freed from the interdependent contexts in which core firms are firmly linked to functionally different SMEs through networking. In Japanese terms, technologies should be transferred from the core to subsidiaries in social contexts that determine the content and timing of transfers and the order of recipients. Hatch and Yamamura correctly point out that Japanese firms, with the help of government vision, have succeeded in nurturing the ability of local producers to adopt sophisticated technology, reduce the cost of production, and enhance their own competitiveness in world markets. They call such efficiency "dynamic technological efficiency," and argue that the pace of technology transfer from Japan to Asia has been dependent on structural change in Japanese industries [Hatch and Yamamura 1996, xii-xiii, 31, 53]. However, what really enhances Japan's efficiency is not hierarchical integration but liberal interdependency among firms, whether they are Japanese or other owned by other Asians. As MITI's official position notes, "restructuring and international specialization are important for Japan not only in terms of international cooperation and contribution to the economic development of developing countries but also in terms of maintaining and strengthening the international competitiveness of the Japanese industry in the medium to long term through capitalizing on the excellent production factors in Asia" [1993b, 146]. At this point, interdependency and dependency converge in the Japanese political economy.

Conclusion

Students of international relations are accustomed to hearing two standardized couplings: one between hierarchical structure (asymmetrical interdependence, or dependency) and national power and competitiveness, and the other between horizontal exchanges (symmetrical interdependence, or interdependency) and collective interests and cooperation. This chapter has offered a new, but odd, linkage between interdependency and national power: national power that arises from interdependency. Unlike structure-driven power, this horizontally derived version cannot be materialized due to constraints imposed by the interdependency. The political consequence of those sociological constraints is what I mean by systemic vulnerability.

The primary puzzle of this chapter has been the Japanese state's preference for open regionalism, despite its dominance in Asia. Recent structural change in Asia was supposed to incline Japan toward the creation of a more exclusive regional economic bloc, and away from open regionalism. The decreasing dependence of Asian (including Japanese) economies on the American market, the increasing intra-regional trade and investment among East Asia, ASEAN, and China, the widening income gap between Japan and the rest of Asia, and the spread of *keiretsu* networks in the region all seem to offer opportunities for the revival of the Japan-centered regionalism of the 1930s. Only examination of the social contexts of Japanese interdependence offers an understanding of the political source of Asian open regionalism. Relying on theories of international interdependence and organizational networks, I have argued that Japan's choice of openness in the regional order has been shaped by a sociological context consisting of an interdependency that realizes national competitiveness. Such interdependency can be identified both at international and domestic levels. Japan's global-scope interdependence, which includes both industrialized and developing countries and Japanese domestic production networks consisting of functionally different firms, causes the Japanese state to opt for openness in preference to exclusive and hierarchical integration. The political power that Japan derives from asymmetrical interdependence with its Asian neighbors in trade, finance, and technology, would be substantially enhanced by the creation of a regional bloc, but is, in fact, constrained by the context of interdependence.

Seeing Japan within the context of interdependency should be distinguished from examining the state from the perspective of conventional social liberalism. In Japanese terms, interdependency can be read as a language of realism. This ambiguous liberalism can be identified in Japanese diplomacy in general. For example, in the North-South dialogues, Japan has been a stubborn advocate of flexibility, conciliation, and pragmatism, while the international liberalism of Western industrialized countries and the economic nationalism of developing countries have collided. Japan's pragmatic liberalism was especially prominent in the discussions of the New International Economic Order (NIEO) [Fukai 1982]. While Japan opposed almost all proposals for the NIEO, and eagerly supported a solution to North-South problems within existing international regimes, it attempted to establish escape clauses on a case-by-case basis for each developing country. As areas of governance by international regimes expand beyond conventional transnational transactions, such as capital and commodities flows, toward new areas like services, technologies, intellectual property rights, immigration, and ecology, Japan's pragmatic liberalism becomes more remarkable. Japan's reluctance, along with developing countries, to support international human right regimes, illustrates this point. While by the mid-1990s Japan had been selected 7 times (Germany, only twice) to a non-permanent seat on the U.N. Security Council, it ratified only 7 out of 25 human right treaties approved in the U.N. General Assembly, fewer than any other state (Germany has ratified 19 out of 25) [Kawabe 1994, 41 and 183-85]. If existing international regimes are designed to realize what John Ruggie calls embedded liberalism, which creates a compromise between international economic liberalism and domestic social welfare [1983], they do not fit the Japanese political economy. What the Japanese wish to see institutionalized is a comfortable coupling of international economic liberalism and what Chalmers Johnson terms developmentalism [1982].

In the 1990s, the Japanese polity and economy have been faced with evidence that the loop connecting interdependency and national power has been coming untied and that systemic vulnerability has prevailed over national power. The Japanese media call the political malfunction "institutional fatigue (*seido hiro*)," which became most evident in the Japanese financial system in the wake of the bubble economy. The so-called convoy system (*goso sendan hoshiki*), in which Japanese banks were supposed to be protected from failure because of their role at a center of economic interdependency, has been on the verge of collapse since the mid-1990s. The systemic vulnerability became evident in a non-economic area, when, following the Hanshin-Awaji Earthquake of 1995, which killed more than 6,000 people, the dense networks through which the Japanese are organized failed to effectively deliver aid to damaged areas [Kato 1998]. The Asian economic crisis of 1997 also made some Japanese realize that interdependence would no longer work in Asia and that only a narrower and deeper regional integration would help solidify the regional order.

As the call for systemic reform increases inside Japan, will open regionalism in Asia also be reconsidered? Probably not. The strategy of interdependency has been and will continue to be firmly embedded in the Japanese political economy, because interdependence has been the source of Japan's national power. International cooperation, national security, and regional integration have always constituted the essential ingredients of open regionalism, and Japanese policy-makers and business elites have never regarded trade in Asia or any other region as a substitute for an open order of global dimensions.[53] Only a combination of big words like "historically, geographically, politically, and economically" made sense of Japan's close relations with Asian countries [Gaimusho 1988b, 340; Japanese Government, 1992; Interview, No. 2, 1 June 1993, Tokyo]. China is said to be the country most likely to modify the interdependent context in Asia. However, China will not be ready, technologically or financially, to replace the United States and other industrialized countries in the Japanese interdependency for decades. Systemic vulnerability has been, and will be, hard to overcome for the networking state, as long as that state creates power by squaring the circle between hierarchy and openness.

NOTES

I am very grateful to insightful and critical comments from Natasha Hamilton-Hart, Peter Katzenstein, and two anonymous readers for the East Asia Program, Cornell University, on earlier drafts of this chapter. Also I owe a great debt to Sumio Hatano, Hiroyuki Odagiri, Kunihiro Ohishi, Hiroki Toya and Tadashi Yamada for their bibliographical information. This research was made possible in part by a grant of the Nippon Foundation to Peter Katzenstein.

1. It is not correct to argue that Japan made these commitments because it was the industrialized country most affected by strong trade and financial linkages with Asian countries. For example, Japanese and European banks' outstanding loans to the five countries most affected by the financial turmoil, that is, Indonesia, Korea, Malaysia, the Philippines, and Thailand, stood at the same level, about $100 billion, at the end of June 1997 [*The Economist* 4 April 1998, 30].

2. Watanabe, Kajiwara, and Takanaka 1991, 2; Clone 1993; Petri 1993.

3. Yamazawa and Hirata, eds. 1990, 98, 104-105; Yamamoto 1989, 176.

4. A similar discussion can be found in Watanabe 1990, 4-30, 48-56.

5. Seki 1993; 1997, 167-201; Hatch and Yamamura 1996, 56-57, 67-72, chap. 10; Katzenstein 1997b.

6. For a comprehensive analysis of Japanese *keiretsu*, see Gerlach 1992.

7. See Nakamura 1981, 171-93 for a summary of the dual structure argument.

8. For a thorough review, see Katzenstein 1997a, 12-22.

9. For example, Tsusho Sangyosho 1992a, 172; Gaimusho 1990b, 316; 1992b, 404-05.

10. Systemic vulnerability also differs from the sensitivity associated with liberal "complex interdependence" [Keohane and Nye 1989, 23-25, 254-57]. In the former, the state's sensitivity continues as long as the state is involved in international exchanges, but the nature of those exchanges do not affect the structure of power at all.

11. I use the term "scope" differently than does Alfred Chandler, who defines it as a variety of production and distribution activities carried out by a single firm [1990]. A discussion of scope that is similar to mine can be found in Stopford and Strange 1991, especially 77-78.

12. See Milner 1988 and Webb 1995 for important works in this line.

13. In the same vein, an anthropological analysis of Japanese inter-personal relations attributes the stable Japanese social order to hierarchical networks among Japanese groups and [Nakane 1970].

14. Ruigrok and van Tulder 1995, especially 154-74; Hatch and Yamamura 1996; Katzenstein 1997b and in this volume; Orr, Biggart, and Hamilton 1997.

15. Hatch and Yamamura 1996, chap. 3, especially 47-48.

16. As seminal works in this line, see Dore 1973, 1986.

17. Dore 1983; Sako 1991; North 1990, 1992; Denzau and North 1994.

18. Aoki 1988; Asanuma 1989; Clark and Fujimoto 1991; Nishiguchi 1994.

19. Williamson 1985, especially, 90-95; Aoki 1988.

20. Especially see Hamilton and Feenstra 1997.

21. Katzenstein 1978, especially 315-16; Pempel 1982; Dore 1986; Samuels 1987; Okimoto 1988 and 1989; Upham 1989; van Wolferen 1990; Kumon 1993; Tsujinaka 1993.

22. This argument is applied to Japanese foreign aid policy in Kato 1996.

23. Akamatsu 1965, chap. 10; Watanabe 1990; Watanabe et al. 1991, chapters 2 and 3 and 179-80.

24. Cohen 1974; Dower 1979, 415-27; Borden 1984; Cumings 1987, 44-83; 1993, 39-40; Rotter 987, especially 5-7, 38-44, 138-39, 166-84; Ikenberry 1989.

25. This part of my argument relies on Dower 1979, 312 and Borden 1984, 214.

26. Borden 1984, 170-71, 179-80; Komiya and Ito 1988, 178-79; Akaneya 1992.

27. The first war reparations treaty was concluded with Burma in 1954 and included a statement that Japan would cooperate with Burma in order to achieve the recovery and development of the Burmese economy and enhance the social welfare of the country. From the Japanese point of view, this was investment. Bilateral reparations payments to Asian countries continued for more than twenty years, until 1981, and totaled Y540 billion ($1.5 billion) [Baisho Mondai Ken-

kyukai 1963; Kajima Heiwa Kenkyujo 1973, vol. 11, 37; Takagi 1995, 11].

28. Yano 1975; A. Watanabe 1987; Igusa 1991.

29. Dower 1979, 451-57, 476-485; Rotter 1987, 30, 42-45; Yoshikawa 1991.

30. Kishi 1983, 85-88, 114-117; Hara 1995, 189-90; Shiraishi 1997, 176-79.

31. Hosoya 1989, 30-31; Tanaka 1991, 55-60; Soeya 1995, 110-11, 158-59, 168-73.

32. Multilateral economic assistance from Japan to Asia began on a limited scale in 1952, when Japan contributed $80,000 to the United Nations Expanded Program of Technical Assistance (UNEPTA), a predecessor of the United Nations Development Program (UNDP).

33. Yoshihara 1978; Ozawa 1979; Sekiguchi 1983; Kojima 1985; Tsusho Sangyosho 1993b, 116-37. To understand the trade-FDI linkage, we should understand Japanese industrial policies that are designed to create comparative advantage strategically (competitive advantage). Under the "sophistication strategy" Japan has sought to target industries able to attain higher income elasticity and then to increase exports from those new industries. To bring about such sophistication, the government liberalized international trade in the 1960s for industrial sectors that had attained a competitive advantage. At the same time, it delayed capital liberalization until the early 1970s, giving new industries time to mature. As is well known, results from such governmental guidance cannot be guaranteed. While state intervention was successful in iron and steel, automobiles, and computer hardware, it failed in petrochemicals, aircraft, and space.

34. Tsusho Sangyosho 1964a, 42; 1968a, 141; 1969a, 105.

35. For a good summary of Japanese FDI history, see Komiya and Wakasugi 1991, 50-53; and Pempel 1993, 116.

36. Tsusho Sangyosho 1971a, 125; 1977a, 174; 1978a, 89.

37. Thomsen and Nicolaides 1991; Sekiguchi 1982, 162-72; Japan External Trade Organization 1997, 259-60.

38. Fallows 1994, 91-108; Hatch and Yamamura 1996, chap. 6; Katzenstein 1997b.

39. See, inter alia, Granovetter 1985; and Katzenstein 1985; North 1990.

40. Fruin 1992, especially 13 and 23.

41. Friedman 1988, 128-161; Nakamura 1992, 1-78.

42. Hatch and Yamamura's data is less convincing. Japanese suppliers' asset specificity (the amount of investment dedicated to primary customers) at 22 percent, was very close to that of their American counterparts, at 15 percent [Hatch and Yamamura 1996, 47, 59, 194].

43. Full-line diversification is a strategy of offering a complete range of goods and services in one or a few related lines of products.

44. Kenney and Florida 1993, especially 44-48; Fruin 1992 270-73.

45. This discussion relies on Piore and Sabel 1984, 224; and Fruin 1992, 272.

46. For a good summary, see Sako 1991, 457-58.

47. This argument was originally made by Franko 1978, 121. Dennis Encarnation claimed that patterns of ownership that distinguished American from Japanese subsidiaries withered away in the 1980s if ownership is measured using sales amounts instead of the actual amount of investment, which was the basis of Franko's argument [1992, pp. 12-14].

48. Japanese electronics companies, unlike the automobile industry, have not yet succeeded in transferring the Japanese model, [Kenney and Florida 1993, 218-53]. It should also be noted that the consequences of rooting the Japanese labor management system on local soil have been mixed. Whereas local white-collar workers expressed dissatisfaction about the lack of delegation of authority from Japanese headquarters and the tendency to appoint Japanese staff to high management positions, local blue-collar workers working for Japanese factories welcomed the "administrative networks" based upon human management [Odagiri 1992, 317-22; Lifson 1993, 240-47; Abo 1994].

49. However, Asian countries' exports of manufactured goods to Japan claimed about 40 percent of total manufactured imports in the mid-1990s. The figure surpassed the American share, 25 percent, and the EU's 22 percent [Tsusho Sangyosho 1995b, 260].

50. For example, T. Aoki 1991, chap. 6; and Ernst 1997.

51. For a good case study, see Minato 1986.

52. As a part of economic assistance in the wake of the Asian crisis, the Japanese government decided to provide two-step loans to Thailand and Indonesia: $600 million and $1 billion respectively [Gaimusho 1997].

53. This argument is originally made by Kosaka 1977, especially 211; and by Scalapino 1977, especially 400.

REFERENCES

Abegglen, James C. 1994. *Sea Change: Pacific Asia as the New World Industrial Center.* New York: Free Press.

Abo, Tetsuo. 1994. *Hybrid Factory: The Japanese Production System in the United States.* Oxford: Oxford University Press.

Akamatsu, Kaname. 1965. *Sekai Keizairon* [International Economics]. Tokyo: Kunimoto Shobo.

Akaneya, Tatsuo. 1992. *Nihon no GATT Kanyu Mondai: Rejimu Riron no Bunseki Shikaku ni yoru Jireikenkyu* [The Problem of Japanese Accession to the GATT: A Case Study in Regime Theory]. Tokyo: Tokyo Daigaku Shuppankai.

Aoki, Masahiko. 1988. *Information, Incentives, and Bargaining in the Japanese Economy.* Cambridge: Cambridge University Press.

Aoki, Masahiko and Masahiro Okuno-Fujiwara, eds. 1996. *Keizai Shisutemu no Hikaku Seido Bunseki* [Comparative Institutional Analysis: A New Approach to Economic Systems]. Tokyo: Tokyo Daigaku Shuppankai.

Aoki, Takashi. 1991. *Ajia-Taiheiyo Keizai no Seijyuku: Nihon to Ajia Taiheiyo Chiiki no Nettowaku Keisei* [Maturing Asia-Pacific Economies: Networks Between Japan and Asia-Pacific Region]. Tokyo: Keiso Shobo.

Asanuma, Banri. 1989. "Manufacture-Supplier Relationship in Japan and the Concept of Relation-Specific Skill." *Journal of the Japanese and International Economies* 3(1) (March): 1-30.

Baisho Mondai Kenkyukai [Reparation Problems Study Group]. 1963. *Nihon no Baisho* [Japan's War Reparations]. Tokyo: Sekai Janaru.

Bernard, Mitchell and John Ravenhill. 1995. "Beyond Product Cycles and Flying Geese: Regionalization, Hierarchy, and the Industrializaion of East Asia." *World Politics* 47 (January): 171-209.

Borden, William S. 1984. *The Pacific Alliance: United States Foreign Economic Policy and Japanese Trade Recovery, 1947-1955*. Madison: University of Wisconsin Press.

Borrus, Michael. 1997. "Left for Dead: Asian Production Networks and the Revival of U.S. Electronics," in Barry Naughton, ed., *The China Circle: Economics and Electronics in the PRC, Taiwan, and Hong Kong*, pp. 139-63. Washington, DC: Brookings Institution Press.

Borthwick, Mark. 1992. *Pacific Century: The Emergence of Modern Pacific Asia*. Boulder: Westview Press.

Caporaso, James A. 1993. "Global Political Economy," in Ada W. Finifter, ed., *Political Science: The State of the Discipline II*, pp. 451-82. Washington, DC: The American Political Science Association.

Chandler, Alfred D., Jr. 1990. *Scale and Scope: The Dynamics of Industrial Capitalism*. Cambridge: Belknap Press.

Chin, Heifu and Takabumi Hayashi. 1995. *Ajia no Gjyutsu Hatten to Gijyutsu Iten* [Technology Development and Transfer in Asia]. Tokyo: Bunshindo.

Clark, Kim B., and Takahiro Fujimoto. 1991. *Product Development Performance*. Boston: Harvard University Press.

Clone, Donald. 1993. "Does Hegemony Matter?: The Reorganization of the Pacific Political Economy." *World Politics* 45(4) (July), 501-525.

Cohen, Benjamin J. 1974. "The Revolution in Atlantic Relations: A Bargain Comes Unstuck," in Wolfram F. Hanrieder, ed., *The United States and Western Europe: Political, Economic and Strategic Perspectives*, pp. 106-33. Cambridge, MA: Winthrop Publishers.

Cumings, Bruce. 1987. "The Origins and Development of the Northeast Asian Political Economy: Industrial Sectors, Product Cycles, and Political Consequences," in Frederic C. Deyo, *The Political Economy of the New Asian Industrialism*, pp. 44-83. Ithaca: Cornell University Press.

———. 1993. "Japan's Position in the World System," in Andre Gordon, ed., *Postwar Japan as History*, pp. 34-63. Berkely: University of California Press.

Denzau, Arthur T., and Douglass C. North. 1994. "Shared Mental Models: Ideologies and Institutions," *Kyklos* 47(1): 3-31.

Doner, Richard F. 1993. "Japanese Foreign Investment and the Creation of a Pacific Asian Region," in Jeffrey A. Frankel and Miles Kahler, eds., *Regionalism and Rivalry: Japan and the United States in Pacific Asia*, pp. 159-214. Chicago: University of Chicago Press.

Dore, Ronald. 1973. *British Factory, Japanese Factory: The Origins of National Diversity in Industrial Relations*. London: George Allen & Unwin.

———. 1983. "Goodwill and the Spirit of Market Capitalism." *British Journal of Sociology* 20, pp. 198-217.

———. 1986. *Flexible Rigidities: Industrial Policy and Structural Adjustment in the Japanese Economy 1970-80*. Stanford: Stanford University Press.

Dower, John W. 1979. *Empire and Aftermath: Yoshida Shigeru and the Japanese Experience, 1878-1954*. Cambridge: Council on East Asian Studies, Harvard University. Harvard University Press.

Encarnation, Dennis J. 1992. *Rivals beyond Trade: America versus Japan in Global Competition*. Ithaca: Cornell University Press.

Ernst, Dieter. 1997. "Partners for the China Circle?: The East Asian Production Networks of Japanese Electronics Firms," in Barry Naughton, ed., *The China Circle: Economics and Electronics in the PRC, Taiwan, and Hong Kong*, pp. 210-53. Washington, DC: Brookings Institution Press.

Fallows, James. 1994. *Looking at the Sun: The Rise of the New Asian Economic and Politica System*. New York: Pantheon.

Fielder, Lennox Gerald. 1969. "After Conflict, Cooperation: Japan's Reparations and Economic Cooperation in an Evolving Postwar International Order in Asia," Ph.D. dissertation, The American University.

Frankel, Jeffrey A. and Miles Kahler, eds. 1993. *Regionalism and Rivalry: Japan and the United States in Pacific Asia*. Chicago: University of Chicago Press.

Franko, Lawrence G. 1978. *The European Multinationals: A Renewed Challenge to American and British Big Business*. Stamford, CT: Greylock Publishers.

Friedman, David. 1988. *The Misunderstood Miracle: Industrial Development and Political Change in Japan*. Ithaca, Cornell University Press.

Fruin, W. Mark. 1992. *The Japanese Enterprise System: Competitive Strategies and Cooperative Structures*. Oxford: Claredon Press.

Fukai, Shigeko N. 1982. "Japan's North-South Dialogue at the UN." *World Politics* 35, 1 (October): 73-105.

Gaimusho (The Ministry of Foreign Affairs, MOFA). Annual(a). *Kaigai Zairyu Hojinsu Chosa Tokei* [Annual Report of Statistics on Japanese Nationals Overseas]. Tokyo: Gaimusho.

———. Annual(b). *Waga Gaiko no Kinkyo* [Diplomatic Bluebook]. Tokyo: Gaimusho.

———. 1997. Ajia Keizai Kiki eno Nihon no Koken [Japan's Contributions to the Asian Economic Crisis]. www.mofa.go.jp, as of May 5, 1998.

Gerlach, Michael L. 1992. *Alliance Capitalism: The Social Organization of Japanese Business*. Berkeley: University of California Press.

79

Granovetter, Mark. 1985. "Economic Action and Social Structure: The Problem of Embeddedness," *American Journal of Sociology* 91(3) (November): 481-510.

Grieco, Joseph M. 1995. "Realism and Regionalism: American Power and German and Japanese Institutional Strategies During and After the Cold War," paper delivered at the Olin Institute Conference on Realism and International Relations After the Cold War, December 8-9.

————. 1997. "Systemic Sources of Variation in Regional Institutionalization in Western Europe, East Asia, and the Americas," in Edward D. Mansfield and Helen V. Milner, eds., *The Political Economy of Regionalism*, pp. 164-87. New York: Columbia University Press.

Hamaguchi, Esyun. 1985. "A Contexual Model of the Japanese: Toward a Methodological Innovation in Japan Studies." *The Journal of Japanese Studies* 11(2) (Summer): 289-321.

Hamilton, Gary G, and Robert C. Feenstra. 1997. "Varieties of Hierachies and Markets: An Introduction," in Marco Orr, Nicole Woolsey Biggart, and Gary G. Hamilton, eds., *The Economic Organization of East Asian Capitalism*, pp. 55-94. Thousand Oaks, California: Sage Publications.

Hara, Yoshihisa. 1995. *Nobusuke Kishi: Kensei no Seijika* [Nobusuke Kishi], Iwanami Shinsho 368. Tokyo: Iwanami Shoten.

Harrell, Edgra Carson. 1973. "Japan's Postwar Aid Policies," Ph.D. dissertation, Columbia University.

Hatano, Sumio. 1994. "onan Ajia Kaihatsu wo meguru Nichi-Bei-Ei Kannkei: Nihon no Koronbo Puran Kanyu wo chushin ni" [Japan-U.S.-U.K. Relations over the Development of Southeast Asia in the 1950s], *Nenpo Kindai Nihon Kenkyu* 16: 215-42.

Hatch, Walter and Kozo Yamamura. 1996. *Asia in Japan's Embrace: Building a Regional Production Alliance*. Cambridge: Cambridge University Press.

Hirschman, Albert O. 1980. *National Power and the Structure of Foreign Trade*. Berkeley: University of California Press.

Hobday, Michael. 1995. *Innovation in East Asia: The Challenge to Japan*. Cheltenham, UK: Edward Elgar.

Hosoya, Chihiro. 1989. "From the Yoshida Letter to the Nixon Shock," in Akira Iriye and Warren I. Cohen, eds. *The United States and Japan: in the Postwar World*, pp. 21-35. Lexington, Kentucky: University Press of Kentucky.

Igusa, Kunio. 1991. "Nihon no Tai-Tonan Ajia Keizai Shinshutsu no Kozu" [Japan's Economic Advancement in Southeast Asia], in Toru Yano, ed., *Tonan Ajia to Nihon* [Southeast Asia and Japan], pp. 204-32. Tokyo: Kobundo.

Ikenberry, G. John. 1989. "Rethinking the Origins of American Hegemony." *Political Science Quarterly* 104,3 (Fall): 375-400.

International Monetary Fund (IMF). 1997. The IMF's Response to the Asian Crisis. www.imf.org, as of May 5, 1998.

Japanese Government. 1992. *Japan's Official Development Assistance Charter* (pamphlet).

Japan External Trade Organization (JETRO). Annual. *JETRO Hakusho Toshihen* [JETRO White Paper on Foreign Direct Investment]. Tokyo: JETRO.

Johnson, Chalmers. 1982. *MITI and the Japanese Miracle: The Growth of Industrial Policy, 1925-75.* Berkeley: Stanford University Press.

――――. 1986. "The Patterns of Japanese Relations with China, 1952-1982." *Pacific Affairs* 59,3 (Fall): 402-28.

Kagaku Gijyutsucho. Annual. *Kagaku Gijyutsu Hakusho* [White Paper on Science and Technology]. Tokyo: Okurasho Insatsukyoku.

Kajima, Heiwa Kenkyujo, ed. 1973. *Nihon no Keizai Kyoryoku* [Japanese Economic Cooperation]. Tokyo: Kajima Kenkyujo Shuppankai.

Kan, Shiyu. 1994. "Nihon Keizai no Ajia eno Kaiki" [Return to Asia of Japanese Economy]. *Bijinesu Rebyu* 42,2: 23-35.

Kato, Kozo. 1996. "Helping Others, Helping Oneself: International Positions, Domestic Institutions, and Development Cooperation Policy in Japan and Germany," Ph.D. dissertation, Cornell University.

――――. 1998. "Hanshin-Awaji Daishinsai to Nihon no Nettowaku: Torihiki Nettowaku to Kihan Nettowaku" [The Hanshin-Awaji Earthquake and Japanese Networks: Transaction Networks and Normative Networks]. *Leviathan* (special issue, summer): 129-52.

Katzenstein, Peter J. 1978. "Conclusion: Domestic Structures and Strategies of Foreign Economic Policy," in Peter J. Katzenstein, ed., *Between Power and Plenty: Foreign Economic Policies of Advanced Industrial States*, pp. 295-336. Madison: University of Wisconsin Press.

――――. 1985. *Small States in World Markets: Industrial Policy in Europe.* Ithaca: Cornell University Press.

――――. 1997a. "Introduction: Asian Regionalism in Comparative Perspective," in Peter J. Katzenstein and Takashi Shiraishi, eds., *Network Power: Japan and Asia*, pp. 1-44. Ithaca: Cornell University Press.

――――. 1997b. "Regional Orders: Technology in Asia and Europe," unpublished paper.

Katzenstein, Peter J., and Nobuo Okawara. 1993. *Japan's National Security: Structures, Norms and Policy Responses in a Changing World.* Ithaca: East Asia Program, Cornell University.

Katzenstein, Peter J., and Takashi Shiraishi. 1997. "Conclusion: Regions in World Politics: Japan and Asia ermany in Europe," in Katzenstein and Shiraishi, eds., *Network Power: Japan and Asia*, pp. 341-81. Ithaca: Cornell University Press.

Kawabe, Ichiro. 1994. *Kokuren to Nihon* [U.N. and Japan]. Tokyo: Iwanami Shoten.

Kenney, Martin, and Richard Florida. 1993. *Beyond Mass Production: The Japanese System and Its Transfer to the U.S.* New York: Oxford University Press.

Keohane, Robert O. and Joseph S. Nye. 1989. *Power and Interdependence* (2nd ed.). Glenview IL: Scott, Foresman and Company.

Kishi, Nobusuke. 1983. *Kishi Nobusuke Kaikoroku: Hoshu Godo to Anpo Kaitei* [Memoir of Nobusuke Kishi]. Tokyo: Kosaido Shuppan.

Kiyonari, Tadao, Toshimi Tanaka, and Tetsuo Minato. 1996. *Chusho Kigyoron* [Analysis of Small and Medium Enterprises]. Tokyo: Yuhikaku.

Koike, Kazuo, and Takenori Inoki. 1987. *Jinzai Keisei no Kokusai Hikaku: Tonan Ajia to Nihon* [Comparative Study on Human Resource Development: Southeast Asia and Japan. Tokyo: Toyo Keizai Shinposha.

Kojima, Kiyoshi. 1985. "Japanese and American Direct Investment in Asia: A Comparative Analysis." *Hitotsubashi Journal of Economics* 26,1 (June): 1-35.

———. 1989. *Kaigai Chokusetsu Toshi no Makuro Bunseki* [Macro Analysis of Direct Foerign Investment]. Tokyo: Bunshindo.

Komiya, Ryutaro. 1988. *Gendai Nihon Keizai* [Contemporary Japanese Economy]. Tokyo: Tokyo Daigaku Shuppankai.

———. 1990. *The Japanese Economy: Trade, Industry, and Government*. Tokyo: University of Tokyo Press.

Komiya, Ryutaro and Motoshige Ito. 1988. "Japan's International Trade and Trade Policy, 1955-1984," in Takashi Inoguchi and Daniel I. Okimoto, eds., *The Political Economy of Japan: Volume 2, The Changing International Context*, pp. 173-224. Stanford: Stanford University Press.

Komiya, Ryutaro, Masahiro Okuno, and Kotaro Suzumura, eds. 1984. *Nihon no Sangyo Seisaku* [Japan's Industrial Policy]. Tokyo: Tokyo Daigaku Shuppankai.

Komiya, Ryutaro and Ryuhei Wakasugi. 1991. "Japan's Foreign Direct Investment." *Annals of the American Academy of Political and Social Science* 513 (January): 50-62.

Kosaka, Masataka. 1977. "The International Economic Policy of Japan," in Robert A. Scalapino, ed., *The Foreign Policy of Modern Japan*, pp. 207-26. Berkeley: University of California Press.

Koshiba, Tetsushu. 1997. "Ajia-Taiheiyo Shokoku ni okeru Nihon Kigyo no Jigyo Netowaku" [Business Networks of Japanese Enterprises in Asia-Pacific Countries], in Rokuro Tsuchiya, ed., *Ajia-Taiheiyoken no Hatten* [Development in Asia-Pacific Region], pp. 89-111. Tokyo: Dobunkan.

Krasner, Stepen D. 1993. "Comment," in Jeffrey A. Frankel and Miles Kahler, eds., *Regionalism and Rivalry: Japan and the United States in Pacific Asia*, pp. 372-76. Chicago and London: University of Chicago Press.

Kumon, Shumpei. 1993. "Japan as a Network Society," in Shumpei Kumon and Henry Rosovsky, eds., *The Political Economy of Japan. Vol. 3: Cultural and Social Dynamics*, pp. 109-41. Stanford: Stanford University Press.

Lifson, Thomas B. 1993. "The Managerial Integration of Japanese Business in America," in Shumpei Kumon and Henry Rosovsky, eds., *The Political Economy of Japan: Vol. 3-Cultural and Social Dynamics*, pp. 231-66. Stanford: Stanford University Press.

Mandelbaum, Michael. 1988. *The Fate of Nations: The Search for National Security in the Nineteenth and Twentieth Centuries.* Cambridge: Cambridge University Press.

Mastanduno, Michael. 1992. *Economic Containment: Cocom and the Politics of East-West Trade.* Ithaca: Cornell University Press.

Maruyama, Yoshinari and Yukinari Narita, eds. 1995. *Nihon Kigyo no Ajia Senryaku: Kokusai Bungyo to Kyosei no Kadai* [Asia Strategy by Japanese Enterprises: International Division of Labor and Economic Symbiosys]. Tokyo: Chuo Keizai-sha.

Milner, Helen V. 1988. *Resisting Protectionism: Global Industries and the Politics of International Trade.* Princeton: Princeton University Press.

Minato, Tetsuo. 1986. "Nihon-gata Seisan Shisutemu no Genchi Tekio Katei" [Adaptation Process of Japanese Production System], in Hideichiro Nakamura and Yoichi Koike, eds., *Chusho Kigyo no Ajia-muke Toshi: Kankyo Henka to Taio* [Japanese Small and Medium Enterprises' Investment in Asia: Environmental Change and Adaptation], pp. 65-85. Tokyo: Ajia Keizai Kenkyujo.

Ministry of Foreign Affairs. Annual. *Diplomatic Bluebook.* Tokyo: Ministry of Foreign Affairs.

Ministry of International Trade and Industry (MITI). 1993. *Prospects and Challenges for the Upgrading of Industries in the Asian Region.* Tokyo: Tsusho Sangyo Chosakai.

Morrison, Charles E. 1988. "Japan and the ASEAN Countries: The Evolustion of Japan Regional Role," in Takashi Inoguchi and Daniel I. Okimoto, eds., The Political Economy of Japan: Volume 2 he Changing International Context, pp. 414-45. Stanford: Stanford University Press.

Murakami, Yasusuke, Shunpei Kumon, and Seizaburo Sato. 1979. *Bunmei Toshiteno Ie Shakai* [Family Society as Civilization]. Tokyo: Chuo Koronsha.

Murakami, Yasusuke and Thomas P. Rohlen. 1992. "Social-Exchange Aspects of the Japanese Political Economy: Culture, Efficiency, and Change," in Shumpei Kumon and Henry Rosovsky, eds., *The Poltical Economy of Japan: Volume 3-Cultural and Social Dynamics*, pp. 63-105. Stanford: Stanford University Press.

Nagatomi, Yuichiro. 1984. *Kindai o Koete: Ko Ohira Sori no Nokorateta Mono, Jo, Ge* [Beyond Modern: Legacies of Prime Minister Ohira, Vols. 1 & 2]. Tokyo: Okura Zaimu Kyokai.

Nakamura, Hideichiro. 1992. *21-seiki gata Chusho Kigyo* [Small- and Medium-Sized Companies of the 21st Centuries] Tokyo. Iwanami Shoten

Nakamura, Takafusa. 1981. *The Postwar Japanese Economy: Its Development and Structure.* Tokyo: Univerity of Tokyo Press.

Nakane, Chie. 1970. *Japanese Society.* London: Weidenfeld & Nicolson.

Naughton, Barry, ed. 1997. *The China Circle: Economics and Electronics in the PRC, Taiwan, and Hong Kong.* Washington, DC: Brookings Institution Press.

Nester, William R. 1991. *Japan and the Third World: Patterns, Power, Prospects.* New York: St. Martin's Press.

Nihon Ginko (Bank of Japan). *Annual. Gaikoku Keizai Tokei Nenpo* [Annual Report on Statistics on International Economies]. Tokyo. Tokiwa Sogo Sabisu.

Nishiguchi, Toshihiro. 1994. *Strategic Industrial Sourcing: The Japanese Advantage.* Oxford: Oxford Universiby press.

North, Douglass C. 1990. *Institutions, Institutional Change and Economic Performance.* Cambridge: Cambridge University Press.

————. 1992. "Institutions, Ideology, and Performance," *Cato Journal* 11, 3 (Winter): 477-89.

Odagiri, Hiroyuki. 1992. *Growth through Competition, Competition Through Growth: Strategic Management and the Economy in Japan.* Oxford: Oxford University Press.

Odagiri, Hiroyuki and Akira Goto. 1996. *Technology and Industrial Development in Japan: Building Capabilities by Learning, Innovation, and Public Policy.* Oxford: Oxford University Press.

Ohira Masayoshi Kaisoroku Kankokai, ed. 1982. *Kaisoroku: Shiryo-hen* [Memoir: Data] Tokyo: Ohira Masoyoshi Kaisoroku Kankokai.

Okimoto, Daniel I. 1988. "Political Inclusivity: The Domestic Structure of Trade," in Takashi Inoguchi and Daniel I. Okimoto, eds., *The Political Economy of Japan. Vol. 2: The Changing International Context,* pp. 305-44. Stanford: Stanford University Press.

————. 1989. *Between MITI and the Market: Japanese Industrial Policy for High Technology.* Stanford, California: Stanford University Press.

Okita, Saburo, ed. 1980. *Report on the Pacific Basin Cooperation Concept.* Tokyo: Okurasho Insatsukyoku.

Organization for Economic Cooperation and Development (OECD). 1989. *OECD Science and Technology Indicators Report No. 3, R&D, Production and Diffusion of Technology.* Paris: OECD.

Orr, Marco, Nicole Woolsey Biggart, and Gary G. Hamilton. 1997. *The Economic Organization of East Asian Capitalism.* Thousand Oaks, CA: Sage.

Ozawa, Terutomo. 1979. *Multinational, Japanese Style: The Political Economy of Outward Dependence.* Princeton: Princeton University Press.

Patrick, Hugh T., and Thomas P. Rohlen. 1987. "Small-Scale Family Enterprises," in Kozo Yamamura and Yasukichi Yasuda, eds., *The Political Economy of Japan: Volume 1-The Domestic Transformation,* pp. 331-84. Stanford: Stanford University Press.

Pempel, T.J. 1982. *Policy and Politics in Japan: Creative Conservatism.* Philadelphia: Temple University Press.

84

———. 1993. "From Exporter to Investor: Japanese Foreign Economic Policy," in Gerald L. Curtis, ed., *Japan's Foreign Policy after the Cold War: Coping with Change*, pp. 105-36. Armonk, NY: M.E. Sharpe.

Petri, Peter A. 1993. "The East Asian Trading Bloc: An Analytical History," in Jeffrey A. Frankel and Miles Kahler, eds., *Regionalism and Rivalry: Japan and the United States in Pacific Asia*, pp. 21-48. Chicago and London: University of Chicago Press.

Piore, Michael J. and Charles F. Sabel. 1984. *The Second Industrial Divide: Possibilities for Prosperity*. New York: Basic Books.

Powell, Walter W. 1990. "Neither Market nor Hierarchy: Network Forms of Organization," *Research in Organizational Behaviour* 12(2): 295-336.

Rix, Alan. 1993. *Japan's Foreign Aid challenge: Policy Reform and Aid Leadership*. London: Routeledge.

Rotter, Andrew Jon. 1987. *The Path to Vietnam: Origins of the American Commitment to Southeast Asia*. Ithaca: Cornell University Press.

Ruggie, John Gerard. 1983. "International Regimes, Transactions and Change: Embedded Liberalism in the Postwar Economic Order," in Stephan D. Krasner, ed., *International Regimes*, pp. 195-231. Ithaca: Cornell University Press.

Ruigrok, Winfried and van Tulder, Rob. 1995. *The Logic of International Restructuring*. London: Routledge.

Samuels, Richard J. 1987. *The Business of the Japanese State: Energy Markets in Comparative and Historical Perspective*. Ithaca: Cornell University Press.

———. 1989. "Consuming for Production: Japanese National Security, Nuclear Fuel Procurement, and the Domestic Economy," *International Organization* 43(4) (Autumn): 625-46.

Sako, Mari. 1991. "The Role of 'Trust' in Japanese Buyer-Supplier Relationships." *Ricerche Economiche* 45(2-3) (Aprile-Settembre): 449-74.

Scalapino, Robert A. 1977. "Perspectives on Modern Japanese Foreign Policy," in Scalapino, ed., *The Foreign Policy of Modern Japan*, pp. 391-412. Berkeley: University of California Press.

Seki, Mitsuhiro. 1993. *Furesetto-gata Sangyo Kozo wo Koete* [Beyond Full-Set, Industrial Structure] Chuko Shinsho, 1153. Tokyo: Chuo Koron-sha.

———. 1997. *Kudoka o Koete: Gijutsu to Chiiki no Saikochiku* [Beyond Hollowing: Rebuilding Technology and Region]. Tokyo: Nihon Keizai Shimbun-sha.

Sekiguchi, Sueo. 1982. "Japanese Direct Invetment in Europe," in Loukas Tsoukalis and Maureen White, eds., *Japan and Western Europe: Conflict and Cooperation*, pp. 166-83. New York: St. Martin's Press.

———. 1983. *ASEAN-Japan Relations: Investment*. Singapore: Institute of Southeast Asian Studies.

Shimizu, Sayuri. 1991. "Creating People of Plenty: The United States and Japan's Economic Alternatives, 1953-58," Ph.D. dissertation, Cornell University.

Shiraishi, Takashi. 1997. "Japan and Southeast Asia," in Katzenstein and Shiraishi, eds., *Network Power: Japan and Asia*, pp. 169-94. Ithaca: Cornell University Press.

Shuchman, Lisa. 1998. "Japanese Auto Companies Map Out New Plans for Asia," *Asian Wall Street Journal*, 30-31 January 1998, pp. 1 and 24.

Soeya, Yoshihide. 1995. *Nihon Gaiko to Chugoku: 1945-1972* [Japanese Diplomacy and China: 1945-1972]. Tokyo: Keio Tsushin.

Stopford, John M. and Susan Strange. 1991. *Rival States, Rival Firms: Competition for World Market Shares*. Cambridge: Cambridge University Press.

Takada, Ryoji. 1994. "Ajia ni okeru Nikkei Shinshutsu Kigyo to Kigyokan Bungyo Kankei" [Japanese Investment Companies and Intercorporate Networks in Asia], in Nihon Chusho Kigyo Gakkai, ed., *Atarashi Ajia Keizaiken to Chusho Kigyo* [Small Business and the Newly Developing Asian Region], pp. 26-41. Tokyo: Dobunkan.

Takagi, Shinji. 1995. *From Recipient to Donor: Japan's Official Aid Flows, 1945 to 1990 and Beyond*, Essays in International Finance, No. 196. Princeton: International Finance Section, Department Economics, Princeton University, March.

Tanaka, Akihiko. 1991. *Ni-Chu Kankei 1945-1990* [Japan-China Relations 1945-1990]. Tokyo: Tokyo Daigaku Shuppankai.

Tanaka, Takashi. 1989. "Facilitating the Recycling of Japanese Funds." *Exim Review* 9, 2 (March): 2-20.

Thomsen, Stephen and Nicolaides, Phedon. 1991. *The Evolution of Japanese Direct Investment in Europe: Death of a Transistor Salesman*. New York: Harvester Wheatsheaf.

Tsujinaka, Yutaka. 1993. "Rengo and Its Osmotic Networks," in Gary D. Allison and Yasunori Sone, eds., *Political Dynamics in Contemporary Japan*, pp. 200-13. Ithaca: Cornell University Press.

Tsusho Sangyosho (MITI). Annual(a). *Keizai Kyoryoku no Genjo to Mondaiten* [White Paper on Economic Cooperation]. Tokyo:Tsusho Sangyo Chosakai.

———. Annual(b). *Tsusho Hakusho* [White Paper on Commerce]. Tokyo: Okurasho Insatsu-kyoku.

———. 1993a. *Prospects and Challenges for the Upgrading of Industries in the Asian Region*. Tokyo: Tsusho Sangyo Chosakai.

———. 1993b. *Sozo-teki Kakushin no Jidai: Chuki Sangyo Keizai Tenbo Kenkyukai Hokokusho* [The Age of Innovative Creation: Report by the Study Group on Midterm Industrial and Economic Development]. Tokyo: Tsusan Shiryo Chosakai.

Upham, Frank. 1989. *Law and Social Change in Postwar Japan*. Cambridge, MA: Free Press.

United Nations Center on Transnational Corporations (UNCTC). 1988. *Transnational Corporation in World Development: Trends and Prospects*. New York: United Nations.

————. 1987. *Foreign Direct Investment, the Service Sector, and International Banking*. New York: United Nations.

————. 1985. *Trends and Issues in Foreign Direct Investment and Related Flows: a Technical Paper*. New York, United Nations.

United Nations Conference on Trade and Development (UNCTAD). Annual. *World Investment Report*. New York: United Nations.

Waltz, Kenneth N. 1970. "The Myth of National Interdependence," in Charles P. Kindleberger, ed., *The International Cooperation: A Symposium*, pp. 205-23. Cambridge: MIT Press.

Watanabe, Akio. 1987. "Sengo Shoki no Nichibei Kankei to Tonan Ajia: Senzengata ankakukosa kara Sengogata antsukiko e" [Japan-U.S. Relations and Southeast Asia in the early Post-War Period], in Chihiro Hosoya and Sadamu Aruga, eds., *Kokusai Kankyo no Henyo to Nichibei Kankei* [Changing International Environment and Japan-U.S. Relations], pp. 27-54. Tokyo: Tokyo Daigaku Shuppankai.

Watanabe, Toshio. 1990. *Ajia Shinchoryu: Nishi Taiheiyo no Dainamizumu to Shakaishugi* [New Waves in Asia: Dynamism in Western Pacific and Socialism], Chuko Shinsho 982. Tokyo: Chuo Koron-sha.

————. *Nishi Taiheiyo Shinjidai to Nihon: Ajia no Hatten ga Nichi-Bei Kankei o Do Kaeruka* [Western Pacific and Japan: Asia and Japan-U.S. Relations]. Tokyo: Japan Times.

Watanabe, Toshio, Hirokazu Kajiwara, and Kimio Takanaka. 1991. *Ajia Sogo Izon no Jidai* [The Age of Interdependence in Asia]. Tokyo: Yuhikaku.

Webb, Michael C. 1995. *The Political Economy of Policy Coordination: International Adjustment since 1945*. Ithaca: Cornell University Press.

Williamson, Oliver E. 1975. *Markets and Hierarchies: Analysis and Antitrust Implications*. New York: Free Press.

————. 1985. *The Economic Institutions of Capitalism: Firms, Markets, Relational Contracting*. New York: Free Press.

van Wolferen, Karel. 1990. *The Enigma of Japanese Power: People and Politics in a Stateless Nation*. New York: Vintage Books.

World Bank. Annual. *World Bank Atlas*. Washington, DC: World Bank.

Yamamoto, Takehiko. 1989. "Keizai Gaiko" [Economic Diplomacy], in Yoshinobu Yamamoto, ed., *Kokusai Seiji no Riron* (Koza Kokusai Seiji, vol. 4), pp. 155-82. Tokyo: Tokyo Daigaku Shuppankai.

Yamazawa, Ippei, and Hirata, Akira, eds. 1990. *Senshin Shokoku no tai Hattentojokoku Boeki Seisaku* [Trade Policies toward Developing Countries]. Tokyo: Ajia Keizai Kenkyujo.

Yano, Toru. 1975. *Nihon no "Nanshin" to Tonan Ajia* [Japan's "Southern Expansion" and Southeast Asia]. Tokyo: Nihon Keizai Shimbunsha.

Yoshida, Shigeru. 1951. "Japan and the Crisis in Asia," *Foreign Affairs* 29,2 (January): 171-81.

Yoshihara, Kunio. 1978. *Japanese Investment in Southeast Asia*. Honolulu: University Press of Hawaii.

Yoshikawa, Yoko. 1991. *Nippi Baisho Gaiko Kosho no Kenky* [Study on Diplomatic Bargaining over Japan-Filipino War Reparation]. Tokyo: Keiso Shobo.

3

Chinese Networks and Asian Regionalism

Ming Yue

The circuitous path of Asian development has led political, journalistic and, to some extent, scholarly assessments to lurch from the Asian "economic miracle" and the "Asian century" before the summer of 1997 to "crony capitalism" and the "Asian basket case" thereafter. In a broader historical perspective Asia's cyclical economic development is not very surprising. Financial crises have been common in the economic development histories of many Asian nations; Hong Kong in 1984 is only one example. However, the present crisis is useful in sharpening our insights into the process of Asian economic development.

Economic development in Asia's Newly Industrializing Countries (NICs) since the early 1960s has relied on cheap labor, a strong work ethic, very flexible market networks, and export-oriented government policies. Put succinctly, the NICs both created and exploited market opportunities by exporting their labor-intensive products world-wide, especially to the US market. Thus the NICs earned the hard currency to purchase high value-added imports that further enhanced their global competitiveness and allowed their economies to take off into sustained high-growth.

The current economic crisis illustrates, however, that market conditions have changed greatly. Taken as a whole Asia's competitiveness has diminished [World Competitiveness 1998]. Once China and Vietnam opened their economies to the outside world, they copied the export-oriented strategies of the NICs and competed against other Asian countries with even lower labor and land costs. The entry of China into world markets, in particular, greatly affected the competitive positions of Thailand, Malaysia, and Indonesia. For an increasing range and volume of products made in China now occupy the shelves of discount retailers in the U.S. In hopes of moving their economies to the next level of development and competing in global markets with higher-value products, the ASEAN countries amassed a large foreign currency-denominated debt, which was to be invested in their industries and infrastructures.

Their plan was that the increased amounts of hard currency to be from the anticipated sales of higher value-added products would enable them to pay off their debts and escape the direct competitive threat of China's enormous pool of low-skilled, low-cost labor. But with the development of new technologies and the globalization of financial markets, economic conditions changed very quickly in the 1990s, and posed an enormous challenge, throughout Asia, to traditional systems of industrial organization and values.

This chapter focuses on the role of Overseas Chinese business networks in Asia. An analysis of their structure and characteristic mode of operations in markets illuminates some of the key characteristics of Asian regionalism, in particular, how network relationships that span the Asian region organize markets. My analysis is based on two general principles. First, economic activities are deeply embedded in social and political environments so that changes in social and political situations alter the nature of entrepreneurial activity. Second, since Asia differs from other parts of the world in its historical traditions, the key analytical issue lies in understanding how systems of production and business networks in Asia organize market competition.

There are two main types of business networks in Asia: Japanese and Chinese. Both are organized along ethnic lines. Measured in terms of control over national GDP, Japanese networks clearly dominate Asia's business landscape. Measured in terms of overall influence, however, the overseas Chinese networks have had the largest and most enduring impact upon Asia.

This chapter surveys the community of Overseas Chinese entrepreneurs in the next section, the textiles and electronics industries in the section following that, and then banking. It concludes with a brief summary and an assessment of likely future developments.

The Overseas Chinese
Markets are a useful starting point for understanding the connections between domestic, regional and international systems. The relationship between markets and the socio-cultural and political institutions in which they are embedded is of particular importance, especially if we wish to understand entrepreneurs and the networks within which they operate. The Overseas Chinese are a good example of entrepreneurs functioning within a variety of socio-cultural and political institutions. They are risk takers with a substantial ability for identifying market opportunities, especially in developing countries in Asia. The conditions that led to the Asian financial

crisis have, however, affected their playing field profoundly. For instance, as one part of a concerted effort to develop or improve their competitiveness, especially in Asian markets, Overseas Chinese entrepreneurs will have to invest more in research and development. They already have a very flexible network of alliances with other firms, which is strong asset in competitive markets, but in adapting to changing market conditions, Overseas Chinese firms most likely will need to develop a more institutionalized presence within those markets.

By all accounts the economic presence of the Overseas Chinese is massive, especially in Southeast Asia. In Thailand, for example, all but one of the 20 largest business enterprises traded on the stock exchange are owned by Overseas Chinese. In the Philippines, with the exception of three Spanish-controlled firms, Overseas Chinese own all of the largest firms. In Singapore the most powerful businesses are state-controlled, but the Overseas Chinese run the second most powerful business groups in that country. In Hong Kong, of the top twenty largest business groups, with the exception of two British groups and the Bank of China, the rest are controlled by Overseas Chinese comprised of Hong Kong Chinese businesses and Overseas Chinese groups from other parts of Southeast Asia. The pattern is similar in Taiwan, with almost every publicly traded business group being controlled by the Overseas Chinese.

The Overseas Chinese are wealthy, both as a group and as individuals. As business groups have developed, they have accumulated property on a vast scale, adding greatly to the personal wealth of families and their members. But economic wealth has not translated automatically into political power. Overseas Chinese have frequently faced resentment and occasionally outright persecution in their adopted South East Asian homelands. Hence they keep a very low public profile and are highly secretive about their personal and business holdings. Thus, it is virtually impossible to determine accurately the extent of their business, real estate, and other financial assets. According to an estimate published by Forbes, in 1994, the personal wealth of 309 Overseas Chinese business persons in residing in Hong Kong, Singapore, Taiwan, Thailand, Indonesia, Malaysia, and the Philippines amounted to more than US$ 100 million each. By 1996, at least 341 Overseas Chinese had reportedly achieved that level of personal wealth. And in 1996, six Overseas Chinese had personal assets in excess of US$ 8 billion. The largest of these fortunes amounted to some US$ 13.5 billion [Tanzer 1997]. Most of this wealth is concentrated in Hong Kong and Taiwan.

The Overseas Chinese influence in Asia derives in part from their substantial wealth but also from the extensive networks that link them to each other. Complicated webs of cross-holdings, combined with a strong sense of obligation based on kinship, dialect, or common place of origin combine to exert a powerful influence on how the Overseas Chinese operate in markets. These networks offer a degree of control over markets and, thus, a competitive advantage, despite the preferential treatment that governments frequently afford indigenous competitors. Even governments cannot do without the economic acumen and capital of Overseas Chinese. For example, although many Overseas Chinese businesses located in Indonesia were destroyed during the May 1998 chaos that led up to President Suharto's resignation, as soon as the riots, which may have been politically incited, ceased, Indonesian government officials quickly called upon Overseas Chinese retailers to return and rebuild their chain store operations throughout the country [Ge 1998, 66].

Place-of-origin, a hometown or province, has often been the basis for Overseas Chinese business networks. Kinship, determined by, blood relationships, family name, or marriage, also matter greatly. Further, there are networking relationships based on membership in guild, trade, or industry associations. Throughout history Overseas Chinese have used such traditional relationships to further their business interests in their adopted countries. Even though the intensity and scope of their use has changed, these traditional bases for networking relationships are still used extensively.

Place-of-origin relationships, for example, are evolving into dialect relationships, which encompass a broader range of possible networking partners. It no longer matters whether a potential partner comes from the same hometown or province, only that he be able to understand and work with others in a common spoken Chinese dialect. Furthermore, traditional provincial guilds have become transnational organizations, so that Hakka people, for example, from anywhere in the world can now cooperate, even though it may have been centuries since their ancestors left Fujian Province. Ethnic Chinese have also maintained their cross-border connections in more formal and non-traditional ways, such as the organized meetings of international ethnic Chinese associations. Most prominent among these are international dialect associations. The worldwide Teochiu Alliance Association, for example, was founded in 1981. It holds meetings biannually and encompasses more than 150 Teochiu organizations. Recent conferences have been held in the United States, Hong Kong, Macau, Canada, France, Thailand, and the Philippines [Department of Foreign Affairs and Trade, Australia 1995].

Blood relationships are also being extended beyond the immediate family. Any person with the right surname is now a potential partner within such expanded kinship networks. As increasing numbers of Overseas Chinese get their education in the West, new types of college- and university-based, rather than 'collegial,' networks are springing up, organized around alumni associations, networking lunches, and the like. The biggest network for ethnic Chinese business people by far, however, remains the World Chinese Entrepreneurs Convention. It is held every two years and attracts more than 1,000 participants. This conference is open to ethnic Chinese regardless of dialect or ancestral origins. The first convention was held in Singapore in 1991, followed by meetings in Hong Kong and Bangkok. Delegates to the Singapore convention came from as far away as the United States, Switzerland, Lesotho, Mauritius, Italy, Guam, Greece, France, Chile, and Japan, as well as from all other parts of Asia [Department of Foreign Affairs and Trade, Australia 1995, 178].

As the economic strength of the Overseas Chinese has steadily increased and the range of their activities, trade, and investment has expanded throughout Asia and beyond, their business networks have been constantly altered and reinforced. These networks have been extended and fortified by the opening up of mainland China's economy and the tremendous growth opportunities this offers to the Overseas Chinese in their native land. Growth opportunities for Overseas Chinese businesses abound further south as well. Overseas Chinese business expansion throughout Southeast Asia appears to follow a sequence of steps that start with domestic expansion, continue with the establishment of a representative office in Hong Kong, and end with investments in China and, subsequently, in other ASEAN countries [Ch'ng 1993, 25].

New Overseas Chinese investment throughout Southeast Asia is facilitated by the presence of already established communities of Overseas Chinese. The advantages that accrue from this support are an important reason why the Overseas Chinese have tended to concentrate their investments in this region. According to a survey by The Institute of Economic Research in Taiwan of Taiwanese investments in the Philippines, for example, additional Taiwanese investments in that country was found to be much more likely because Taiwanese investors were already present. Seventy-five percent of the respondents indicated that they received useful information about market developments from the Overseas Chinese present in the Philippines; fifty percent reported help from local Overseas Chinese in securing the necessary relationships with the Filipino government. An additional 38 percent reported that their enterprises received managerial help from local Overseas Chinese businesses in the Philippines [Taiwan's Investment in Southeast Asia 1995].

The most striking feature of the Overseas Chinese business network is that it is composed almost entirely of small- and medium-sized family businesses. In Japan a company is always identified by its name. In the Chinese communities, by contrast, the name of the firm's founder is the accepted identifier during the networking process. Close examination of the organizational charts of typical Overseas Chinese businesses reveals that nearly all key positions are held by family members. And this structure is perpetuated across generations.

For many generations, emigrant Chinese entrepreneurs have been operating comfortably within networks of family and clan, laying the foundations for stronger links among businesses that span national borders. Chinese-owned businesses in East Asia, the United States, Canada, and even farther afield are increasingly becoming part of what John Kao has called the "Chinese Commonwealth" [1993, 24-32]. This commonwealth is primarily a network of carefully nurtured entrepreneurial relationships between many individual enterprises. The commonwealth offers the kind of global network that Western transnational corporations have tried to create in their own organizations, often without great success in Asia. As a result, these same Western companies are often casting about for partners for joint ventures in Asia.

Overseas Chinese business networks also extend to private and informal capital markets, organized along the lines of family or clan association, in which financial resources are pooled for new ventures without the intervention of commercial banks, professional venture capital companies, or government investment agencies. Unlike Japanese corporations, the Chinese commonwealth has, in the language of computer programming, an "open architecture." In a variety of environments it offers access to local resources like information, business connections, cheap raw materials, low labor costs, and different business practices. In contrast to Japanese *keiretsu* structures, the Chinese commonwealth is an interconnected and open system that offers new mechanisms for conducting global business. Eventually, both Chinese and non-Chinese may come to take advantage of opportunities in North America and Europe through Chinese networks operating in those regions.

The new Chinese management model, like the Overseas Chinese commonwealth that underpins it, is grounded in both traditional Chinese values and such Western practices as professional management and marketing. The combination encourages flexibility, innovation, and the assimilation of outsiders. It is clear that Confucianism in its many guises is remarkably persistent within these networks. For most Chinese entrepreneurs, no matter how Westernized, the enterprise is still a means for exerting control and achieving security in a disorderly world. That yearning for security is easily understood. In a 1993 study conducted by researchers at Harvard University, 90 percent of Overseas Chinese entrepreneurs who were first-generation emigrants had experienced war; 40 percent had gone through a political disaster like the cultural revolution; 32 percent had lost a home; and 28 percent had weathered economic disasters that resulted in significant loss of wealth [Harvard Business Review March-April 1993].

Such personal experiences make the nine maxims of Chinese business intelligible: thrift ensures survival; extremely high levels of savings, regardless of immediate need, are desirable; hard work to the point of exhaustion is necessary to ward off the many hazards of an unpredictable world; the only people you can trust are family members, and a business enterprise is created to be a family life raft; the judgement of an incompetent relative in the family business is more reliable than that of a competent stranger; obedience to patriarchal authority is essential in maintaining enterprise coherence and direction; investment must be based on kinship or clan affiliations—not abstract principles; tangible goods like real estate, natural resources, and gold bars are preferable to intangibles like illiquid securities or intellectual property; and keep your bags packed at all times, day or night [Harvard Business Review March-April 1993, 25]. These maxims help explain the typical business choices of first-generation Overseas Chinese entrepreneurs: real estate, light industry and import-export companies.

Often, even quite large Chinese enterprises maintain only rudimentary organizational structures. Chinese entrepreneurs manage traditional enterprises much as a Chinese emperor managed his empire. Thus, business assets are usually passed on exclusively to family members, and even in global companies, such as Li Ka Shing's Cheung Kong Holdings of Hong Kong, the Malaysian Robert Kuok's Shangri-La Hotel chain, or Liem Sioe Liong's Salim Group of Indonesia, control will most likely remain in the hands of family members. As reassuring as this form of business dynasty is for family members, it leaves outsiders very insecure. Key advisors never know the family insiders as well as these know each other. And knowledge is power. The typical Chinese entrepreneur will keep a poor manager simply because "he's family."

As Overseas Chinese companies start to grow, the conventions of traditional Chinese business, especially this deeply ingrained caution toward outsiders, becomes a clear competitive liability. The quickly changing global economy has created strong pressures for organizational changes, but the break with deeply held traditional views does not come easily. Strong paternalisms tends to stifle innovation within traditional organizations. In the words of one Overseas Chinese: "in Chinese culture, you have to respect your father and mother; this respect kills creativity. If you have to respect what your father says, then you tend to kill your own thinking" [Kraar 1994]. The need for organizational change is nowhere more pressing than in technology-intensive industries. In businesses where individual intellectual contributions and proprietary knowledge are the key to success and survival, individual contributions from outside of the family are strategically important and can be disregarded only at great risk to the entire firm.

The need for individual organizational reforms has even greater implications for the Overseas Chinese business network as a whole. Few Chinese entrepreneurs have any political power or influence to help them through difficult times. While some large Taiwanese and Singaporean companies have close relations with the government, and can count on support from economic bureaucrats, the Chinese entrepreneurial network as a whole is too dispersed to allow for the type of massive government assistance that the governments of Japan and Korea have traditionally granted to their *keiretsu* and *chaebol* corporate groups.

Many Overseas Chinese business patriarchs are aware of the need for organizational change, and for the health of their companies and the good of the next generation, they are willing to implement far-reaching reorganization. Thus, while they have been reluctant to share power with family members, these first-generation business pioneers worry about how to cope best with the consequences of their success. Most Overseas Chinese shy away from publicity and cling to their own community. Even their public companies are small parts of family-controlled conglomerates that rarely reveal the full details of their finances or the true extent of their ownership. To further complicate matters, their businesses tend to be in fields like trading, real estate, and finance. Their lack of brand-name products keeps them out of the public's eye.

However, this lack of visibility, and public accountability, is changing as the Overseas Chinese expand into high-tech growth fields such as telecommunications and computers. However, there is no Overseas Chinese equivalent to high profile executives like Bill Gates of Microsoft, or Akio Morita, the leader of Sony. This, too, is likely to change as Overseas Chinese business organizations evolve to become more transparent and less patriarchal.

Despite these difficulties, undoubtedly made worse by the present Asian financial crisis, the Overseas Chinese have proven themselves repeatedly to be able to adapt to changing business conditions. The core values that have given them this distinctive ability to thrive, rather than merely survive, under the most trying circumstances, include an abiding belief in hard work, strong family ties, frugality, and education.

The most crucial element in the economic success of the Overseas Chinese seems to be their shared memory as emigrants. According to Overseas Chinese billionaire Lee Shau Kee, "the success of the Overseas Chinese is the result of bad times in China itself. The Chinese who left the mother country had to struggle, and that became a culture of its own, passed on from father to son through each generation. Because we have no social security, the Overseas Chinese habit is to save a lot and make a lot of friends" [Kraar 1994]. The uncertainties and hardships of immigrant life have reinforced the Overseas Chinese penchant for a guarded style of business that does not cede control easily. Major deals are usually closed by the patriarch, and he makes such deals only with people he knows and trusts. In that sense, just about every Chinese business proprietor, no matter how large his organization, is a hands-on entrepreneur. This may explain the remarkable success of the

Overseas Chinese in combining their innate sense for "smelling profit" with the ability take business decisions very quickly. By being pragmatic rather than legalistic, they are able to close large deals in a matter of a few days, whereas the same transaction in the United States could easily take several months.

The Overseas businesses also benefit from their considerable patience. They are typically more willing and able than widely held public corporations to take a long-term view, without worrying about impatient shareholders. This, in turn, gives them a competitive advantage in those areas or projects where it is not possible to realize an immediate return. Instead of impatient investors and the high level of institutionalization relied upon in the West, Overseas Chinese rely upon their *guanxi*, or personal connections, to preserve their network ties. In Mainland China, for example, Overseas Chinese use their *guanxi* to make up for weaknesses in the rule of law and lack of transparency in rules and regulations. In an uncertain business environment, speaking the same language and sharing important cultural values are often crucial.

Today, people and contacts are still the foundation of Chinese business. As members of a new generation of Overseas Chinese come to power, many with education in the West, a new model for Chinese enterprises is gradually emerging. This new model relies more on Western management techniques while retaining the traditional strengths of a family-owned firm. It is probable that each of these first-generation entrepreneurial firms will have to make the transition to a more professional style of management in order to remain viable in the face of ever-increasing competition from Japanese corporations and Western multinationals.

The Overseas Chinese and the Hong Kong Textile and Electronics Industries
Hong Kong's industrialization was unique among the postwar East Asian growth "miracles" because the state played a very limited role. Historically, industrialization in Hong Kong has been propelled by small and medium-sized companies. The average number employed in these firms declined even as their numbers climbed and industrial growth accelerated, thus illustrating the ease with which new enterprises were formed. In 1994, 95.6 percent of Hong Kong's 34,068 manufacturing establishments employed fewer than 50 people. The Chinese who enter into industrial competition take great pride in proprietorship and disdain salaried employment, and the patterns of entrepreneurial familism in Hong Kong's first wave of industrialization have survived largely intact. They are reflected in today's domination of the Hong Kong Stock Exchange by listed companies that remain under family control. Indeed, by 1988, ten family groups controlled 54 percent of Hong Kong's stock market capitalization; seven were ethnic Chinese, and only three were

British [Department of Foreign Affairs and Trade, Australia 1995, 93]. Hong Kong confronts the same issue as do Western industrialized states: can the mass-manufacturing industries that fueled growth in the first stages of industrialization remain viable in changing markets? With its small domestic market, geographical, cultural, and political access to low-cost labor on the mainland, and unparalleled experience in transferring and coordinating production in that vast hinterland, this issue is particularly acute for Hong Kong.

Textiles are an area of particular concern to Hong Kong. With sales of US$ 21 billion out of a world total of US$ 153 billion, Hong Kong has been the world's largest exporter of clothing [Hong Kong's Manufacturing Industries 1995]. After Germany, it was also the world's second largest exporter of textiles. The experience of other high-wage countries suggests that textiles and clothing need not become "sunset" industries for Honk Kong. In the United States, for example, this sector continues to rank among the top four industries in terms of employment, sales, contribution to manufacturing GDP, and in recent years, productivity increases. As in the United States and Western Europe, however, the number of employees in textiles and clothing manufacturing in Hong Kong has declined rapidly over the past decade. But even in its reduced dimensions, this sector continues to be very important, both as the largest segment of Hong Kong manufacturing and as the coordinating hub of production networks that carry a high volume of business into and out of China and beyond.

To a substantial degree Hong Kong clothing and textile manufacturing businesses retain the traditional organizational structure of ethnic Chinese enterprises: control and management remain squarely in the hands of the founder or the founder's family, and even in companies that have gone public, the senior family figure remains the dominant influence in the firm's management.

Despite their outmoded organizational structures, these firms retain a high degree of flexibility. They display an unusual capacity to turn out a wide range of products and to switch product lines rapidly. These firms have learned how to produce an increasing number of products from within a single plant in order to satisfy the demand for a greater variety of goods. For example, some firms with as few as 200 employees are able to work on 20 different styles at one time, providing customers with orders as small as 150-350 pieces. There can be little doubt that this flexibility has been a great competitive advantage for manufacturers whose outmoded organizational structures might otherwise have failed the rigorous demands of global competition.

Strength also comes from the ability of Hong Kong's clothing and textile manufacturers to understand the very different needs of customers in different markets. From its beginnings in the 1950s, Hong Kong's manufacturers realized that American and European buyers had different demands and different ways of doing business. American buyers had highly detailed specifications and emphasized price, but they also wanted long production runs and high-volume business. American buyers also tended to bring models that they wanted copied exactly. European buyers, on the other hand, solicited design ideas from Hong Kong manufacturers and focused more on consistency and quality and remaining loyal to their suppliers. Europe is not one big market, however, but a composite of distinct smaller markets. Twelve thousand pieces may be a small order for the United States; five hundred pieces is a large order for Europe. Clearly then, the organization of production for these markets differs greatly. Hong Kong firms avoided specialization and learned instead how to serve both types of customers simultaneously. Through their astute ability to recognize customer needs, Hong Kong's textile and garment manufacturers were able to become globally competitive.

For the future, Hong Kong textile and garment manufacturers are looking use the capabilities developed over the course of many years of doing business in American and European markets to leverage a move into new markets. They are most keen to succeed in Japan and China, and while there is great potential in both, there are also enormous obstacles.

Japan has very affluent consumers who are extremely demanding in terms of quality. And the Japanese retail system is dominated by small shops and department stores with sales counters controlled by individual brand name producers. Although Japan, unlike the United States and Europe, does not have country-of-origin rules limiting imports made by Hong Kong companies in plants located in the Peoples Republic of China, access to the Japanese market virtually requires a Japanese corporation. Cultivating relationships with Japanese partners is a very lengthy process that requires careful fulfillment of multiple small orders.

For those who wish to sell to the Chinese market, there is virtually unlimited potential. As in Japan, some daunting obstacles must to overcome, but after the 1997 reunification with China, Hong Kong producers are no longer outsiders. Ethnic ties and geographic proximity will help Hong Kong firms to overcome obstacles more easily than producers based in other countries. Retail sales have been growing at about 12 percent per year in China. There is a rapidly growing number of consumers who are willing and able to spend greater amounts of money on good quality clothing. Brand name recognition is also high in China, and those Hong Kong companies that have implemented brand-name strategies in China have done well, despite the high costs of advertising. The key challenges for the Hong Kong textile and clothing industry are the absence or weakness of retail outlets, regulations that make it virtually impossible for Hong Kong retailers to establish their own shops, and very high rents. Hong Kong textile and clothing manufacturers have overcome these difficulties by selling their products in department and franchise stores, and persisting in attempts to open their own retail shops in China.

Once a name brand is established in China it becomes a tempting target for copying. While piracy is a continual source of headaches for Hong Kong producers, their customers in China are at the top of the income scale and resist buying inferior pirated goods. Thus, although they damage the brand's image, pirated goods are probably not cutting deeply into the market of Hong Kong producers.

Some of the most highly valued attributes of Hong Kong textile and clothing products derive from the location and reputation of the city itself. Hong Kong's role as the one-stop shopping center for Asia, like New York City's role in the West, depends on a concentration of activities and a comprehensive industry, all parts of which are readily accessible from within the city. Hong Kong's small size makes it possible for business executives to manage the whole value chain. Sales outlets are in Hong Kong; factories are owned, managed, and financed by Hong Kong personnel; and the profits accrue in and to Hong Kong. In this manner Hong Kong's textile firms have functioned as the "nerve center" of the city's manufacturing industry.

Despite these strengths and the vast potential for future sales in China and other emerging and developed markets, ethnic Chinese textile and clothing manufacturing firms in Hong Kong remain vulnerable on several fronts. Nearly all firms remain under the control of the firm's founder or the founder's family members. Only a few firms have non-family members in key positions. All family firms must solve the problems of succession and of finding strong leadership in the second and third generation, but this universal dilemma is compounded by a traditional pattern spreading the inheritance of family business assets among the male siblings. This can lead to a fragmentation of the business, and it makes it even harder to bring qualified outsiders into management positions. In these firms many competent mid- to senior-level managers sense correctly that they have little chance of rising to the top, no matter how hard they work or how good their record.

In U.S. and European manufacturers the most severe job cuts have been made at the middle levels of the organizations. In these countries, however, the thinning of middle management have been compensated for somewhat by providing better opportunities to lower ranks through better training and more responsibility. No such knowledge transfer is taking place in Hong Kong firms or their China production sites. As a result Hong Kong producers remain extraordinarily dependent upon strong control from the top, and, beyond the founder's generation, these firms cannot assure the dynamic leadership needed to ensure their future success [Berger and Gartner 1997, 140-69].

The specific characteristics of the Hong Kong textile industry are evident in a brief comparison with the city's electronics industry, which exemplifies new, rather than old, money. Electronics is also one of the city's top manufacturing industries. Even though electronics accounted for only 3.5 percent of all manufacturing establishments in Hong Kong, it employed 10.5 percent of Hong Kong workers in manufacturing and contributed 26.2 percent to Hong Kong's total domestic exports [Tuan and Ng 1995]. In order for Hong Kong's electronics industry to grow at a rate of approximately 5 percent annually (the growth rate of Hong Kong's real GDP), one or more of the following must occur: the number of multinational corporations in Hong Kong needs to increase; the number of Hong Kong-based companies must increase; or the size of the present companies in Hong Kong must increase.

Most electronics companies in Hong Kong have adopted a low-cost, flexible manufacturing strategy. This is true for both component and end-product manufacturers. Their emphasis has been on producing established electronic products at lower cost. Hong Kong producers have been able to follow this strategy when the original developer of a product decides that it can no longer earn an acceptable profit margin making the product itself. If demand for the product remains strong, Hong Kong manufacturers quickly step in to fill the gap and use low-cost, flexible manufacturing systems to produce a higher profit margin. It is of course true that profit margins will erode for Hong Kong electronics manufacturers, but they are sufficiently flexible to shift quickly to other products with better margins.

Although the electronics industry has been growing at a healthy pace, the continuation of well-tested strategies is risky. Other low-cost manufacturers in newly industrializing countries may begin to chip away at Hong Kong's competitive advantage in this sector. Since they do not rely on a migrant workforce, producers in other regions of mainland China, such as Shanghai, have lower labor costs and a more stable workforce than do producers operating in Guangdong province. They also enjoy access to relatively skilled labor and a very competitive transportation infrastructure of shipping ports and roads. Furthermore, even if Hong Kong electronics manufacturers adopt a strategy of significantly improving their production processes, the industry will not reach its full potential. Instead, they must learn how to create new products. The formation of new companies is, thus, very important if Hong Kong's electronics producers wish to move into new industry segments. New companies would bring innovations in product and technology and avoiding the trap of operating simply as original equipment manufacturers producing mature products.

Finally, an increased presence of multinational corporations is important to the continued growth of Hong Kong's electronics industry. One of the major reasons why multinationals come to Asia is to gain access to both low-cost labor and expanding markets. No market is more promising than China's. Compared to mainland China and other countries Hong Kong is at a distinct disadvantage in its efforts to attract the investments of multinational corporations. It does not offer incentives such as tax holidays, low land prices, or reasonable costs for housing and office space.

While there are many challenges, Hong Kong's electronics producers also have plenty of opportunities. This is true especially if ethnic Chinese enterprises in this sector move towards a strategy of product innovation and begin to view China and multinational corporations as valuable partners, especially in the marketing and distribution of innovative products [Reif and Sodini 1997].

In both textiles and electronics, networks provide the Overseas Chinese with a base from which to conduct their business throughout Asia and, increasingly, the rest of the world. Business activities are always embedded in the context of the norms of specific locales, and networks institutionalize business norms and provide a comfortable framework within which the Overseas Chinese can operate.

Overseas Chinese Banking in Asia

The Overseas financial and banking system has a strong impact on capital markets in Asia. Hong Kong is the financial capital of Southeast Asia, and Taiwan and Singapore are important secondary nodes. Personal connections and interpersonal trust are central to the Chinese banking system. Whether a financial system based on personal trust can remain viable as levels of institutionalization in the financial industry increase in a modernizing Asia is the most vexing issue for the future of Overseas networks.

Hong Kong

Historically Hong Kong has had many advantages that account for its role as Asia's financial hub. In the last two decades, its role as the natural gateway to mainland China, with its booming economy, has served Hong Kong markets extremely well. Its bilingual culture greatly facilitates communication with North American, European, and Japanese investors, all of whom typically rely on English as their language for international commerce. Finally, members of the Hong Kong financial community also derive an advantage from their familiarity with Chinese customs. They know how to navigate the tangled web of bureaucratic rules that surrounds anyone doing business in China.

A local Hong Kong business partner is often seen as the crucial component in the arrangement of a business deal in China. Although manufacturing facilities have increasingly moved onto the mainland, their headquarters and regional offices remain in Hong Kong. The financial community is not particularly interested in being in close proximity to manufacturing operations, but prefers ready access to representatives from firms' headquarters. Access is a definite advantage that Hong Kong continues to offer.

Ethnic Chinese hoping to start up a new business venture in Hong Kong typically avoid the formal financial markets and, instead, rely on family funds for financing. Although family financing is not unique to Hong Kong companies, it is virtually unheard of in Hong Kong to find a company that did not start out with family money. Members of the investment community rarely see applicants for new venture start-ups. Entrepreneurs tend to fear a loss of control if they turn to non-family financing and sometimes suspect that they would not be able to secure outside funding for their ventures.

While the financial sector in Hong Kong is large, active, and sophisticated, it does not supply capital in sufficient quantities to technology start-ups to support a vibrant high-tech sector in Hong Kong. This capital shortfall is part of a cycle in which the lack of investors and the lack of entrepreneurs feed on each other. There are three main reasons for this funding bottleneck. First, although this is now changing, there have been few entrepreneurs in Hong Kong who focused on high-tech. Second, would-be investors in the high-tech sector have had many lucrative opportunities in other areas, such as local real estate and the increasingly rapid expansion of Hong Kong manufacturing firms in the Pearl River Delta region of the mainland. Finally, and perhaps most importantly, there are few viable exit strategies for potential investors.

Software companies exemplify the challenges facing high-tech start-up firms in Hong Kong. Most are initially self-financed. Few receive venture capital or are able to secure extended bank loans. In order for these firms to grow and thrive, they need expansion capital, for which the flow of internal funds is crucial. Due to the lack of external capital, many have been unable to expand rapidly and, as a result, are looking for ways to facilitate contacts with large firms that require their services. Such contacts may help establish partnerships able to infuse the capital needed for sustained growth. In general, however, these firms continue to rely on personal finances and software sales. Group Sense is one company that has been successful with this strategy. This software company was founded in 1988, using only personal and family funds. The company grew by reinvesting its profits. Rather than inventing the technologies it uses, the company adapts existing technologies for local markets. The history of Group Sense shows that Hong Kong firms can succeed without funding from capital markets. Small, self-financed companies are viable if they take advantage of Hong Kong's considerable local strengths while drawing on outside expertise.

Chinese banks, however, are much less likely to make loans to high-tech companies than to other industries. In many cases, the primary product of such a company is an idea or new way of doing business. The high value that Chinese attach to tangible forms of wealth, such as real estate or gold bars, makes it difficult to obtain financial backing on the basis of an idea. Furthermore, these high-tech firms face stiff international competition. Software firms, for example, must compete immediately with U.S. and European firms which attract capital market funding more readily. They must also compete with software companies from emerging countries, such as India, which may have a considerable cost advantage.

The financial structure of Hong Kong's large high-tech firms is quite similar to that of smaller, start-up firms. Larger firms also tend to rely heavily on internal financing or short-term bank loans. Even though they have much greater access to Hong Kong's sophisticated capital markets, it is still rare for larger firms to access these markets for long-term project financing. Most large firms continue to rely on internal funds as the primary source of expansion capital.

Nevertheless, Hong Kong banks are the first contact most firms have with the financial sector, usually through trade credit arrangements. Manufacturing and related industries tend to account for only a small percentage of the banking business in Hong Kong, and the portfolios of domestic banks are heavily weighted in the property and retail sectors. Before 1978, regulations restricted most foreign banks to operating only a single branch, effectively barring them from operating a large-scale retail business under their own name. In general, foreign banks have affiliates of multinationals from their home countries as their major customers. Foreign banks also finance a small number of local property deals, but many fewer than do local banks [Bernard and Hallward-Driemeier 1997].

The Bank of East Asia and the Evolution of a Modern Chinese Banking System
Officially opened on January 4, 1919, the Bank of East Asia offers a concrete illustration of the evolution of Chinese banking. It was hardly a coincidence that a modern Chinese bank appeared at this juncture in Hong Kong's history. The economic expansion in the colony during the early twentieth century and an evolving social and economic structure combined to both create a demand for a new type of bank and allow the accumulation of the Chinese capital needed to form a bank to fill that demand.

In the decades leading up to the bank's founding, Chinese businessmen in Hong Kong had been moving up the economic ladder and branching out into all types of businesses. In practice, by the mid-1910s, ethnic Chinese were no longer excluded from any area of commerce. Chinese-owned, Chinese-managed, and Chinese-staffed joint stock companies were doing business in fire, marine, and life insurance, as well as in shipping, ship-building and repair, and real estate. A small number of Chinese were even beginning to have seats on the boards of directors of both small and large British firms. And they were becoming more willing to invest in industrial ventures.

As Chinese businessmen in Hong Kong moved into new areas of business and up the hierarchy of authority and power, many found existing financial organizations inadequate. At the same time, they were eager to invest their funds in profitable ventures. A few began to realize that modern banking could provide them with those opportunities.

Previously, most Hong Kong banks had a very narrow capital base and were owned by only one proprietor or a small number of partners with a small capital base. People made deposits in these banks based solely on the proprietor's reputation. Although the interest rates were quite high, so too, were the risks the depositors faced. As a result, depositors were almost always related in some way to the proprietor. They were either direct family members, distant relatives, friends, or persons from the same region or hometown. It was highly unlikely that anyone would make a deposit in the bank of a total stranger.

Personal relationship was also the basis for determining whether the bank would grant a loan. These banks accepted a wide range of collateral, such as real estate, jewelry, gold bullion, or antiques; loans were frequently made against only a baidan, or "white bill." These I.O.U.'s had no security other than a man's reputation. Thus, the risks of bad loans were high, and one way to minimize those risks was to confine the bank's lending business to a tight circle based on personal connections. The result was an inflexible and, to outsiders, closed money market.

The first modern Chinese-owned bank in Hong Kong, the Bank of Canton, opened in 1912. It was formed by Chinese returning from San Francisco. In 1919, The Bank of East Asia started operations and was the first public, Chinese-capitalized bank to be traded on the stock exchange. The bank had nine founders, but the original idea had sprung from three key figures: Kan Tong-po and Li Koon-chun and his brother Tse-fong. The two families had been close friends and these social ties developed into a valuable business relationship.

The nine founders became permanent directors. This structure provided continuity by making the Bank a life-long commitment for all of them. Seven of the permanent directors were still serving on the board at the end of the Second World War, and the last founder did not pass away until 1978. Continuity was also maintained through business and family ties. The business relationship between the three key founders, originally built on social connections, continued into the next generation. The children of the founders grew up as friends, schoolmates and neighbors, and a series of marriages between the families further sealed the relationship. Strong ties were especially important as the second generation joined the bank. Through trade and industry, the nine directors also formed important and profitable overseas ties, especially with Japanese and French businessmen in Indochina.

Local Chinese Banks in Hong Kong

The evolution of banks such as the Bank of East Asia no doubt helped to propel Hong Kong to its current status as a modern and sophisticated regional financial center. But older native banks, or *yinhao*, did not simply vanish. The *yinhao* had had dealings with foreign banks, and they developed close relationships with the newly established modern, Chinese banks, even though those banks were to take much of their business.

The modern banks provided much needed safety and a variety of new financial services to the older, native banks. The native banks, in turn, with their intimate knowledge of local commercial activities at all levels, provided them with indirect access to the local market. Thus, the original local banks became "feeders" to such modern Chinese banks as the Bank of East Asia. This system has perpetuated itself [Sinn 1994].

Hong Kong's banking sector has been influenced greatly by fluctuations in the domestic economy, in particular, the cyclical nature of the real estate sector. Despite past problems, local Chinese banks have played an important role in the post-war economic development of Hong Kong. They not only financed foreign trade, but were also involved in making loans to industry. Although bank loans to industry are technically short-term, the debt is generally not called, and thus, serves as a form of long-term financing. This has been important because Hong Kong has no industrial development bank to provide such capital.

All local Chinese banks started as family businesses. As discussed previously, some were founded in the early 1910s, while others were established in the late 1940s when private business was driven out of China in the aftermath of the Communist victory. A few banks were set up in the 1950s and 1960s, and only one was established in the 1981, the Sun Hung Kai Bak, founded by the Fung family (see Table 3.1). Several founders of Chinese banks had humble origins as money changers or gold traders.

During the rapid economic development of the 1960s and 1970s, local Chinese banks flourished and became modern banking institutions. Some have gone public. Others have imported modern management and financial expertise by entering into a variety of arrangements with international banks. Despite these changes, local Chinese banks are still predominantly organized along family lines and are run in the traditional Chinese patriarchal manner.

Table 3.1
Membership List of the Chinese Banks' Association, Hong Kong

Bank of China Hong Kong	Wing On Bank, Ltd.
Bank of East Asia, Limited	Hong Nin Bank, Ltd.
Shanghai Commercial Bank, Ltd.	Dah Sing Bank, Limited
Bank of Canton, Ltd.	Liu Ching Hing Bank, Ltd.
Nanyang Commercial Bank, Ltd.	Commercial Bank of Hong Kong
Bank of Communications	Chung Khiaw Bank, Ltd.
Sin Hua Trust Savings & Commercial Bank, Ltd.	Tai Sang Bank, Ltd.
Wing Lung Bank, Ltd.	Overseas Trust Bank, Ltd.
National Commercial Bank, Ltd.	Hongkong Industrial & Commercial Bank, Ltd.
Kwangtung Provincial Bank	Ka Wah Bank, Limited
China and South Sea Bank, Limited	Po Sang Bank, Ltd.
Kincheng Banking Corporation	Chekiang First Bank, Limited
China State Bank, Ltd.	Hong Kong Chinese Bank, Ltd.
Yien Yieh Commercial Bank, Ltd.	Far East Bank, Limited
Chiyu Banking Corporation, Ltd.	Dao Heng Bank, Ltd.
Hua Chiao Commercial Bank, Ltd.	Sun Hung Kai Bank, Ltd.
Overseas-Chinese Banking Corporation, Ltd.	Wing Hang Bank, Ltd.

Source: The Chinese Banks' Association, Hong Kong, 1986

In contrast to foreign banks which have concentrated on wholesale banking, local Chinese banks specialized in retail banking, that is, money lending, mortgage, trade finance, and money exchange. Local banks serve a predominantly Chinese community, and have established long-term links with small businessmen. These close relationships are strengthened further when bank executives and clients speak the same Chinese dialect. For example, Liu Ching Hing Bank in Hong Kong has established good relationships with small businessmen who speak the Tiewchow dialect. Although retail banking is still their specialty, recent years have seen some larger and well-established Chinese banks expand into wholesale banking by linking up with international banks to arrange syndicated loans for overseas borrowers.

The major impediments to the further development of Chinese banking are the complicated links that bind companies to other businesses operated by the banks' owners and other members of their families. Personal connections between family members and friends have a profound impact on the lending practices of local Chinese bankers, as loans are readily available to those with personal connections. This discounting of an individual's creditworthiness increases the commercial risks banks run and makes them especially vulnerable during periods of economic downturn, as was demonstrated during the Asian crisis of the second half of 1997.

Taiwan

After Hong Kong, Taiwan is a second major center of Chinese banking in Asia. In Taiwan, over 90 percent of businesses are small- and medium-sized and are owned by family members [Taiwan Economic Research 1998]. In these firms, the necessary capital usually comes from immediate family, more distant relatives, or family friends. This system of financing new business ventures is deeply ingrained in the Chinese social order and its underlying value system, allows for a high degree of autonomy in the management of firms, and makes transfers of ownership relatively rare. However, avoiding the use of capital from the public or banking sector limits opportunities to spread business risks and expand firms.

In the West, managers have a contractual relationship with their companies, and the manager's job performance usually determines his pay, promotion, and job security. This is not the case in Taiwan. The power of appointment is held by the *laoban*, or "boss," typically the family patriarch, who may choose to appoint many family members to key positions within the organization.

The importance of family in Taiwanese business has important legal ramifications. In particular, the Taiwanese "limited corporation" does not have the same well defined legal liabilities as its Western counterpart. The crisis of the Tenth Credit Cooperative Association is a good example of what can happen. The crisis began with a cash flow problem. The chairman of the board of the Tenth Credit Cooperative Association was also the vice president of the Cathay Plastics business group, and when Cathay Plastics ran a deficit and needed a large amount of money quickly, its funds were tied up in real estate. In order to get the funds, the vice-president obtained a loan from the Tenth Credit Cooperative Association and borrowed through informal financial channels and from employees' deposits in his enterprises. In principle, if his "credit" had been good, it would have just been a technical problem of getting cash to be solved by tapping his personal networks. But when the government decreed that the Tenth Credit Cooperative Association should stop business for three days, his personal credit, based on the trust he enjoyed in his personal network, was fatally damaged. The result was the bankruptcy of the entire business group. Because of a small cash flow problem in one business, all other Cathay businesses suffered. Cathay Plastic, Cathay Trust, and Sun-Lai business groups, all owned by a single family, went bankrupt and were subsequently taken over or sold. In effect, all the branches of "Cathay" that had been inherited from the group's founder disappeared.

While this degree of personal liability is unthinkable in Western corporate law, in Taiwan it is thought quite natural that relatives should share liability. Thus, there is an expectation of joint-liability for a family business. The family is viewed as a corporation of unlimited liability. Under these circumstances, Taiwanese enterprises cannot possibly become legal entities, and corporate law merely defines the formal criteria of a company's establishment, not its modus operandi.

Western companies can be viewed as legally defined entities that satisfy their capital needs with funding from various sources in institutionalized, formal financial sectors, such as banks and the stock market. By contrast, Taiwan's enterprises can be viewed as socially defined entities which raise capital from within the society, particularly from within the family. Thus, the fundamental differences between the two systems rest on the different ways in which businesses create and maintain capital. In the West, the system relies on a foundation of secured credit. In the East, the foundation is personal trust.

The importance of personal connections is also apparent in the Taiwanese stock exchange. From 1985 to 1989, more than 35 percent of Taiwan's total population invested in the stock market. Increased investment in the market was due in large part to personal connections among investors. The main criterion for entry into the stock market in Taiwan is not credit rating or personal wealth, but rather a personal connection to a stock broker. Stock brokers, in turn, exploit their own personal networks, which further speeds up the rate of investment in the market. Although these networks have no legal standing in financial markets, they are important parts of the social order.

Formal social insurance and security are not well established in either in Taiwan or Hong Kong or, indeed, anywhere in Asia. People know they must take care of their own needs both on a daily basis and for old age. In addition Chinese families normally provide for their children's education, marriage, and even housing. Thus high levels of family savings are regarded as essential. The amount of savings for children and old age can be estimated, but the amount needed for emergencies is impossible to predict. Thus families tend to save as much as possible. After daily needs are met, many families save most of the remainder of their income.

Capital for investment is available only after very high savings have been accumulated to cover a family's various short- and long-term needs. In recent years, the fluidity of investment funds in Taiwan indicates that the accumulation of wealth has surpassed the psychological threshold for minimum savings. There has also been an increase in the number of channels that lead investments to the stock market. It is also possible that families, seeking speculative gains, are beginning to ignore the psychological boundaries separating personal wealth from investment capital.

There exist no close links between the formal and informal financial sectors, but both are part of a system that is based upon a single set of social norms of personal connections. These connections are unique to the Taiwanese financial system, although similar systems based upon personal connections and trust are found in Chinese societies throughout Asia. They determine the available range of investment channels, formal, informal or both, and the possibilities for and limits of the creation and circulation of capital in financial markets. Personal relationships and personal trust combine with practical and material interests, each reinforcing the other in daily life. Because this combination is so deeply rooted within the social structure of Taiwan, it is virtually impossible to destroy these personal networks without also destroying the entire financial system [Lin 1984].

Ethnic Chinese Banking in Southeast Asia

Chinese banking stretches beyond Hong Kong and Taiwan throughout Southeast Asia. A large number of Chinese banks were established after the region recovered from the Great Depression, when some Chinese banks were forced to close or to merge. During World War II, all colonial regimes were disrupted, as was the regional economic system of the Overseas Chinese. Chinese banks were forced either to suspend service or to take refuge elsewhere, in places such as Australia or India. After World War II, the colonial powers faced difficulties in reestablishing their rule, and the French and Dutch eventually granted independence to their colonies in Indochina and Indonesia. While Chinese banks continued to flourish where decolonization had not yet occurred, increased economic nationalism in the new states threatened their operations.

The banks' difficulties were due to the large size of the Chinese controlled sector both in the national economies of the new states and in the regional trading system. The new states imposed limits on Chinese banks that badly disrupted foreign trade. Chinese banking had traditionally provided financial services for trading operations, which were mainly operated by ethnic Chinese. Political demonstrations, including violence, against ethnic Chinese by the indigenous populations was common and resulted, at times, in legislation that further impeded the operation of Chinese-owned banks within these countries.

The politics of independent countries has often made it difficult to define "Chinese bank" precisely, especially in places where many Chinese banks have been forced to take on local partners. These cases differ from outright nationalizations, in which Chinese banks were absorbed into the national bank of a country. A "Chinese bank" can be defined loosely as a bank that originated from an individual or group of Chinese, with ownership shared solely or largely among Chinese business clients.

Generally speaking, Chinese banking in Southeast Asia has continued to grow and prosper only in Singapore and Hong Kong, where there are overwhelming Chinese majorities. In Singapore, for example, the Overseas Chinese Bank Corporation, Lee Wah Bank, Four Seasons Communications Bank, Overseas Union Bank, and United Overseas Bank are major banks established in or before the 1940s. In the 1950s, Asia Commercial Bank, Chung Khiaw Bank, and Far Eastern Bank were also set up. In the 1960s and 1970s, Development Bank of Singapore and the Industrial Bank of Singapore emerged. By 1986, there were 13 Chinese banks incorporated in Singapore. Before there was any significant foreign direct investment, these banks played a very important role in channeling private wealth into industrialization.

Similar developments occurred in Hong Kong. Up to the 1980s, most of the industries in Hong Kong were financed by Chinese banks. Without the safe and convenient service provided by local, Chinese banks, it would have been unimaginable for local industries to collect 90 percent of their investment capital from local funds [Chan 1989].

The Future of Chinese Banking in Asia
High-speed technological innovations and new product developments introduced into the banking sector in recent years have brought both new opportunities and novel threats for Chinese banks in Asia. If the banks are to survive and prosper in an era of increasing competition and organizational change, it is important for them to base their strategies on a thorough analysis of the banking environment that identifies clearly viable, competitive strategies. Chinese banks need to identify those market niches for which they are best suited. Since local Chinese banks are typically small, they need to husband their limited resources and concentrate, as a core business, on one or a limited number of groups within an industry or financial sector. Most local Chinese banks already have clear identities and rely on news tools, such as management by objective, to implement their strategies [Nyaw and Lau 1989].

Just as in the United States and the United Kingdom, the banking industry in Hong Kong is undergoing a marketing revolution. 1978, when the Hong Kong government lifted the moratorium on bank licenses, was key. Foreign banks rushed into the market and generated intense competitive pressures on local banks. Because Hong Kong's policy no longer discriminated against foreign banks doing local currency business, foreign banks could easily enter into the traditional core businesses of local Chinese banks. The early 1980s was, thus, an extremely difficult period for local Chinese banks. With the support of the Exchange Fund, the Hong Kong government took over three local Chinese banks and extended standby-credit to several others. The government also gave financial guarantees to financial institutions acquiring two ailing banks [Ho 1989]. However, those local Chinese banks that did survive have been exposed to the competitive pressures of international finance for twenty years now, useful preparation for the difficulties that lie ahead.

The many difficulties and bankruptcies notwithstanding, local Chinese banks will play an important role in Asia's new banking environment. The previously discussed Bank of East Asia is a good example. Soon after 1978 the bank launched various projects in cooperation with banks in the United States, Great Britain, Japan, and even China. Under highly professional management, the bank took advantage of a rapidly changing business environment and utilized its comparative advantage, a thorough knowledge of the local environment in Hong Kong and China, to form strategic alliances with foreign partners in profitable business ventures [Lee 1989].

If the local, traditionally managed and operated Chinese banks are to survive globalization and the opening up of mainland China's economy, they will need to follow the example of the Bank of East Asia in forming linkages with China and the international community. Furthermore, they will have to establish within their organizations mechanisms for more open and professional styles of management without sacrificing the personal connections and specialized market niches that made them so successful in the first place. This requires a delicate balance, but it is one they must strike if they are going to survive and prosper in the twenty-first century.

In this chapter, I have argued that East Asian economic development has been organized and achieved by mean of the business and production networks. In order to understand the characteristics of East Asian regionalism this paper provides an in-depth analysis of Overseas Chinese networks by focusing on the three sectors of textiles, electronics, and banking in Hong Kong, Taiwan and other East Asian countries.

It is unquestionable that Overseas Chinese business networks play a very important role in East Asian economic development. "Although they are fewer then ten percent of the population of East Asia, ethnic Chinese outside China make up 86 percent of its billionaires. They control much of the region's non-land capital and its retail trade, and are major stakeholders in most of the region's economies" [Department of Foreign Affairs and Trade, Australia 1995]. Most Overseas Chinese businesses are on the small or medium side, and typically, they are family owned. There are many factors, including entrepreneurship and a spirit of hard work, that contribute to their success, but the main strength of Overseas Chinese business is its networks and their capacity to adapt. The networks provide access to domestic markets, allowing Overseas Chinese businesses to expand efficiently and without regard to borders.

Business networks, however, are also a source of weakness for Overseas Chinese entrepreneurs. They create the conditions for flexibility, allowing businesses to react quickly to ever-changing market conditions, but their lack of formal institutions, managerial professionalism, the rule of law, and financial transparency have become more problematic in recent years. The increased intensity of global competition has revealed weaknesses in the form of economic organization preferred by the Overseas Chinese. The challenge for the future, then, lies in strengthening processes of institutionalization in business affairs without sacrificing the advantages of the business networks that have worked so well for the Overseas Chinese.

REFERENCES

Berger, Suzanne with David Gartner and Kevin Karty. 1997. "Textiles and Clothing in Hong Kong," in Suzanne Berger and Richard K. Lester, eds., *Made by Hong Kong*, pp. 140-69. Hong Kong: Oxford University Press.

Bernard, Andrew B. and Mary Hallward-Driemeier. 1997. "Capital Market in Hong Kong," in Suzanne Berger and Richard K. Lester, eds., *Made by Hong Kong*, pp. 294-316. Hong Kong: Oxford University Press.

Ch'ng, David C.K. 1993. *The Overseas Chinese Entrepreneurs in East Asia: Background, Business Practices and International Networks*. Melbourne: Committee for Economic Development of Australia.

Chang, Chak-yan. 1989. "Localization and Chinese Banking in Southeast Asia," in Nyaw Mee-kau and Chang Chak-yan, eds., *Chinese Banking in Asia's Market Economies*, pp. 7-17. Overseas Chinese Archives, CCAS, The Chinese University of Hong Kong.

Department of Foreign Affairs and Trade, Australia. 1995. *Overseas Chinese Business Networks in Asia*. Canberra: AGPS Press

Ge, Lei-shi. 1998. "New President Visited the Chinese Community, *International Chinese Newsweekly*, 22(12) (July 1-July 7). Japan Print (Hong Kong), p. 44.

International Institute for Management Development (IMD). 1998. *World Competitiveness Year Book*. Swiss.

Kao, John. 1993. "The Worldwide Web of Chinese Business," *Harvard Business Review* 71 (March-April): pp. 24-32.

Kraar, Louis. 1994. "The Overseas Chinese: Lesson from the World's Most Dynamic Capitalists." *Fortune* (October 31) pp. 91-113.

Lee, Kam-hon. 1989. "Competition Among Commercial Banks in Hong Kong— A Strategic Marketing Review for Local Chinese Banks," in Nyaw Mee-kau and Chang Chak-yan, eds., *Chinese Banking in Asia's Market Economies*, p. 94. Overseas Chinese Archives, CCAS, The Chinese University of Hong Kong.

Lin, Pao-an. 1991. "The Social Sources of Capital Investment in Taiwan's Industrialization," in Gary Hamilton, ed., *Business Networks and Economic Development in East and Southeast Asia.* pp. 66-77. Hong Kong: Centre of Asian Studies, University of Hong Kong.

Nyaw, Mee-kau and Lau, Ho-fuk. 1989. "The Banking Environment and Competitive Strategies for Local Chinese Bank in Hong Kong," in Nyaw Mee-kau and Chang Chak-yan, eds., *Chinese Banking in Asia's Market Economies*, pp. 57-71. Overseas Chinese Archives, CCAS, The Chinese University of Hong Kong.

Sinn, Elizabeth. 1994. *Growing with Hong Kong: The Bank of East Asia 1919-1994*, pp. 1-15. Golden Cup Printing Co. Ltd. Hong Kong: Bank of East Asia, Ltd.

Tanzer, Andrew. 1997. "The Global Power Elite," *Forbes* 160(2) (July 28), pp. 90-96.

Yan-ki, Ho. 1989. "The Performance of Chinese Banks in Hong Kong," in Nyaw Mee-kau and Chang Chak-yan, eds., *Chinese Banking in Asia's Market Economies*, p. 113. Overseas Chinese Archives, CCAS, The Chinese University of Hong Kong.

4

Regional Capital and Cooperation in Asia

Natasha Hamilton-Hart

This chapter describes the transnational banking relationships, capital flows, and limited moves towards cooperation that have contributed to an uneven regionalism in Asia. The unevenness of Asian regionalism helps explain the political controversy that has surrounded the idea for most of this century. The complex and sometimes opaque processes that define the region also constrain the emergence of a regional order, making it politically problematic and, in some ways, intellectually puzzling.

Perhaps the most basic problem concerns where the region begins and ends. Other regions do not have static boundaries but in Asia regional boundaries are particularly fluid, varying from issue to issue. In this study Asia comprises the countries of the Western Pacific from Indonesia to Japan. But, as suggested by work on the "Asia-Pacific" or "Pacific" region, many important processes cover a wider sphere and Asia is unlikely to disengage from these external ties.[1] Most importantly, the influence exercised by the United States is a factor that has deeply colored the nature of intra-Asian relationships [Cumings 1997]. Nonetheless, there are transnational economic flows and relationships that differentiate Asia from the wider Pacific. These include the increasingly regional nature of trade and direct investment, as well as regionally-based production structures and inter-firm ties.[2] Asian countries are also distinguished by shared features of their domestic political economies, creating the grounds for regional cooperation or, at the least, making cooperation in broader Pacific settings difficult.[3] In the account that follows, actors and initiatives incorporating the wider Pacific area are frequently significant but there is also a concentration of economic, and to some degree political, exchange in the region.

How to explain the degree of economic integration in either the Asian or Pacific areas is a second issue confronting studies of the region. The most common statement about integration in Asia and the Pacific is that it has been "market-led" rather than the product of interstate cooperation.[4] Economic integration may not, in fact, present a collective action problem when economies are increasingly internationalized [Drysdale and Garnaut 1993]. Asian countries have faced economic incentives and bilateral political pressure to liberalize their economies, further limiting the need for multinational cooperation to achieve the same end.[5] But the record in the rest of the world leaves room to ask why things turned out the way they did in Asia.

There are two major lines of explanation for this outcome. On the one hand, consultative groups such as APEC (Asia-Pacific Economic Cooperation) and its related dialogues may constitute a process-based cooperation structure or "meta-regime" that has eased international cooperation problems.[6] Alternatively, the network character of regional business can explain economic integration. The intra-Japanese ties among firms and official agencies, and their relationships with host country firms and governments, are one aspect of regional networks. Another is the spread of ethnic Chinese business across the region and the interaction between Chinese, Japanese, western, and other business.[7]

Doner [1997] has argued that the informal support structures carried by Japanese networks make formal mechanisms such as investment guarantees, market access negotiations or agreements on investment liberalization less necessary. As structures that economize on information and other costs, business networks explain the concentration of economic activity in the region in ways that add to rather than replace "market driven" explanations. The evidence presented below tends to support explanations of integration that build on the character of regional business and its relationship with political actors. Not only are collaborative, network-like ties evident in the spread of regional banking and business, the current level of integration in the region has its roots in economic exchanges and transnational ties that clearly predate consultative processes such as APEC.

A third issue raised in studies of the region is why the level of formal cooperation remains at a low level. Formal and substantive cooperative commitments are limited and the consultative structures promoting economic integration do not deal with a whole range of other issues. In particular, the absence of cooperation on issues of financial and economic management is noticeable, a deficiency that was dramatically brought to light with the currency and financial crisis that hit the region in 1997.

The outcome of limited cooperation to manage the effects of economic integration can be explained in a number of ways. First, the region includes countries at different levels of development, which means that national interests often diverge [Kahler 1988, 336; Soesastro 1983]. However, in contrast to trade issues, there are fewer reasons to suppose that countries at different stages of development should have divergent interests in most areas of financial and monetary management. The exception lies in the area of access to the national financial market. But the regional spread of financial intermediation described here suggests that, in practice, this has not been a significant obstacle for regional actors. Secondly, low cooperation in Asia could be the product of rivalry and mistrust in a region which, unlike Europe, has not built up habits and institutional structures that support collective action by reducing levels of suspicion.[8] Formal organization clearly is at a comparatively low level in Asia but the extensive economic ties that define the region do not fit easily with explanations of non-cooperation that stress the underdeveloped nature of regional institutions. If collective action problems or mistrust are that important, why is it that they have not impeded the process of economic integration? If consultative regional structures facilitate cooperation on some issues, why not on others?

Global cold war politics and American hegemony over much of Asia help explain these anomalies but, as discussed in the conclusion, not in all cases. Some analyses which emphasize global bipolarity and American hegemony are consonant with realist international relations theorizing, which holds that cooperation requires a hegemonic state to monitor and enforce compliance.[9] In this view, the region's dependence on American leadership in security and economic terms blocks the possibility of Japanese leadership and thus the possibility of greater regional cooperation. While realist explanations are compelling on some counts, the detail given in the next two sections shows that they do not erase the scope for significant intra-Asian processes. Further, even in their most persuasive forms, explanations that focus on the cold war and American hegemony pose additional questions. If the cold war in Asia had yet to end as of 1997 [Johnson 1998, 660]—more than 25 years after the Sino-Soviet split and the normalization of Sino-American relations—this is not something that the structural factors identified by realist theories can explain.

The first part of this study shows that transnational, regionally-focused ties among bankers and bank-related businesses have been the norm in Asia for most of the last century. For capital flows, a regional concentration is now evident for bank lending and direct investment but not for portfolio flows. The second part of the study describes regional cooperation attempts in the area of monetary and financial management. There has been some demand for cooperation in this area but little collective action, a record that stands in contrast to the high level of economic integration. The currency and financial crises of 1997 and 1998 illustrate both aspects of the region. The interdependence of regional economies meant that what started as a currency crisis in Thailand developed rapidly into a matter of region-wide concern. Attempts to deal with the crisis on a regional basis, however, either stalled or never materialized. The final section offers two complementary interpretations of the integration and cooperation described in this chapter. One interpretation is that wide differences among regional states in terms of their governing capacities go some way to explaining extensive economic integration but limited ability to manage its effects. A second interpretation is that external factors, particularly the role of the United States, present significant obstacles to greater regional cooperation.

Banking and Capital Flows in Asia

This section looks at the foreign activity of Asian banks, the geographic origins of foreign banks operating in Indonesia, Singapore and Malaysia, and the geographic distribution of capital flows. The history of regional banking activity presented here shows that there are close, often collaborative, ties among many bank-related groups and that these ties and transnational interests are far from new, indicating the effective mobility of regional capital for most of this century. Among bank-based business groups in particular, the ethnic Chinese are prominent regional actors. Frequently described as "colleagues not competitors at the top," most of the large Chinese conglomerates are connected with other business groups through a web of collaborative ventures [DFAT 1995, 154-61].

Pre-war Regional Banking and Business Relations

At the end of the nineteenth century a multi-currency open monetary system operated in Asia. The region operated on a de facto silver standard at this time but around the turn of the century most areas converted to gold, with the exception of Hong Kong and China. The trade and foreign exchange operations of the major banks ensured a continuous flow of notes and specie between Europe and the Pacific.[10] The regional flow of money was also based on trade and emigration between China and India, with Singapore and Hong Kong acting as commercial and financial centers. The hinterlands around Singapore (both Sumatra and Malaya) provided produce for the export trade and the destination for large numbers of Chinese emigrants whose remittances, combined with trade finance opportunities, supported the regional flow of funds and the regional extension of banking business [Hamashita 1994; Hicks, ed. 1993].

At the beginning of the twentieth century formal banking organizations began to be established by the Chinese living in the region. One of the first Chinese banks in Southeast Asia was Kwong Yik Bank, established in Singapore in 1903 by a Cantonese building contractor and gambier planter.[11] The Oversea-Chinese Banking Corporation (OCBC) was established in 1932 from the merger of three Chinese banks in Singapore which were all suffering from the effects of the depression, the Japanese invasion of Manchuria and sterling devaluation in September 1931. The Singapore Chinese banks were caught in an overbought Sterling position but also suffered because their exchange operations were based mainly in Hong Kong and Shanghai and they had large deposits in Hong Kong dollars, which remained tied to the silver standard [Wilson 1972, 3-6].

OCBC inherited a number of regional ties. Business in China was important and many of the bank's founding directors were China-born. One of OCBC's predecessors, the Chinese Commercial Bank, had close ties with the Bank of China, which at one time held 30 percent equity in the bank. Another predecessor bank, Ho Hong, had branches in Sumatra, Batavia (Jakarta), Hong Kong and Shanghai, as well as in Malaya and Singapore. The largest of the predecessor banks, the Oversea-Chinese Bank, had been established with equity partly provided by two Java-based merchants, Oei Tiong Ham and Oei Ik Tjoe.[12] Its branches extended beyond Singapore and Malaya to Rangoon, Sumatra and Amoy. When OCBC was incorporated it thus had 17 branches in Malaya, China, Java and Burma [Wilson 1972, 25] and connections with many of the largest Chinese rubber traders and merchants in the region. In the 1930s OCBC opened branches in Bangkok, Surabaya, Haiphong (French Indochina) and "reactivated" the branch in Sumatra. In 1938 it arranged with the Director-General of Postal Remittances and the Savings Bank of China to become the sole agent of the Savings Bank of China for family remittances to China [Wilson 1972, 50].

The other principal Chinese bank active in Asia before the war was the Bank of China. Its Singapore branch opened in 1936, with the chief function of earning foreign exchange from Chinese remittances for the Chinese government. Until then the remittances had been handled by OCBC, British and American banks [STI April 1972]. The Bank of China also had branches in the Netherlands Indies, Malaya and elsewhere in Southeast Asia. Smaller Chinese banks included the predecessor of today's United Overseas Bank, the United Chinese Bank (UCB), incorporated in Singapore in 1935. Its founding directors had ties with other banks in the region, including OCBC and Bian Chiang Bank in Kuching, and were mostly businessmen with interests in Malaya, Singapore and Sarawak [UOB 1985, 11-16]. UCB, however, did not branch outside of Singapore until after the war.

Dutch and French banks in the region at this time were mostly involved in, respectively, the Netherlands East Indies and French Indochina. They also had branches in Singapore, which was known for the variety of foreign banks represented there, although its financial system remained oriented to its role as a staple port [Huff 1994, 86-89].[13] The British banks were the largest regional players, with branches from India to China established in the second half of the nineteenth century. The Hong Kong and Shanghai Banking Corporation (HSBC) had pre-war branches throughout Asia [King 1987-1991]. As well as being the largest bank in most of the British colonies, it had branches in Saigon, the Philippines, the Netherlands Indies, Bangkok, Japan and China. The other long-lived British bank was the Chartered Bank of India, Australia and China, now Standard Chartered, which had branches across coastal China, Southeast Asia and India by the end of the nineteenth century [MacKenzie 1954].

Other banks operating in Asia before the war were also international operations: from the small, trade-focused Indian banks in Singapore to the Japanese banks which supported the Japanese commercial push into Asia. This advance was influenced by commercial motives but it was also, as Barnhart has described, part of Japan's pursuit of national security, in which military and economic concerns were inextricably linked. Japan's attempt to escape dependence on the world market—and the American economy in particular—by creating an American-style continental empire was always a precarious venture, at odds with the demands of Britain, America, and increasingly assertive Chinese forces [Barnhart 1987]. In some ways, however, Japanese economic expansion in the pre-war era followed a pattern of regional integration that was far from unique, being focussed on colonial possessions and nested within wider global ties. After the acquisition of Korea and Taiwan, the Japanese government established the Bank of Taiwan and Bank of Korea, which combined note issue in these colonies with commercial and government business (the Bank of Korea took over note-issuing functions in the colony that were initially carried out by Dai-ichi Bank).[14] The economic relationships developed at this time integrated the colonies in cross-cutting webs of interdependence. According to Woo, by 1923 only 35 percent of total investment by the Bank of Chosen (Korea) was in Korea, while 47 percent was in Manchuria.[15] And with the push to locate heavy industry in Korea in the 1930s, Japanese capital flowed to the colony while Taiwan became a net creditor to Japan [Woo 1991, 28-32]. Even before the 1920s, the Bank of Taiwan was "moving a large amount of its resources to the Chinese mainland, the Malayan straits area and even beyond" [Tamaki 1995, 124].

The government-related Yokohama Specie Bank was a major operator in Manchuria, and also supported Japanese trade in other parts of the region, including Southeast Asia [Ishii 1994]. The Specie Bank's most important function, however, was to raise finance on the London market and take over the financing of Japanese exports in order to channel the proceeds back to Japan [Tamaki 1995, 70-73, 94-97]. Singapore was the site of its first branch in Southeast Asia, in 1916. The Mitsui group also had banking offices in Southeast Asia supporting its trading and shipping ventures, and the Bank of

Taiwan had a branch in Singapore [Yoshihara 1988, 21; Tamaki 1995, 124]. But despite an early twentieth century concentration of overseas branches in the Far East, in terms of economic importance, the foreign relations of Japanese banks focused first on London and North America, then China [Tamaki 1995, 102-03, 128-130]. The Japanese attempt at a "yen bloc" before 1941 was limited to Northeast and North China [Nakamura 1996].

The Japanese commercial presence in Southeast Asia was small compared to its presence elsewhere and compared to total business activity in the region. However, the pre-war years saw the consolidation of official Japanese management of its overseas citizens, replacing scattered groups of small traders, prostitutes and shopkeepers with more consciously Japanese communities of businesspeople, tasked with securing Japanese economic interest and, in the words of an official at the time, Japanese civilization [Yuen 1978, 175; Shiraishi and Shiraishi 1993].

Thus by the 1930s most of the large (and many of the not-so-large) businesses in the region operated transnationally, or across colonial borders. This was true of western businesses which had ties to their metropolitan centers and, particularly in the case of British business, interests in other territories. The Japanese commercial presence had become significant in the region, even beyond the area of Japanese colonization. And ethnic Chinese living in Southeast Asia, many of whom were China-born, were active in business concerns that cut across colonial and national boundaries.

Post-war Regional Banking and Business Relations to the 1970s
By the 1970s many of the pre-war relationships which had been disrupted by war and nationalist policies had re-emerged. Many had been less disrupted than is commonly thought. The most significant change from the pre-war situation was the division of the region into communist and non-communist spheres, dominated by the global superpowers. Hence the relative closure of China and the Indochinese countries as regards economic integration in the region. With respect to China, this had begun to change in the 1970s and, by the late 1970s, most of the fundamental cleavages in the region were not a product of global bipolar rivalry. Other aspects of the current regionalism had also taken shape: Singapore, for example, had already become a significant regional financial and business center. As early as 1971, Eurodollars were being funneled to the Singapore offshore market for loans to Asian businessmen, who also used the Singapore market as a safe place for their money [*STI* January 1972].

Much of the regional activity of ethnic Chinese entrepreneurs continued after the war. The sectoral diversification of business groups increased as, in addition to banking activity, earlier interests in mining, plantations and trade were added to, or replaced by, new ventures in property, newspapers and industry. In some cases the diversification was out of banking, as with the Aw family, which had established a diversified chain of companies concentrated in Singapore, Malaysia and Hong Kong by the end of the 1950s [*Singapore Trade* July 1961, 33]. The family's bank, Chung Khiaw, had been founded in Singapore in 1950. In 1970 Chung Khiaw Bank was sold and the family's interests became centered on Hong Kong. Chung Khiaw Bank and the Aw family's Haw Par conglomerate were acquired by another Singapore banker, Wee Cho Yaw of UOB. UOB was listed in Hong Kong from 1972 (until 1998) as well as Singapore and, in 1974, held a minority share in a Californian bank owned by Hong Kong businessman and shipping magnate, C.Y. Tung [UOB 1985, 82]. Some connection with China was made in 1971, when Wee Cho Yaw led a delegation from Singapore's Chinese Chamber of Commerce to China, to discuss trade opportunities and prospects for breaking the cartel of European shipping firms.[16]

Major Chinese banks to expand in the region at this time included the Thai-based Bangkok Bank, at one time the largest local bank in Southeast Asia. The principal figure associated with the Bangkok Bank was Sino-Thai entrepreneur Chin Sophonpanich (Tan Piak Chin) who had close ties with a number of regional businessmen, Japanese as well as Chinese [Yoshihara 1988, 197; Hewison 1989, 192-303]. One example of the support that could be extended by these businessmen dates from when, in the late 1940s, the Bangkok Bank was having trouble finding premises for a branch in Singapore. Singapore-based Lien Ying Chow, who already had the idea of establishing his own bank, provided one of his properties to the Bangkok Bank, free of charge, for about a year. Lien describes this as a "gesture of friendship which we people from China want to extend to each other in Southeast Asia. We always like to cooperate with each other" [(Lien 1992, 107)].

The Bank of China opted to serve the new regime in 1949, as did the Singapore, Malayan and Indonesian branches (the Australian, New York and Thai branches stayed with the Chiang Kai-shek government).[17] The Malaysian government consequently closed its branches in Penang and Kuala Lumpur in 1959, ostensibly because of restrictions against banks owned by foreign governments, but these almost certainly had their origins in Malaysia's poor relations with China and its own communist insurgency. In 1964 the bank's offices in Indonesia were closed after the Indonesian government suspended activities such as foreign exchange handling (the bank had already been substantially taken over). This left the Singapore branch as the only one in Southeast Asia. During the period of amalgamation with Malaysia (1963-1965) this branch was under threat, although the Singapore government was said to have argued vigorously to retain it on the grounds that closure might lead to loss of trade with China. In the early 1970s the bank was playing an important role in Singapore-China trade but its regional presence was diminished compared to the pre-war period. However, even then this "communist" bank was an accepted member of the Hong Kong banking fraternity [(*Insight* August 1973, 28-30].

Banks established in Singapore set about restoring or creating regional ties soon after the war. OUB, founded in 1949, illustrates the process. The bank's founder, Lien Ying Chow, came to Singapore as a teenager and became established in commerce in the 1930s. He maintained ties with family members in Thailand and China, spending time during the war in the Chinese wartime capital of Chongqing where he established both a bank and ties with Nationalist and Communist leaders, including Chiang Kai-shek and Zhou Enlai. As a representative of China he also went to London during the war, where he made contact with a number of British companies with interests in the Far East. After the war Lien's bank in China closed and business contact was only taken up again in 1978, when he started negotiations to build a hotel in Beijing. This was built some time later with the help of the Bank of China. Lien raised the initial deposits and capital for OUB from friends and relations in Thailand, Hong Kong and Vietnam [Lien 1992, 34-48]. In 1966 he served as Singapore's High Commissioner to Malaysia, where he and the then Prime Minister, Tunku Abdul Rahman, were described as "old chums." Lien also had close relations with the Sultan of Johor, Thai royalty and a number of Thai Prime Ministers. His Thai relationships included a long-standing friendship with Chin Sophonpanich, chairman of the Bangkok Bank, and he cooperated with other Thai banks in ventures that included promoting barter trade between Singapore and Thailand [Lien 1992, 101-08].

Lien's international orientation was mirrored by that of his senior staff and other directors of the bank. Chi Owyang, Lien's long-serving manager (1947-1968), had personal ties and banking experience in China, Hong Kong and Thailand. Chi Owyang was also able to develop OUB's relationship in new areas, such as in Burma from the 1950s onwards. Through the State Commercial Bank there, OUB handled all the Burmese business in Singapore at that time and, later on, in Hong Kong as well [Owyang 1996, 87]. Yos Kupasrimonkol, the general manager in the early 1970s, had thirty years of banking experience in Hong Kong and Thailand before joining OUB as the Penang branch manager in 1958. Many of OUB's early directors were China-born and almost all came to the bank with business interests in a number of different countries [OUB 1974].

Another Singapore-based bank, OCBC, was associated with many Malaysian businesses [Lim 1981]. The bank was also closely connected with businessmen based in Hong Kong. For example, Hong Kong-based tycoon Runme Shaw was a director of OCBC from 1962 until 1982. Runme Shaw and his brother owned numerous entertainment outlets across Asia in the

1960s and 1970s. Among other positions, Runme was a director of Robert Kuok's Shangri-La hotel company, along with other OCBC directors [SEMS, vol. 5]. Another director of OCBC from 1978 until 1983 was Lamson Kwok, the China-educated chair of Hong Kong's Wing On Life Ltd. (an associate company of OCBC's since 1974) and "a prominent leader of the business community in Hong Kong" [OCBC, *Annual Report* 1978].

Ethnic Chinese entrepreneurs operating in the region at this time included almost all the prominent ethnic Chinese businesses in the 1980s and 1990s. A few examples show their early sectoral and international diversification. The Jack Chia group of companies was established by a China-educated Thai citizen whose group started in Thailand in 1948. By 1974 it had invested in Singapore, Malaysia, Hong Kong, Indonesia, Taiwan, Australia, North America and Japan. The group's interests ranged from pharmaceuticals in Australia (from the mid-1950s) to publishing, hotels, manufacturing and dredging operations [*STI* June 1973; *STI* January 1974]. Robert Kuok (Kuok Hock Nien), originally based in Malaysia, moved in 1976 to Hong Kong from where he ran one of Asia's largest business empires, active in a range of sectors, including financial services, hotels and shipping. Robin Loh was another prominent entrepreneur in the 1970s with interests from Indonesia to China and extending to the Middle East. By the late 1970s he was based mainly in Hong Kong, where Loh was, among other things, a part owner of Chin Sophonpanich's Commercial Bank of Hong Kong [*Insight* March 1978].

Regional interests and relationships included individuals from Indonesia as early as the 1960s, despite restrictive policy in Indonesia [Hamilton-Hart 1999, 77-78]. In addition, many Indonesian Chinese left the country, with Singapore a destination for the wealthier individuals and thousands more going to China and Hong Kong [DFAT 1995, 181-82]. Those going to Singapore very often retained family or business connections in Indonesia. Goh Tjoei Kok, for example, was a rubber trader who left in 1954 for Singapore, where he later established Tat Lee Bank. Before the establishment of his bank in 1974, his rubber trading business meant that ties with Indonesian producers and merchants were maintained. He later formed a joint-venture bank in Indonesia with one of these associates. Ng Quee Lam was a China-born, Singapore-based rubber trader with close ties to Indonesian businesses [*STI* June 1972]. He also founded the Hong Kong-registered Far Eastern Bank in 1959 and had interests in shipping and real estate. Ong Tjoe Kim was another Sino-Indonesian who left Indonesia in 1957 to found a major retail business in Singapore. Again, ties to Indonesia were maintained, including by marriage into an Indonesian family which owned a chain of department shops, in which Ong invested in the 1990s.

Singapore-based individuals also renewed or established contact with Indonesian officials and traders. UOB, now one of Singapore's largest banks (then called UCB), decided in 1960 to move into trade financing. Only banks designated as "first class" were able to issue shipping guarantees for Indonesia-Singapore trade and at that time only the British banks and OCBC were recognized as first class. Having no luck with the Singapore authorities the bank's new managing director, Wee Cho Yaw, tried the Indonesian side, with whom "his frequent visits and appeals finally paid off" [UOB 1985, 33]. In 1963 Indonesia's opposition to the formation of Malaysia resulted in the prohibition of Indonesia-Malaysia trade, which reduced the bank's foreign exchange business by 70 percent. Consequently, "[e]nterprising businessmen from the two countries decided to get over the economic blockade by trading through third countries." The bank's branch in Hong Kong was established mainly to circumvent the Indonesian economic boycott [UOB 1985, 35-9].

Indonesian bankers had started their regional expansion by the 1970s. Liem Sioe Liong (Sudono Salim), later to gain notoriety as president Suharto's primary business partner, controlled two banks in Indonesia by the early 1970s. He established a finance company in Hong Kong in 1975 in cooperation with a long-term business partner, fellow Indonesian banker Mochtar Riady. Riady had on his own account built up foreign business interests by the end of the 1970s, including rather controversial attempts to buy into U.S. banks [*Insight* September 1978]. Another Indonesian conglomerate, the Sinar Mas group, had family business interests in the region from the early 1970s. Sinar Mas and its associate bank, Bank Internasional Indonesia, are headed by Sino-Indonesian Eka Tjipta Widjaya (Oei Ek Tjhong). Oei's son, Peter Oei Hong Leong, was educated in China and remained there from 1960 until 1969, during which time he is said to have had a lot of contact with Communist Party cadres. Around 1970 he went to Singapore to start Sinar Mas's first overseas operations. As well as Sinar Mas's operations he also bought into other businesses, including United Industrial Corporation [*Asia Inc.* August 1993], of which Lee Kim Yew, brother of Singapore's Prime Minister, was a director.

British banking expanded in the region after the war but declined relative to local banks from the late 1960s. The geographically-diverse HSBC started a concerted drive in Southeast Asia after it lost its Chinese branches (except Shanghai) in 1949 [King 1979, 51-68; *FEER* 30 July 1959]. It opened a number of new branches in the region as well as taking over those of another British bank, Mercantile, in 1959. Chartered Bank also increased its area and scope of operations in Southeast Asia and the Middle East in the 1950s. Like the other British banks it was heavily concentrated in the main commercial centers and in Malaya was described as having "a fairly marked predominance, thanks notably to its close association with the big tin companies which, having their head offices in London, like to deal with a bank similarly oriented" [*FEER* 30 July 1959].

American banks were also increasing their regional presence in the 1950s and 1960s. Only Citibank (then First National City Bank), which opened in Singapore in 1902, was significant in the retail market.[18] Some, like First National City Bank of Chicago, were using Singapore as a regional base to finance international business activities. This bank decided to set up in Singapore in 1970 and announced that the Singapore branch "will be the key to our Asian operations. All bank financing from Japan to Australia will be channeled through it" [*STI* November 1970]. This strategy was also adopted by some Japanese banks which were significant global players by the early 1970s. Dai-Ichi Kangyo, for example, the largest bank in Japan and the fifth largest in the world in 1972, decided to use Singapore as the base for its new trade and investment consulting department. According to its chairman, the bank saw Singapore as a focal point for internationalizing its activities and for expansion in Southeast Asia [*STI* April 1972].

The first post-war wave of Japanese investment in Southeast Asia was a reason for the extension of Japanese banking activity in the region, as the banking relationships established in Japan moved overseas. In the post-war period Japanese businesses had started to return to Southeast Asia as part of an American-supported policy of "economic cooperation," aimed at establishing export markets for Japanese goods and securing supplies of raw materials [Shiraishi 1997, 176-78]. As well as using official Japanese support schemes, Japanese businesses developed or resurrected relationships with influential local contacts, particularly in Indonesia [Nishihara 1975; Malley 1989]. Outward manufacturing and natural resources investment in Southeast Asia from Japan was well underway by the mid-1970s and, often through the Japanese trading houses, the provision of credit was an important component of the process.[19]

Japanese banks were restricted in terms of retail branching in the region. The Bank of Tokyo (the reformed and initially much smaller Yokohama Specie Bank), for example, had 76 branches in Southeast Asia at the end of the war [Peattie 1996, 198], most of which were lost. Much Japanese financing was thus provided through representative offices, locally-based joint venture merchant banks and Japanese banks active in the offshore market in Singapore.[20] Japanese institutions established many joint venture financial companies in Southeast Asia in the 1970s, including merchant banks in Singapore and Malaysia and investment finance institutions in Indonesia. Some of these relationships have been long term, such as the consortium investment bank established in Indonesia in 1975 by Liem Sioe Liong's bank, Bank Central Asia (BCA), and the Long Term Credit Bank (LTCB) of

Japan. When joint venture commercial banks were permitted in 1989, BCA and LTCB were among the first to establish one.

Regional Banking and Business Relations in the 1980s and 1990s
Regional business and banking relations since the 1980s are essentially a continuation of these trends, with the major change being the incorporation of China and Indochina into the regional sphere. Other new developments were, first, the continuing demise, or takeover by local interests, of the British agency houses and resource-based multinationals. Second, Japanese investment in the region escalated in the mid-1980s and rose again in the first half of the 1990s. Third, regional governments took an increasing role in supporting the outward investment of their nationals or investing abroad themselves. Inter-firm alliances and joint investments abroad are so frequent as to be almost the norm.

Bank groups from Singapore, Malaysia and Indonesia have concentrated their outward expansion in the region. Many banks set up offices in the 1960s or early 1970s in the financial centers of London and New York and Indonesian banks opened offices in financial havens such as the Cayman Islands. But these offices were largely limited to booking loans or, in the case of London and Tokyo offices, lending in the local interbank market [Owyang 1996, 98-99]. Retail banking, trade finance and project loans abroad have all been centered on Asia, although not exclusively so. The outward expansion of Singapore banks now represents something of a return to pre-war branching patterns. Interviews with banks in Singapore suggested that regional expansion depends on business generated by Singaporean trade and investment. Operations in Malaysia are an exception, since Singapore banks were established early in the Malaysian banking market. The picture is similar for some of the larger Malaysian banks but, compared to the Singaporean banks, they have much shorter histories in the region. They also seem to have focused more on Indochina and less on China than the Singaporean banks. The outward expansion of Indonesian banks has mainly been through Hong Kong affiliates. Again, a regional concentration in branching and subsidiaries is evident although Indonesian bankers have also taken shares in American (particularly Californian) banks.

The Sinar Mas group of which Bank Internasional Indonesia is a part has, along with other Oei family companies, been very active in the region. Until 1991, Peter Oei was president and CEO of Singapore-based United Industrial Corporation (UIC) [SES 1994]. For some time in the late 1980s UIC held a significant stake in Malaysia's D&C Bank, associated at the time with the family of former finance minister Henry Lee [Gomez and Jomo 1997, 62]. Sinar Mas has a significant concentration of interest in China, mainly through Singapore or Hong Kong companies. Between 1991 and

1994 the Oei family had invested about $400 million in China to acquire a controlling interest in between 80 and 196 Chinese state-owned companies (accounts vary).[21] Peter Oei is said to have capitalized on the relationships formed during his time in China in the 1960s, using these ties to acquire state companies cheaply. Sinar Mas's ties include a partnership with the Singapore GLC, Singapore Power, [*BT* 7 January 1998] and co-investments and cooperation with Hong Kong-based Li Ka-shing.[22] The family also has investments in the U.S. and Eka Tjipta Widjaya (Peter Oei's father) was named Emerging Markets CEO of the Year in 1996—on which he was congratulated by President Clinton.[23]

Another of the regional bank groups is the Lippo group, controlled by the Riady family of Indonesia, where the group's bank is Lippo Bank. Lippo group has investment holding companies in Hong Kong through which it has invested in China and the Philippines, as well as other countries. The group holds a stake in the Hong Kong Chinese Bank, in which a large share is also held by the Chinese government-linked China Resources, which has helped the bank's expansion into China [Ramu 1995, 252; DFAT 1995, 177]. By the mid-1990s Lippo had invested about $1 billion in China and was said to be planning $10 billion worth of investments there [DFAT 1995, 235]. Its relations in Hong Kong include joint investment in a large finance company with Liem Sioe Liong and a tie-up with a subsidiary of Malaysia's MUI group.[24] Riady had begun investing overseas in the 1970s and Lippo added to its overseas assets in the early 1980s. Although the group has concentrated on Asia it also took over a Chinese-run bank in California in 1984.[25] This bank, like its other overseas assets, has been brought into a trade finance network that includes Daiwa Bank, LTCB and Tokai Bank [*FEER* 15 February 1990]. The group has concentrated in banking and financial services but also has interests in property, trade, manufacturing and other activities.

The Salim group is another large regional conglomerate with its origins in Indonesia. Indonesia's largest private bank, Bank Central Asia (BCA), was a part of the group until the bank's takeover by the Indonesian authorities in 1998. The group is controlled by Liem Sioe Liong and his family. It consists of over 400 companies operating throughout Asia whose combined 1993 sales were estimated at $9 billion, about 35 percent of which were earned outside of Indonesia.[26] In 1983 Liem established a Singapore holding company, KMP, which was the vehicle for his already substantial operations there, mainly in property. But more extensive assets had already been built up in Hong Kong, and most expansion overseas during the 1980s was through two Hong Kong holding companies.[27] The group did have industrial ventures overseas but at this stage concentrated on trade and finance [Robison 1986, 308] and property. Salim's early 1980s interests included a bank in California (now sold to the Liem family in its personal capacity), a large finance company in Hong Kong and securities firms in Hong Kong and the U.S. By the 1990s the group had operations in 25 countries. At the end of 1990 Liem acquired the Sinar Mas-related share of UIC's investment in Singapore Land. Salim has also been a major investor in China since the early 1990s. In 1992 the group announced it had invested over $500 million in the country and said it planned further investments of $1 billion over the next five years, mainly in Liem's home province of Fujian.

As well as significant management or ownership ties with other Indonesian businessmen, Liem has ties to Robert Kuok and the Koo family of Taiwan. The Bangkok Bank, reportedly on the personal advice of its chairman, provided important external finance for Liem's early venture in cement in 1973, with other finance coming from a Taiwanese cement company. More recently, Salim has entered into at least eight separate projects with Singaporean GLCs, including in the Batam and Bintan industrial parks (as part of the Singapore-Indonesia leg of the southern "growth triangle") and in China. In China he has also been a co-investor with other Singaporean companies, including the United Overseas Bank group's property arm, United Overseas Land. Other China projects include a joint venture for vehicle production with Mazda and a group of Chinese companies, announced in 1994.

The Singapore banks started to intensify their efforts in China from the mid-1980s [DBS 1986]. However, they were accused of being overly conservative as regards financing in China and less supportive of Singaporean investment than Japanese banks [*BT* 11 January 1993]. Tat Lee Bank's activity in China (where it has a representative office) in fact included an agreement with a state-owned Chinese bank to direct clients investing in China to the Chinese bank [*BT* 22 December 1993]. The property wings of the big four Singapore banks have large investments in the region, especially Hong Kong, where they have joined up with leading Hong Kong developers and China-backed firms. DBS Land has probably been the largest Singapore bank-related property investor in China, with seven developments by 1996 [*ST* 10 September 1996]. Other Southeast Asian bank-related groups with investments in China include the Bangkok Bank group, the Dharmala group of Indonesia and the Hong Leong group of Singapore and Malaysia.

Japanese banks greatly increased their regional (and international) role in the 1980s and 1990s [Nakao 1995, 125-47]. Japanese banks had 99 banking offices (branches, affiliates and representative offices) in Asia in 1980, 313 in 1990 and 363 in 1994 [PEO 1995, 233]. Asia accounted for a quarter of the total overseas network in 1980 and a third in 1994. The most significant increases in banking representation over this period were into China and Hong Kong. The role of Japanese banks in financing the outward investment of Japanese companies has been significant and is reflected in Asia's increasing share of foreign lending by Japanese banks from the late 1980s, along with increasing direct investment in Asia.[28] At the end of 1993, long term loans accounted for 70 percent of funds raised by Japanese affiliates in Asia. Loans from Japanese banks accounted for 23 percent of all funds raised and a further 43 percent of funds were sourced from financial institutions in the host country [PEO 1995, 234]. This category includes an unknown amount of lending by Japanese financial institutions (or joint ventures) in the host country [Tokunaga 1992, 154].

The financial crisis that started in 1997 has begun to affect regional banking interests. On the one hand, it has led to many joint ventures unraveling as projects are put on hold and investors liquidate assets in a bid to reduce debt. On the other hand, the stressed situation of the finance sectors of Thailand, Indonesia, Malaysia, Korea and Japan, combined with foreign pressure to liberalize, saw considerable easing of restrictions on foreign investment in local financial firms. Western investors have been fairly quick to seize on under-valued industrial and commercial assets, especially in Korea, and Taiwan has supported acquisitions in the region, including through a government-linked fund [AFR 17-18 January 1998]. Most investment in ailing financial sector firms in Southeast Asia, however, has come from Singaporean government-linked institutions.[29] The Malaysian government also announced it was taking a share in Indonesia's troubled Islamic bank [BT 17 June 1998].

Foreign Banking in Three Countries

In Singapore, banks from Asian countries were established early and so make up a large number of the banks with full licenses, since these were not issued after the early 1970s. In 1959, 13 (16 if one counts the three Indian banks) of the 27 banks not incorporated in Singapore were Asian [Ministry of Finance 1961]. Most of these have retained their offices (two have become locally-incorporated) and, as of 1995, Asian banks accounted for about half of the full-license foreign banks. The British banks which dominated in the early post-war period [Owyang 1996, 80] have been replaced by American banks which are now pre-eminent among full-license foreign banks in terms of total assets. Japanese banks account for a much larger share of lending out of Singapore than in the past. It should be noted that, as a measure of strength in the local market, total assets are misleading because they include offshore operations. The table below shows that there is some regional concentration in the Singapore market for loans and profits.

In Malaysia the dominant role of British banks still shows, with Hong Kong Bank (formerly HSBC) and Standard Chartered being the largest foreign banks and the sixth and eighth largest banks overall.[30] Singapore banks have been increasing their presence since the 1980s, with the largest, OCBC, moving from fifth to third place among the foreign banks between

Table 4.1
Top Five Full-license Foreign Banks in Singapore

Total assets	(S$)	Loans	(S$)	Net profits	(S$)
BAM	76.4	Sakura	4.0	Malayan	0.057
Chase	48.6	Tokyo	3.3	China	0.048
BIZ	33.2	China	3.2	Tokyo	0.028
ABN	20.6	Malayan	3.0	Bangkok	0.027
Tokyo	16.9	BAM	2.0	ABN	0.021

Note: Figures are in billions of Singapore dollars and relate to 1995.

ABN: ABN-AMRO	China: Bank of China
BAM: Bank of America	Malayan: Malayan Banking
Bangkok: Bangkok Bank	Sakura: Sakura Bank
BIZ: Banque Indosuez	Tokyo: Bank of Tokyo
Chase: Chase Manhattan	

Source: SRMS, 1996, 48-53.

1985 and 1995. Four of the top seven foreign banks at the end of 1995 were Singaporean. Foreign banks from Asian countries accounted for 28 percent of total foreign bank assets in 1985 and 40 percent in 1995, with most of the increase attributable to the Singaporean banks. Of the other Asian banks, Bangkok Bank and Bank of Tokyo saw their share of the market fall.

The decline of the Bank of Tokyo (now Tokyo-Mitsubishi) in Malaysia is noticeable. In 1985 it was the fourth largest foreign bank in Malaysia with total Malaysian assets 37 percent the size of Hong Kong Bank's; by 1995 it was the eighth largest foreign bank and its assets were 17 percent of Hong Kong bank's. It is the only Japanese bank in Malaysia. The decline in the Bank of Tokyo's position was attributed by bank staff to the loss of many Japanese clients on which it had relied. This was due to the quasi-compulsory Malaysianization of the management of Japanese FDI in Malaysia and of the Bank of Tokyo's staff. It is also related to regulatory limits on the amount of business foreign companies can give to foreign banks in the country. However, Japanese banks have moved into the Malaysian market in other ways. As of 1990, Japanese banks held equity in eight of the twelve merchant banks in Malaysia and had started investing in Malaysian banks. Despite these arrangements they reportedly still found it difficult to service Japanese companies in the country due to regulatory constraints and the small size of the Malaysian merchant banks [*FEER* 24 May 1990]. Some Japanese bankers interviewed were also unhappy with their relationships with Malaysian partners and the central bank.

In Indonesia, the market share held by foreign banks has become increasingly fragmented. For nearly 20 years until the late 1980s American banks had the greater part of this market. The table below shows the relative decline of the early-established foreign banks after many new joint venture banks were set up after 1989. The table does not reflect the inroads made by Japanese banks collectively because of the relatively even distribution of assets among a large number of banks. Japanese banks led the return of foreign banks after liberalization in 1989 and accounted for eight of the nine largest joint venture banks in 1994.[31] The role played by banks and merchant banks with only representative offices in Jakarta is unknown but likely to be significant. Many large operators such as Morgan Guaranty have been in Indonesia since the 1970s and have been, in their own eyes, generally unrestricted [interview, Morgan Guaranty, Jakarta, April 1997].

Figures are available on the largest brokerages on the Jakarta stock exchange, which publishes quite comprehensive information about trading and traders. In 1996 the largest brokerages in terms of value of trading were two Indonesian firms. The next six largest were all European or American firms (including a joint venture, BZW Niaga Securities). Non-Indonesian Asian firms accounted for an insignificant share of brokerage activities, giving some support for the view that foreign portfolio flows have been mainly due to European and American investors. It is noticeable that in both the banking and capital market, Indonesia—a country with substantial market imperfections—is not more open to any particular national or ethnic inter-mediary. The ability to penetrate patrimonial relationships thus does not appear to be confined to specific groups.

Table 4.2
Top Foreign and Joint Venture Banks in Indonesia

	1982			1994	
	%	rank		%	rank
Citibank	27	1		9	1
Bank of Toky	13	2		4	3
Chase	12	3		2	18
Bank of America	10	4		2	17
European	10	5	(Deutsche)	4	5
ABN	5	7	(ABN-Amro)	4	4
HSBC	5	8		7	2
Total (Rp.)	1,252			27,909	

Note: Total (Rp.) refers to total assets of foreign and joint venture banks, in billions of Rupiah.

Source: Bank Bumi Daya (*Kinerja bank-bank devisa*), various issues.

Capital Flows in Asia

Overall, the evidence points to U.S. investors as the most significant source of portfolio flows, Japanese and European banks as the most important sources of bank lending and Asian investors collectively as the most important source of direct investment (FDI) in the region.[32] However, information on the geographic sources and distribution of capital flows is very incomplete, especially for portfolio flows which have been significant. There is particular uncertainty about the purchasers of bonds issued by regional countries in the 1990s.[33]

Based on BIS estimates, Europe and Japan have been the most important sources of bank lending to the region in the 1990s [BIS 1997]. The BIS estimates, however, exclude lending by Singapore banks, which was significant. They also exclude lending from Hong Kong, which in early 1998 totaled $547 billion, including $4.3 billion to Indonesia and $2.2 billion to Malaysia. Of the external claims of Hong Kong banks, Asian countries accounted for 37 percent in 1980, 80 percent in 1993 and 76 percent in early 1998.[34] The U.S. dollar is the dominant currency in international lending to the region.[35]

Japan remains the single largest source of bank lending and FDI in the region, despite falling behind Korea, Taiwan, Hong Kong and Singapore collectively in FDI flows.[36] Japanese banks accounted for 34 percent of the $810 billion in loans to the region by BIS reporting area banks as of 1997 [*BT* 2 March 1998], which is considerably higher than their 22 percent share of world-wide international lending [BIS 1997, 122]. However, in 1996 lending to Asia by Japanese banks still accounted for only 25 percent of all Japanese international lending, although this is a higher proportion than only three years earlier. Similarly, Europe and the U.S. still account for most of Japanese outward investment. Japanese portfolio investors (purchasers of equities and bonds) were not that important in the region in the early 1990s, especially compared to the large portfolio flows from the U.S.[37]

For Indonesia, capital inflows from Asia range from 45 percent of direct investment (1967-1996) to over half of all reported bank lending and 36 percent of all official lending.[38] No aggregate figures are available for outward capital flows from Indonesia. Anecdotal evidence from Indonesian business activity abroad shows a regional focus for direct investment but nothing certain can be said about portfolio and real estate purchases. There are accounts of real estate purchases by Indonesians in the U.S., Canada and Australia and U.S. records of foreign purchases of equity include large amounts from Hong Kong and Singapore, both intermediating points for Indonesian capital. Estimating how large these flows are in comparison with total flows is impossible due to the lack of monitoring by the Indonesian authorities and the extent to which Indonesians use foreign-registered companies to channel their investments.

The regional concentration of capital flows in the Malaysian case is noticeable in the 1990s. Of total inward direct investment receipts of $8.4 billion (1992-1996), 66 percent came from Asia. The very large portfolio flows Malaysia experienced in the first half of the 1990s, however, are likely to show a much higher proportion of non-regional sources. Outward investment (portfolio, direct, real estate and loans) of $9.2 billion from 1992 to 1996 was concentrated in Asia, with 61 percent of total flows destined for the region. The sources of bank lending to Malaysia are not as clear but if the amounts from Hong Kong ($2.2 billion outstanding in early 1998) and Singapore ($14 billion at the end of 1997) are added to the $10.5 billion BIS estimate of lending from Japan, then about 63 percent of all external debt (of $42 billion) is sourced from the region.[39]

Capital flows for Singapore also show a regional concentration in outward direct investment. Of a total stock of S$37 billion in direct investments as of 1995, 58 percent was in the Asian region.[40] Official figures on the distribution of outward portfolio flows are not available but it is likely that a much higher proportion goes to Australia, the U.S. and Europe: press reporting and figures from the U.S. show that Singaporeans are significant stock market and property investors there with, for example, $3 billion in net purchases of U.S. equities in the first two quarters of 1996 [BT 21 October 1996; ST 5 January 1996]. About 60 percent of cumulative inward portfolio investment was from the region as of 1994 but net inward portfolio flows are a very small part of total capital inflows (about 3 percent). There is no regional concentration for inward direct investment—if anything, the trend is towards U.S. predominance but this is not yet clear.

Singapore is a net lender internationally and its banks' loans are heavily concentrated in the region. When foreign lending by Singaporean banks was first disclosed in early 1998, the six local banks had S$41 billion, 18 percent of their total assets, in Malaysia, Indonesia, Thailand, the Philippines and Korea. About two thirds of this (S$28 billion) was concentrated in Malaysia, of which $5 billion was in the assets of Malaysian branches and subsidiaries—the rest, presumably, booked in Singapore. Exposure to Indonesia was the next most significant at $5.5 billion, followed by Thailand at $4.2 billion and Korea at $2.5 billion [BT 15 January 1998; BT 28 January 1998]. These official figures do not include lending to Hong Kong or China. The omission of lending to Hong Kong is likely to be significant since Singapore has for a long time been a source of funding for Hong Kong banks.[41]

Summary: Extent of Regionalization
Overall, there is a definite regional concentration in some of the indicators covered: outward capital flows, outward internationalization of financial intermediaries and (with the exception of Indonesia) a trend towards a

regional concentration of foreign financial intermediaries in the domestic market. Inward capital flows offer a more mixed picture of regionalization: very little, if any, regional concentration for short-term flows but some for bank lending and FDI. The source of bank lending is quite obscure but it is safe to say that at least half of all foreign bank lending in the region comes from regional countries which, compared to Asian banks' share in total international bank lending, is a significant regional concentration. The U.S. dollar is the dominant currency in the region in terms of trade invoicing, bank lending and exchange rate baskets.

Cooperation Agendas and Outcomes
Perhaps the most noticeable aspect of regionalism in Asia is the comparative absence of cooperation on financial issues. There has been some demand for cooperation but achievements to date are limited. This section discusses six types of cooperation: capital controls, macroeconomic coordination, adjustment support, harmonization of standards, externally oriented coordination, and liberalization. The only group of states to achieve significant cooperation on all of these measures is the European Union. The following account does not expect Asia to show the same kind of capacity for regional cooperation but the European case raises questions about realist analyses of Asia that emphasize U.S. hegemony and the lack of Japanese leadership to the exclusion of other factors. Europe has no obvious regional hegemon and laid the early foundations of regional cooperation under conditions of dependence on the United States. Further, cooperation on the issues of financial and monetary management discussed here has not been limited to European or Europe-U.S. settings but, at various times, has been pursued elsewhere.[42]

Capital Controls
With reliance on strategies of capital import and export, few Asian countries have an interest in preventing the international movement of capital. On the other hand, and as increasingly acknowledged in the wake of the region's financial crisis, it does not follow that a completely open capital account is desirable [Bhagwati 1998]. Regional countries plausibly have an interest in ad hoc restrictions during periods when portfolio inflows or the accumulation of foreign debts threaten to destabilize the domestic system. While this remains a unilateral option, as demonstrated by Malaysia in 1994 and again in 1998, mobilizing diplomatic support for such actions might have eased the criticism that was leveled at Malaysia. Many governments would also have benefited from cooperative monitoring of currency trading and capital flows, given the information deficits that came to light in 1997—and which in some cases were recognized *before* the crisis [interview, Bank Indonesia official, Jakarta, March 1997]. Finally, to the extent that currency volatility is

attributable to turnover unrelated to trade or investment, governments have an incentive to throw "sand in the wheels of international finance" to reduce the payoffs from low-margin, high-volume arbitrage or speculative activity [Eichengreen et al. 1995].

Capital controls are not on the agenda in Asia and only in the wake of the currency crisis of 1997 were proposals tabled for greater monitoring efforts. The call for transparency and some regulation of currency trading was made by the Malaysian Prime Minister, Mahathir, but, apart from a commissioned study on the issue, the proposal has not been taken up. Initially, most Asian leaders acceded to the IMF-led view that the appropriate response to the crisis included allowing for greater capital mobility. However, ASEAN did lend some support to Mahathir's views by issuing a communiqué in July 1997 that expressed "serious concern over well-coordinated efforts to destabilize ASEAN currencies" [*ST* 26 July 1997] and there is the perception that Mahathir does represent the views of many politicians, officials and business people in Asia [*AFR* 27-28 September 1997].

On 1 September 1998 Malaysia announced a range of capital controls that would ban offshore trading of its currency and stocks, and heavily discourage portfolio capital flows. Concurrently, the currency was pegged to the U.S. dollar. No other country followed Malaysia's lead but reactions in the region were mixed. At the time of the Malaysian announcement, the Hong Kong Monetary Authority was engaging in a major stock-buying exercise, along with regulatory restrictions, to thwart the activities of foreign hedge funds. Singapore, whose banks and brokerages were most affected by the Malaysian decision, refrained from public criticism. Japan's vice-minister for economic affairs in the Ministry of Finance, Sakakibara Eisuke, offered qualified support for Malaysia with the comment that the move "wasn't wrong as an emergency measure" [*BT* 31 October 1998]. Largely as a result of Malaysian efforts, but with some support from Japan, the November 1998 APEC summit in Kuala Lumpur was to consider anti-speculation measures [*BT* 29 October 1998]. With international opinion on the issue of international financial regulation changing rapidly during 1998, Japan was among the G7 countries most supportive of a stronger regulatory regime at the international level [*International Herald Tribune* 30 September 1998].

Given the role of non-Asian actors, the scope for an Asia-only agreement may be limited. The sources of portfolio investment are hard to determine but it is clear that American investors have been much more important purchasers of equities than Japanese investors and the operators of the hedge funds whose short-selling activity was reportedly behind large currency falls in 1998 are not from the region [*BT* 22 January 1998]. Further, those countries receiving IMF-administered emergency financing as a result of the currency crisis—Indonesia, Thailand and Korea—were effectively barred from emulating the Malaysian move. With the United States widely considered to be the primary force behind IMF conditionality [Wade and Veneroso 1998], the importance of external powers is again apparent. On the other hand, U.S. influence is hard to relate to the absence of cooperative monitoring of currency flows. Further, identifying American investors and the U.S. government, which supported investor interest in market-access in the years before the crisis, as major destabilizing forces serves to highlight the potential gains to be had from intra-Asian cooperation. In all the crisis-hit countries, savings were high and less volatile sources of foreign finance were readily available, making for a situation where the recognized risks of huge inflows of short-term capital were not justified by any structural need for portfolio capital [Dean 1996].

Monetary Policy Coordination and Currency Agreements
Given the role of the U.S. dollar and the importance of the U.S. economy for regional countries, there is limited potential for Asian currency and macro-economic cooperation until regional countries alter exchange rate and foreign reserve policies. For most ASEAN countries, interest and exchange rates are most heavily influenced by the U.S. dollar and U.S. interest rates, with a more moderate influence exercised by the yen.[43] The U.S. market also has the most significant influence on stock market movements for regional exchanges while the Japanese market appears to have no influence on ASEAN equity markets [Janakiramanan and Lamba, cited in Tan and Ng 1997]. Cooperation on monetary issues involving a regional country has largely been confined to periodic U.S.-Japan efforts from the mid-1980s onwards.[44] Outside of the U.S.-Japan relationship, macroeconomic or currency coordination was not on the agenda in Asia until very recently, apart from vague discussion of macroeconomic policy at meetings of regional central bankers.

The possibility of providing a greater role for the yen in the region has been periodically raised, more often by the press and academics than by regional officials.[45] Increasing seriousness was given to the idea in Japan from late 1980s and, in 1994 and 1995, the Japanese Ministry of Finance, MITI and the Economic Planning Agency all released reports mentioning the desirability of greater international and regional use of the yen [Kwan 1996, 3]. Even before the regional currency crisis, one of the main intellectual proponents of some kind of a yen bloc, C.H. Kwan, argued that the idea was "no longer ahead of its time" [Kwan 1996, 15]. Spurred on by the events of 1997, the idea gained more prominence among academic commentators and extended to the official and political levels. Greater use of the yen as a regional currency has been impeded by the lack of liquidity in the market for yen-denominated assets such as government securities.[46] In this context, liberalizing Japanese financial markets as part of Japan's bundle of financial reforms to come into effect in April 1998 was explicitly connected to proposals for greater regional use of the yen. Senior LDP politicians endorsed the idea of greater yen use in the region in early March 1998 [*BT* 2 March 1998]. Senior finance official Sakakibara noted that part of the reason for the currency crisis had been over-dependence on the U.S. dollar. His visits to Malaysia, Singapore and Thailand in March 1998 included discussion of increased use of the yen as part of the efforts to resolve the problems of regional economies [*BT* 3 March 1998]. Malaysia's then finance minister, Anwar Ibrahim, had already urged Japan to consider denominating more of its regional trade in yen and the idea of a yen bloc was endorsed in an editorial in Singapore's *Business Times*. The editorial also noted that "the U.S. will not like the idea of losing some of its currency hegemony but Asia must not let that stand in the way of reform" [*BT* 5 March 1998].

Malaysia also announced that the Singapore dollar could serve as a major currency for intra-ASEAN trade, a proposal which was not greeted with much enthusiasm by Singapore [*BT* 10 February 1998; *FEER* 19 February 1998]. The ASEAN meeting in February did, however, endorse the idea of greater use of regional currencies in intra-regional trade and has since commissioned a study on the merits of currency cooperation. An Asia-wide currency union has also been raised as an agenda item for the future by the head of the Hong Kong Monetary Authority [*Financial Times* 31 December 1998]. One sign of regional currency use is the increasing, but limited, amount of Indochinese-area trade and financial transactions settled in baht, which has been encouraged by the Thai authorities [Tantramongkol 1995]. Somewhat at odds with these currents, Indonesia's short-lived hopes for a currency board in early 1998 involved fixing the currency to the U.S. dollar. Malaysia's capital controls did in fact fix the currency to the dollar.

Many of the actions to increase the yen's role in the region could be taken unilaterally by regional central banks, commercial banks and traders [Kwan 1996]. Beyond this, some kind of institutional structure for cooperation among regional central banks and finance ministries would be necessary and, to date, remains limited. The idea of an Asian Clearing House and Asian Reserve Bank circulated in the late 1960s but for a number of reasons, including opposition by Japan, never amounted to anything [Vorachattarn 1977, 34]. There is an ASEAN committee of central banks and monetary authorities, but the SEACEN (Southeast Asian Central Banks) and SEANZA (Southeast Asia, New Zealand, and Australia) groupings have been more active. The SEACEN has organized meetings of central bank governors and officials from ASEAN, Indochina, Nepal and Sri Lanka since the 1960s. Through the Kuala Lumpur training center, it has organized numerous courses and seminars for officials since 1972. The SEANZA grouping of central banks was formed in the 1950s and has included Japan and South

Korea since the 1960s. The most recent central bank group is a dialogue forum established at the initiative of the Bank of Japan in 1991, the Executive Meeting of East Asia and Pacific Central Banks (EMEAP) which has held bi-annual meetings at the senior official level since then.[47] The first meeting of EMEAP central bank governors was held in July 1996. Apart from training initiatives, these groups have served primarily as a means of exchanging views. In September 1995 the governor of the Reserve Bank of Australia raised the idea of "Asian BIS" which would provide funding facilities [*JP* 17 April 1996] but this idea has not been developed.

In 1995 Japan began floating the idea of regional monetary cooperation more actively. In February 1996 an agreement was reached with the Singapore and Hong Kong Monetary Authorities on intervention in currency markets in support of the Bank of Japan to help maintain stable yen-U.S. dollar cross-rates and prevent further appreciation of the yen. Malaysia, on the other hand, rejected the idea on the grounds that "poor, developing countries" should not be compelled to help manage the Japanese currency [*FEER* 29 February 1996; *ST* 18 March 1996]. More progress has been made with a series of bilateral repurchase agreements among Asian countries which were concluded in 1995 and 1996.[48] Although not directly related to these recent agreements, a precedent had been set by the ASEAN Swap Arrangement established in 1977 [Skully 1985; Soedradjad and Esmara 1985, 12]. The bilateral pacts were endorsed by the APEC Finance Ministers but remain outside the APEC framework.[49]

The events of 1997 provided an early testing ground for the recently-concluded support arrangements. Although details of the support provided during the currency crisis have been kept under wraps, some cooperative intervention has been acknowledged. When the Thai baht first came under pressure in mid-May, the Singapore Monetary Authority (MAS) and the Thai central bank intervened jointly. It is not known how much was committed by the MAS, or even whether it just acted on behalf of the Thai central bank rather than using its own funds [*ST* 31 July 1997]. The bilateral repurchase agreements do not appear to have been used during the currency crises but before the baht was floated in July, the central banks of Malaysia, Singapore and Hong Kong reportedly bought baht in swap arrangements with the Thais, a faster method of response according to Bank Indonesia's governor [*ST* 10 July 1997]. The MAS, Bank of Japan and Bank Indonesia also coordinated their interventions in the first week of November, which contributed to stabilizing the rupiah, if not for long [BNM, *Quarterly Bulletin* October 1997, 68].

The rescue packages that were put together for Thailand, Korea and Indonesia, although devised under IMF auspices, show that Asian countries were prepared to offer mutual support. The $17 billion package for Thailand was largely made up of commitments from regional countries.[50] The larger scheme for Indonesia was made up of two components: a first line of support of $23 billion from the IMF, World Bank, ADB and Indonesia's own fiscal reserves, backed up by a second line of support consisting of $16 billion pledged by regional countries and the United States.[51] The IMF took the single biggest part ($21 billion) of an even larger package for Korea announced in December.

Overall, however, the countries of Asia have taken a back seat to the IMF in the rescue packages, especially since they have pledged that their commitments be released only in accordance with IMF timetables and very little had actually been made over as of early 1998. While other factors are also at work, this relative inaction had something to do with U.S. influence. Japan looked like it would take the lead in a rescue package for Thailand but then amended this to an agreement to support the IMF. This was followed by a Japanese proposal for an emergency rescue fund of $100 billion to be financed and used by the countries of Asia. Taiwan also offered to anchor an Asia-only $50 billion fund, an idea which was welcomed by those in need and vetoed by the U.S. and China [*AFR* 29-30 November 1997]. Despite U.S. opposition to an Asian fund, it agreed to discuss it at the Manila APEC meeting of senior finance officials [*AFR* 3 November 1997]. What this meeting produced, however, was a rejection of the idea and, in what was called the Manila Framework, commitment to giving primary responsibility for dealing with the crisis to the IMF.

With the lid on ideas for Asia-based solutions to the currency crisis, some bilateral moves have still been made. A $10 billion line of support was thought to have been committed by the Bank of Japan to the Bank of Korea before the IMF deal was worked out [Macquarie Bank, *International Weekly* 24 November 1997]. Japanese measures to support its banking industry, announced at the end of 1997, can be seen as a de facto support package for the region in that a portion of the 30 trillion yen package for Japanese banks would, according to the finance ministry, be used to roll-over loans to Asia [*BT* 13 January 1998]. In February 1998 Japan announced that it was committing 300 billion yen in new loans for Asia through the Export-Import Bank of Japan. These funds would be untied, that it, available for trade finance not related to Japan and would also in part be used to provide "two-step" loans to central banks for onlending to domestic borrowers [*BT* 21 February 1998]. Later in 1998 Japan announced a $30 billion aid package for crisis-hit countries in the region. It has also, in conjunction with the Asian Development Bank, helped crisis-hit countries raise funds internationally by guaranteeing bond issues.

Singapore, partly in collaboration with Japan, has helped coordinate negotiations with creditors exposed to Indonesia and efforts to arrange multilateral export guaranties for Indonesia. Singapore was also among the first to promise support for Indonesia, with its offer of $5 billion which Bank Indonesia said might be used in credit to small-scale businesses [*Weekend Australian* 29-30 November 1997]. When the offer was made public (according to some it was never meant to be) Singapore qualified it and hitched it more firmly to the IMF package. As of early 1998, none of the pledge had been disbursed. Singapore attempted to coordinate an international trade finance guaranty facility of around $8 billion for Indonesia. Unable to gain support for the idea, Singapore later announced it was going ahead with a $2 billion package alone, which would draw on its $5 billion commitment under the IMF scheme. Also on the table was an American-backed idea for a $10 billion fund to support Thai, Korean and Indonesian imports [*AFR* 21-22 February 1998]. In early 1998 other countries announced official support for exports to Indonesia, Korea and Thailand but many of these packages are simply bilateral deals to secure market share for home country exporters. By one account, the Singaporean plan was the one that appeared most helpful to Indonesia [*FEER* 5 March 1998] and was one of the few that would actually involve real financial commitments as opposed to second-line guarantees. However, as of June 1998, the Singapore scheme remained stalled due to delays on the Indonesian side.

Adjustment Support

Adjustment support measures in the region have taken a number of different forms. In the case of Indonesia and the Philippines, they have involved a large role for the international organizations in which non-regional countries are dominant, mainly the World Bank and the IMF. Apart from this, longer-term adjustment support has been proposed and implemented on a regional basis through initiatives associated with Japanese foreign aid, Japan-ASEAN cooperation, Japanese-led initiatives within APEC and some intra-ASEAN initiatives.

Japanese aid is substantial and remains concentrated in Asia, where it has also been a component of Japan's regional investment strategy.[52] Japan-ASEAN cooperation has for some time revolved around the idea of combining aid, technology transfer and private investment. Support for such cooperation was upgraded in the 1970s as part of the "Fukuda doctrine" of greater engagement and support for ASEAN [Sudo 1992]. Since then, there have been a number of ASEAN or APEC-related schemes under which Japanese investment would be used to support industrial development in the region.[53] Loosely under the APEC banner there are also a number of Japanese-led projects for human resources development and technology transfer.

As a complement to these schemes there are Japanese-instituted funding mechanisms, the earliest of which (not counting bilateral reparations agreements) was the Asian Development Bank, opened in 1966 following low-profile but substantial Japanese efforts [Yasutomo 1983, 3-7, 23-65]. The ASEAN Development Fund started taking shape in 1980 with a Japanese business association (Keizei Doyukai) mission to Jakarta, led by an adviser to the Sanwa Bank, Murai Shichiro. Murai announced at the conclusion of this mission that Japan was happy to assist ASEAN economic development through a fund to be jointly financed by Japan and the ASEAN countries [*FEER* 15 February 1980]. This idea was put to the ASEAN Banking Council but the ASEAN view was that Japan should make the approach to an ASEAN institution on an "equal footing" and that they did not want a Japanese-dominated institution with "ASEAN credentials" [*FEER* 15 February 1980]. What resulted was the establishment in July 1981 of the Japan ASEAN Investment Company (JAIC) by the 137 members of the Keizei Doyukai, with Murai Shichiro as its president. At the end of 1984 the OECF became a shareholder in the company until it sold its share back to Japanese private companies in October 1989. In 1991, the company's name was changed to the Japan Asia Investment Company. As of 1995 total assets of the company were at 75 billion yen ($842 million), having increased sharply from 1994 [JAIC, *Annual Report* 1995]. The JAIC was also to be used as a channel for investment in the region in conjunction with the ASEAN-Japan Development Fund, which was announced in 1987 as part of Japan's capital export program. Partly because of opposition from the IMF and World Bank, however, some of the operations originally intended for the Fund were not pursued [Shiraishi 1997, 191].

An early government-supported private sector initiative was the Private Investment Company for Asia (PICA), which dates back to 1969. It had a fragmented shareholding structure of financial institutions from the U.S., Japan, Europe, Australia and Asia. While meant as a venture capital company, most of its disbursements were in the form of loans and these were very modest. Total assets amounted to only $57 million in 1978, the year the group's first dividend was declared [*FEER* 1 February 1980]. A recent public-private initiative is ASIA Ltd. (Asian Securitisation and Infrastructure Assurance), a financial guarantee company that "rents" its credit rating to borrowers. Its shareholders include American International Assurance, the ADB, Malaysia's Employees' Provident Fund and the main investment arm of the Singapore government, the GIC [*Economist* 6 July 1996]. The APEC Private Financiers Group is among the bodies pursuing efforts to develop regional bond markets, although with limited results compared to activity on the Hong Kong market [Tan and Ng 1997].

The first ASEAN initiative in the financial area was the establishment in 1972 of the Central Banks and Monetary Authorities Committee. Later, the Committee on Banking and Finance held its first meeting in 1977, after which it met quite frequently: eleven times by April 1983 [Skully 1985, 10]. Private sector cooperation in ASEAN has revolved around the ASEAN Banking Council, established in 1976. The Council is made up of representatives from ASEAN private and state sector banks. It met twice a year until 1982, thereafter yearly. The reduction in meetings was due to the increase in the Council's permanent committees on issues such as banking education, an ASEAN Bankers Acceptance market and publication of financial directories [Skully 1985, 36]. Like the other ASEAN bodies it was considered "much more productive in new ideas or recommendations to other groups than in tangible results from their own efforts" [Skully 1985, 43].

The council's most tangible product is the ASEAN Finance Corporation (AFC), incorporated in 1981 in Singapore.[54] The AFC grew out of schemes proposed at an ASEAN Bankers' Council meeting in Jakarta by both Indonesian state banks and Chinese bankers from the Malaysia and Singapore Chinese Chambers of Commerce. The draft proposal by the Chinese Chambers of Commerce and Industry of Malaysia and Singapore [*FEER* 1 February 1980] appears to be the one which, with a few modifications, was taken up. The AFC was to function as a guarantor of bond issues and a channel for equity and loans from outside the region such as from Keizei Doyukai [*FEER* 15 February 1980]. It owns 50 percent (S$500,000) of the ASEAN-Japan Development Corporation with the JAIC as the other shareholder. Overall, the AFC's achievements have been very limited: total assets in 1985 were only S$121 million. Diffuse ownership, the limited number of eligible ASEAN projects and potential competition from the shareholding banks were cited as among the reasons for its limited growth [Shulze 1988].

Harmonization of Government Intervention Standards
Globally, international negotiations on market access and investment are tackling core regulatory issues such competition law, government contracting and financial subsidies [Underhill 1993; Ruggie 1995]. In the area of finance, common prudential standards for banks have been pursued as part of the BIS regime and, on a regional basis, in Europe [Kapstein 1994; Underhill 1991]. With deliberate harmonization of policy very much on the international agenda, the absence of regional cooperation in Asia that might fall into this rubric in noticeable.

As regards prudential regulation of banks, Asia is converging on global BIS standards rather than any regional version. The IMF and World Bank have also played a role in promoting common standards by providing "technical support" for regulatory reform. Regional efforts have been almost nonexistent. APEC Finance Ministers have only met since 1994 and have yet to come up with substantive agendas. The APEC Finance Ministers' meeting in 1996 agreed that members should help the IMF efforts to develop standards of greater disclosure and endorsed the idea of cooperation among APEC regulators to develop supervisory principles and practices that conform to international standards [APEC Finance Ministers' Joint Ministerial Statement 18 March 1996]. ASEAN Finance Ministers (as opposed to "economic ministers") met for the first time in 1997 but this meeting too was limited to an exchange of views and endorsement of macroeconomic stability.[55]

Lower-profile efforts have been carried out through the SEACEN and SEANZA groupings. SEACEN in particular has for the past two decades carried out many training programs and seminars aimed at upgrading the skills of central bank officials and, possibly, promoting a common outlook among regional officials. Informal contacts among regional central bankers have supplemented the meetings of the SEACEN and later EMEAP. However, a number of sources suggest that informal contacts and working relationships among senior central bank officials in ASEAN were closer in the 1960s and 1970s than they are today.[56] Considerable differences in the regulatory styles of regional countries have remained and, according to interviewees, prospects for greater cooperation or convergence through deliberate harmonization are limited.

With regard to more general business regulation or government intervention there has been little in the way of formal cooperation, despite the potential for common standards to avoid the negative effects of competitive deregulation or FDI incentives [Pangestu 1994; Konan 1996]. When the head of Indonesia's Investment Coordinating Board suggested ASEAN harmonize investment incentives the idea was considered by private sector individuals to be a remote possibility [*ST* 27 June 1992]. ASEAN investment agencies do meet but their cooperative agenda goes no further towards harmonization than support for regulatory transparency and exchange of information.[57] APEC's non-binding investment principles agreed to in November 1994 are loosely worded and stress liberalization and treatment "no less favorable" than accorded to domestic investors. The only element which could be construed as a move towards the harmonization of incentives was the principle that health, safety and environmental regulations not be relaxed as an incentive to foreign investment.[58]

A degree of de facto harmonization may be brought about by active dissemination of economic institutions and government advice, complemented by deliberate copying of institutional structures. There may be no "Asian model" of economic development in reality but there has been some convergence among regional countries on a different "species of capitalism" through emulation of Japan [Johnson 1993, 49-56] or through the more direct influence of the Japanese regulatory systems [van den Berg 1995]. Similarities in economic and government systems may also lay the ground for regional cooperation that would be premised on sustaining this type of

"Asian" capitalism.[59] The more commonalties among Asian countries in terms of concerns, practices and values, the more there is a basis for regional cooperation to maintain these characteristics [Funabashi 1993].

There has been deliberate diffusion and copying of institutions, the pursuit of intergovernmental and public-private cooperation that rests on common institutional attributes and the assertion of commonalties. Countries such as Malaysia and Korea embarked on industrialization programs with the Japanese model explicitly in mind and with substantial Japanese involvement. Singapore too appears to be something of a model for regional countries. The Japanese government has been promoting the development abroad of institutional structures that would in some ways be a replication of its domestic institutions. Singapore has also taken on this role, both through its own outward investment and through an active advisory service carried out by officials and former officials particularly in China but also in Hong Kong, Vietnam and other countries.[60] Another possible channel of diffusion of administrative styles and structures is through intra-ASEAN cooperation among administrative services.[61]

The assertion of a common regional political economy is easily exaggerated, espoused in rhetoric more than reality, but areas of commonalty are not entirely illusory. On the other hand, many strategies of emulation have produced arrangements that are quite different from those in Japan [MacIntyre 1994]. Further, these strategies and statements of common purpose are sometimes at odds with the unilateral liberalization that is occurring (as well as bilateral and regional efforts towards this goal). Features distinctive to the region may remain but it is not at all clear that they will persist or that the common political economy that emerges will not actually be one rather closer to that prevailing in the United States.

Externally-oriented Coordination
Despite coming under pressure in multilateral settings such as the WTO and bilaterally, particularly in negotiations with the U.S., Asian countries have done little to develop the institutional structure for coordinated diplomacy. Japan, Taiwan and Korea have been the primary objects of U.S. pressure to liberalize foreign access to the financial services sector and to deregulate aspects of the domestic financial system [Haggard and Cheng 1989] but other regional countries have not been exempt from this kind of pressure. For example, regulatory controls on the operations of foreign banks and the government-controlled savings funds in Malaysia and Singapore have been among the targets of American criticism. Given the importance of these funds for Malaysia and Singapore and their points of similarity with systems such as the Post Office savings system in Japan, there is the potential for such countries to find common cause in defending the legitimacy of their

domestic institutions. As yet, they have done little to coordinate resistance to foreign demands on these or other issues.

The most prominent Asia-only forum in the region is the East Asian Economic Caucus (EAEC), which grew out of a Malaysian proposal made at the end of 1990 for a regional body. It has been described as an institution that promotes the common domestic policies, values and institutions that differentiate Asian countries from others in the wider APEC group [Higgott and Stubbs 1995]. However, the EAEC shows little sign of being able to promote coordinated resistance to outside pressure. The EAEC has been hampered in even laying the grounds for such a future role by the strong opposition leveled at the idea of an Asia-only group, particularly by the U.S. [Haggard 1997, 29-30]. Given this opposition, countries such as Japan have been extremely cautious in supporting the EAEC, although Japan has not been opposed to the idea.[62] The EAEC has begun to function as a dialogue forum, most prominently in the Asia-Europe (ASEM) meetings since 1996.[63] The ASEM meetings have been seen as a means for countries like Japan to sidestep U.S. criticism of the EAEC. As a less controversial forum, the ASEM has received a fair amount of support from regional governments.[64]

Regional Liberalization

The initiatives and outcomes described so far are not insignificant but they are less prominent than the regional agenda for liberalization. In trade and investment, including financial sector investment, regional countries are now committed to the principle of further liberalization. Under the ASEAN Framework Agreement on Trade in Services, concluded in December 1995, members made a general commitment to end discrimination and market access limits and pledged to reach an agreement on liberalization that would go beyond their offers under the WTO agreement on trade in services by mid-1998.[65] Agreement on the WTO pact was finally concluded in December 1997, with all regional countries putting forward commitments that entailed greater (but not unrestricted) foreign access to domestic banking, insurance and securities markets.

Both the Pacific-wide APEC group and the EAEC have been promoted as means to further global liberalization or to prevent closure elsewhere.[66] Any potential role for the EAEC in this regard, however, has effectively been eliminated in favor of APEC-based efforts. The agenda of APEC remains contested but it is clearly dominated by liberalizing efforts in trade and investment. APEC has been described as subscribing to norms more liberal than those of the GATT regime [Aggarwal 1993] and individuals associated with the APEC process have frequently made pronouncements on the desirability of free trade and investment [APEC EPG 1993; Garnaut 1996]. A common interpretation of "economic cooperation" in this context is liberalization of Asian economies in order to maintain access to the American market. But despite the general concurrence on the need for openness and the increases in regional trade and investment flows—and despite the involvement and interest of the U.S.—APEC has yet to conclude any binding agreement and many of its members have a strong preference for "unilateral liberalization" and loosely-worded, non-binding statements [Soesastro 1995].

Interpreting Regional Relations

This chapter has shown that an Asian regionalism of sorts does exist. The region has significant internal ties that unite it as an economic area, although it is far from being an exclusive economic bloc. Formal regional cooperation, however, remains extremely limited in comparison with the degree of economic integration. The network-based analyses referred to at the start of the chapter offer an explanation of integration without formal cooperation that accords with the account of regional banking given here. What remains in need of explanation is the low level of cooperation to manage the effects of this integration. This section outlines two complementary explanations: first, differences among regional countries in terms of their domestic state systems; secondly, the influence of the United States.

Commonalties in domestic structure or development path are likely to explain certain features of Asian regionalism.[67] However, differences among regional states are also significant. In particular, there is variation in the extent to which domestic state systems are institutionalized and regularized.[68] These features provide for what may loosely be called governing capacity, a factor which is not evenly distributed in a region that brings together the patrimonial governing systems of Indonesia and the Philippines with the relatively regularized systems of Japan, Taiwan and Singapore, along with intermediate cases such as Malaysia and Korea. This uneven distribution of governing capacity is an important factor behind the particular pattern of regionalism in Asia.

It is fairly straightforward why a government such as Indonesia's, with a mixed ability to enforce declared policy, should be a poor cooperator on many issues. If policy is not hijacked at the negotiation stages, the low credibility of its commitments will make potential cooperation partners wary about Indonesia's ability to deliver on its promises. Harold Crouch was one of the first to make this explicit when he noted that coordinated foreign investment policies to prevent investors playing one country off against another would be virtually impossible to implement "where vested interests exercise substantial influence on government decisions not only at the level of policy formulation but also at the level of implementation" [Crouch 1984, 99]. Given the technical tasks involved in financial sector cooperation, such as monitoring currency trading or enforcing common prudential standards, creaky administrative machinery can fail even without direct intervention by vested interests.

What is perhaps less obvious is why a low level of governing capacity is conducive to economic integration with the region, particularly at certain times and in certain ways. One reason is that countries with less regularized governments, such as Indonesia and the Philippines, find their attempts to enforce a degree of economic insulation costly and unsustainable [Bowie and Unger 1997]. When policy is forced to shift, as it was in Indonesia in the 1960s and 1980s, the government is in no position to follow a middle path or negotiate concessions from investors or lending agencies [Winters 1996]. Policy thus becomes much more permissive as regards integration. More consistently, weak governing capacity in some states has not been an obstacle to integration because regional partners have been able to cement integration through personal negotiations and the provision of benefits to particular power-holders or brokers—a pattern that has characterized the flow of aid and investment from Japan to Indonesia from the 1950s to the present.[69]

In contrast, the region's more regularized states have been able to meet a greater range of objectives in domestic and foreign economic policy. Through a combination of personal and informal relationships, business alliances and official support, the regional spread of Japanese business has been secured and, to some extent, coordinated. In this way, the institutions of Japanese economic management are transported overseas without the need for formal cooperation. Singapore's regionalization policy is in many ways similar.[70] To the extent that countries such as Singapore and Japan are able to internationalize policy, through the adaptation of governance mechanisms with regard to domestic firms and through the manipulation of points of vulnerability in foreign systems, they have no interest in pursuing the same objectives through formal government-to-government cooperation. Further, when faced with a government that is unable to make a credible commitment to implement a cooperative agreement, outsiders have an additional incentive to seek out informal means of making side-payments at the sub-national and sub-agency level.

There are limitations to this type of regionalization. The requirements of financial and monetary management are not analogous to those of financial integration [Helleiner 1994b]. Consequently, informal regionalism and externalization of policy have not been very effective in these areas. As economizers of information and other transaction costs, the region's informal institutions are oriented to providing economic goods. While they may carry out some of the functions associated with public authority (particularly in the enforcement of economic contracts) they have limited ability to act as transnational carriers of regulatory capacity or to provide public goods such as currency stability.

Overall, differences in governing capacity have led to an uneven demand for cooperation and an uneven ability on the part of regional states to cooperate on certain issues. Differences in domestic governing capacity have smoothed the path to economic integration but they also present a challenge to many kinds of cooperation, including that required for effective monetary and financial management. States with low levels of governing capacity are too much part of the regional economy for meaningful cooperation to take place without them but these states face significant domestic obstacles to cooperation. These obstacles operate independently of the factors that "supply" cooperation, whether these factors are conceived of in realist terms, as hegemonic powers, or in liberal-institutionalist terms, as regimes. Further, one of the legacies of the previous pattern of integration was to create entrenched interests in the status quo. If aspects of regional integration are based on differences in the political economies of regional countries[71] then the advantages which this confers on some constitute an incentive not to promote more regularized governments and state-to-state cooperation.

There are other obstacles to greater intra-Asian cooperation. The first and clearest difficulty is that politically and economically Asia does not stand alone. It is tied to a world financial system that remains anchored in Europe and, even more, America. The concentration of many aspects of economic activity in Asia means that there is, in theory, scope for the region to cooperate more than it has. But, without drastic and costly disengagement, regional solutions to problems of monetary and financial management will be nested within, and to some extent contingent on, broader global regimes. The agenda at the global level remains driven by the United States more than any other country [Oatley and Nabors 1998; Underhill 1993]. Complementing this wider regime-setting influence, America has enormous bargaining power in bilateral relationships, thereby affecting the cost-benefit calculations of regional states.

The U.S. serves Asia as a market, as a guarantor of security, and—less beneficently—as the likely source of the much of the short-term capital flow to the region in the first half of the 1990s. The region's dependence on the United States, a country with different public policy priorities, helps explain the limited results of initiatives for greater regional cooperation. Much of this influence, and its implications for Asian cooperation, can be traced to the post-war settlement in the region. That is, the global bipolar competition of the cold war divided the region and entrenched American hegemony over the non-communist countries [Cumings 1997; Johnson 1993, 39-41, 45-46]. Under American leadership, the region's non-communist countries adopted bilateral economic and security relations with the U.S. rather than multilateral relations with each other.[72] From the 1980s, the U.S. increased its use of bilateral pressure on regional countries [Haggard and Cheng 1989]. In financial services, Japan, Taiwan and Korea have all come under sustained U.S. pressure to open up their markets and dismantle the domestic institutions that were mainstays of their financial systems.[73] U.S. opposition to Malaysia's initiative for intra-Asian collaboration was a major factor behind its slow development [Haggard 1997, 29-30]. U.S. pressure was also one obstacle among others to regional action on the currency crisis.[74]

The legacy of the cold war and ongoing American influence are significant but, as the preceding sections show, there have been processes occurring at an intra-Asian level that are not simply derivative of global politics. In the case of many of the early Asian initiatives for cooperation on financial issues, not only is there no evidence of American opposition to such cooperation, it is hard to imagine why there should have been. The U.S., in fact, sometimes supported regional cooperation in both Asian and Pacific settings but was unable to create effective multilateral structures that would formalize cooperation.[75] Thus even if we shift analysis to a Pacific region that includes the U.S., Asia's dependence on the United States does not completely explain regional outcomes. The low level of formalized cooperation in Asia is not compensated for by more cooperation at the Pacific level, even towards the goal of liberalization in which the U.S., the region's presumed hegemon, has expressed most interest. Bilateral bargaining has partly compensated for this absence but not, as recurrent cross-Pacific disputes testify, completely to the satisfaction of the United States. Indeed, looking at the cooperation issue from a Pacific perspective, some writers have explained low levels of cooperation by reference to the *declining* salience of cold war cleavages and *declining* U.S. hegemony [Kahler 1988, 333-34].

The decline in U.S. hegemony is frequently over-stated but the realist emphasis on hegemony as a precondition for cooperation is also over-stated. Other types of leadership and paths to cooperation exist.[76] Within the "diffuse, outer-limit leverage" exercised by the United States over Japan and most other Asian countries [Cumings 1997, 136], there was scope for an Asian sphere of action—not an independent sphere but not one that was entirely dictated by global forces either. This regional sphere of action manifested itself primarily in terms of economic integration but it also included attempts to set up inter-governmental organizations, many of which were quite compatible with the requirements of "outer-limit leverage" set by Washington. In addition to the attempts described here, several other initiatives for inter-governmentalism in Asia have been made, even before the revival of the idea in the 1990s [Schubert 1978]. After twenty or thirty years of operation, most of these organizations remain, at best, only marginally effective in terms of formal management tasks. Successful cooperation, such as Japanese-led adjustment support to the region, or ASEAN's role in containing political disputes, tends to operate on a diffuse, largely ad hoc, organizational basis that is effective on some issues but precludes concerted action to provide regulatory goods. Neither U.S. hegemony nor the cold war dictated this organizational weakness. We need to look elsewhere to understand why, after thirty years of operation, a relatively successful organization such as ASEAN is unable to deal with transboundary regulatory problems in its own backyard.[77] Similarly, in the wider Asian region described here, internal factors have combined with external forces to produce the contours and limits of an uneven regionalism.

NOTES

1. Frankel and Kahler, eds. 1993; Higgott et al., eds. 1993; Mack and Ravenhill, eds. 1994.

2. Kwan 1997; Kohsaka 1996; Bernard and Ravenhill 1995; Hatch and Yamamura 1996; Katzenstein and Shiraishi, eds. 1997.

3. Fruin 1995; Higgott and Stubbs 1995; Stubbs 1995; Beeson and Jayasuryia 1998; Pauly 1994.

4. See, for example, Garnaut 1996; Bergsten and Noland, eds. 1993; Frankel and Kahler, eds. 1993; Low and Toh 1993.

5. Bello and Cunningham 1994; Frieden 1993; Ito 1993; Ravenhill 1995; Rosenbluth 1993, 1996.

6. Mack and Ravenhill 1994, 14-15; Acharya 1997; Aggarwal 1993; Crone 1993.

7. On intra-Japanese relations, see Gerlach 1992; Tokunaga 1992; Morris-Suzuki 1992; Aoki 1992; Seki 1994; Arase 1995; Hatch and Yamamura 1996; Hamilton, ed. 1996; Doner 1997; and Katzenstein and Shiraishi, eds. 1997. On Chinese business, see Mackie 1992; Kao 1993; DFAT 1995; Suryadinata, ed. 1995; Menkhoff and Labig 1996; Hamilton, ed. 1996; and Selden in Katzenstein and Shiraishi, eds. 1997.

8. Friedberg 1993/94; Betts 1993/94; Buzan 1994.

9. Gilpin 1987, 72-91 reviews realist thinking on international cooperation.

10. On monetary arrangements, see van den Berg 1996; Hamashita 1991, 1994; and Lee 1990, 7-16; as well as banking histories such as Checkland et al., eds. 1994; King 1987-1991; MacKenzie 1954; and Tamaki 1995.

11. See Tan 1961 on the Chinese banks established in Malaya and Singapore. Huff 1994, 218-35 places the development of Chinese banks and industry in Singapore in the context of their trade and rubber interests which grew enormously at the beginning of the twentieth century.

12. The Oei family ran a major, diversified and multinational enterprise before the war [Yoshihara, ed. 1989; Mackie 1991; Panglaykim and Palmer 1970].

13. On the French banks see Bonin 1994 and Meuleau 1990. Van Laanen 1990 and Allen and Donnithorne 1957, 182-94 describe the Dutch and other banks in the Netherlands Indies.

14. These and other Japanese banks and industry laid much of the social infrastructure for the post-war paths to industrial development and economic integration with the region taken by Korea and Taiwan [Johnson 1987; Cummings 1987; Woo 1991].

15. According to Tamaki, however, the Bank of Korea was primarily concerned with financing in Korea itself [1995, 125].

16. The initiative was supported by the Singapore government. An agreement was reached for the Chinese to send China Ocean Shipping Company vessels to Singapore as an alternative to the European firms. Wee later led a large delegation to China in 1979 [*Insight* May 1980].

17. This paragraph is drawn from the account in *STI* April 1972.

18. Other American banks with retail business were American Express (from 1925), Bank of America (from 1955) and Chase Manhattan (from 1964) [*SI* April 1970, 46-47].

19. Yoshihara 1978, 1982; Doner 1997, 207-08; *FEER* 1 February 1980.

20. Japanese foreign aid funds and organizations such as the OECF, established in 1961, were important for many projects [Doner 1997, 204-5]. Tokunaga 1992, 153-89 and Yoshihara 1978, 10-12 discuss financing of FDI. Anecdotal reports suggest that Japanese investors (like most others) preferred to deal with banks they were familiar with. At the end of the 1970s over half of Japanese banks' overseas lending was directed at developing countries [*FEER* 18 April 1980] which implies a concentration in Asia. Japanese banks moved early into the Singapore offshore market which directed the largest part of its funds (52 percent of lending in 1975, excluding transfers within the market) to Asian countries [Monetary Authority of Singapore, *Annual Report* 1976, 90].

21. Many of the group's China investments go through a Hong Kong company, China Strategic Holdings (CSH). Expansion plans in China include a $1 billion investment in a pulp and paper mill and a share in a $889 million pipeline project. The sources for this section are *Asia Inc.* August 1993, *Singapore Business* August 1990, and DFAT 1995, 242-43.

22. Li Ka-shing's wealth was estimated by *Forbes* in 1997 $11 billion. In 1990 he was said to control 40 percent of the capitalization of the Hong Kong stock market [*Singapore Business* August 1990], although the basis for this probably over-generous estimate was not given. He was involved in a S$1.5 billion property project in Singapore through a consortium with other Hong Kong businessmen, including Runrun Shaw, Frank Tsao and Cheng Yu Tung. As well as major property development in Canada he was also said to be the single largest shareholder in the Canadian Imperial Bank of Commerce [*Singapore Business* August 1990].

23. The letter from Clinton was reproduced in a Chinese-language magazine *Inni Yu Dongxie* (Indonesia and ASEAN) in November 1996. I am grateful to Edwin Yang Tsung-Rong for bringing the item to my attention.

24. MUI's Hong Kong connections include shares in Robert Kuok's Kerry Financial Services and Shangri-La hotels. MUI has a number of manufacturing projects in China and various finance sector companies in Hong Kong. Riady's overseas assets and business relationships from 1960 to the early 1980s are described in *Asian Finance* 15 September 1983. Kuok's other international ties include a sugar and palm oil ventures with an Indonesian banker, Hashim Djojohadikusmuo [Ramu 1995, 255]. For other details on Kuok's businesses and relationships see DFAT 1995, 185; Ramu 1995, 267-8; and *Forbes* July 1997.

25. Also in 1984 the Riadys bought into an Arkansas bank in partnership with U.S. investment banker Jackson Stephens, with whom they had established ties through a Hong Kong company in the 1970s. U.S. regulators have been critical of the Riadys' banking practices and by the 1990s the group's California bank was reportedly in a poor position. The family was the subject of investigations into political party funding in 1997, at which time it was alleged that the Riadys had close ties with the Chinese government [*JP* 25 April 1997; *JP* 3 March 1997; *BT* 17 July 1997].

26. The sources for this account of the Salim group are DFAT 1995, 163-75; Sato 1993; *Asia Inc.* August 1993; and Schwarz 1994, 109-15.

27. First Pacific Enterprises and First Pacific Investments, both Liberian-registered companies. Liem's overseas group structure in 1983 is given in *FEER* 7 March 1983.

28. As well as direct investment, foreign lending by Japanese banks increases markedly after the yen appreciation in the 1980s. Although the proportion of bank lending going to Asia remains small compared the amounts going to developed countries, it rises noticeably in the late 1980s [PEO 1995, 232].

29. Investments include a takeover by DBS of Thai Danu bank, which was the first takeover by a foreign bank in Thailand [*BT* 27 January 1998], a 15 percent ($258 million) share in Thai Farmers Bank by the GIC [*BT* 30 April 1998], stakes by the GIC and Temasek in the Bangkok Bank and other companies [*BT* 29 April 1998] and takeover of a Thai brokerage by DBS [*BT* 17 June 1998]. In addition, the GIC was negotiating a stake in Malaysia's Arab Malaysian financial sector group [*BT* 11 May 1998].

30. End 1995. Bank assets for this section are sourced from the Arab-Malaysian Merchant Bank (AMMB) and Association of Banks in Malaysia (ABM) annual banking directories.

31. These joint venture banks are essentially foreign banks: local equity interest does not generally exceed 15 percent and reportedly often involves no actual investment.

32. All figures in this section should be read with caution as estimates vary hugely. The World Bank put net portfolio investment in East Asia in 1994 at $26 billion, net FDI at $43 billion and net bank lending of $3.4 billion [World Bank 1996, 134-35]. In contrast, the Institute of International Finance put net bank lending to just five Asian countries (excluding China and Hong Kong) at $23.4 billion in 1994. Net private capital flows to these countries in 1996 were esti-

mated by the Institute at $12.4 billion in portfolio flows, $6.3 billion in FDI and $97.1 billion in lending [cited in *FEER* 16 July 1998].

33. International issues by Malaysians came to nearly $5 billion between 1990 and 1995, while Indonesians issued $7 billion over the same period. These amounts do not include funds raised by foreign-incorporated but Indonesian or Malaysian-owned companies. Singapore recorded only $175 million in international bond issues over the same period [OECD 1996].

34. Calculated from Hong Kong Monetary Authority, *Monthly Statistical Bulletin*.

35. The proportion of medium and long term debt denominated in dollars rose from 50 percent in 1992 to 72 percent in 1996 for Malaysia [BNM, *Annual Report 1996*]. For Indonesia, U.S. dollar-denominated long term debt declined from 43 percent in 1980 to 21 percent in 1995 [World Bank, *Global Development Finance 1997*] and the yen accounted for 35 percent of long term debt. But these figures do not capture the much larger amounts of short-term and unrecorded Indonesian debt as well as Indonesian issues of bonds, which are all thought to be mainly dollar-denominated.

36. On the increasingly intra-regional nature of FDI flows see Pempel 1997; Chen 1996; and Kwan 1997.

37. Japanese investment in equities on regional stock markets in the 1990s was less significant than investment from the U.S. and Europe, with net Japanese purchases in 1993, a boom year for regional bourses, at $463 million compared to $10.6 billion by U.S. investors [Khan and Reinhart, eds. 1995, 72-74]. Other sources for Japanese capital flows used here are BIS [*BT* 2 March 1998] and Securities Dealers Association of Japan [PEO 1995, 207, 224-43].

38. Figures are suspect for bank lending and non-existent for portfolio flows. Sources used here are *FEER* 15 January 1998; *IFS* January 1997, Table VI.5; PEO 1995, 179; and World Bank, *Global Development Finance 1997*.

39. Based on preliminary estimate of end-1997 total foreign debt (including short term debt) from BNM, *Annual Report 1997*. Other sources for this paragraph are BNM, *Monthly Statistical Bulletin*, Table VIII.2; *FEER* 15 January 1998; BNM, *Annual Report 1996*, Table A.23; and Hong Kong Monetary Authority, *Monthly Statistical Bulletin*.

40. Sources for this paragraph are Department of Statistics, 1995, 1997; *Yearbook of Statistics*; EDB, *Yearbook 1995*; Krause et al., 1987, 35; and PEO, 1995, 429.

41. About U.S.$42 billion was owed by Hong Kong banks to banks in Singapore at the end of 1997 [Hong Kong Monetary Authority, *Monthly Statistical Bulletin*]. However, this includes lending from the Singapore offshore market and there is no way of telling what part of it was accounted for by local Singapore banks.

42. On regulatory cooperation in finance on a non-European basis, see Kapstein 1994, and Herring and Litan 1995. Examples of cooperative currency arrangements and international currency use are given in Cohen 1998, 48-65, 69-

74. The global regime providing for limited capital mobility until the late 1960s is described by Helleiner 1994a.

43. Frankel concludes that while Japanese interest rates exert some influence on rates in some other Asian countries, the U.S. dollar is the currency that predominates in exchange rate policies, official reserves and trade invoicing [1993, 69-79]. See also de Brouwer 1997, and Chinn and Frankel 1995.

44. Leaver 1993; Henning 1994, 140-75; Cohen 1993; Frieden, 1993.

45. Emmott 1989, 189-206; *FEER* 11 October 1990; Fujii 1992; Ito 1994; Kwan 1994, 1996, 1997.

46. Fujii 1992; Ito 1994; Frieden 1993.

47. The group comprises Singapore, Malaysia, Indonesia, Thailand, the Philippines, China, Hong Kong, South Korea, Japan, Australia and New Zealand. A review of EMEAP and other regional central bank meetings is given in BNM *Annual Report 1997*.

48. These agreements form a net of bilateral arrangements among ASEAN countries, Hong Kong, Japan and Australia. The agreements provide for the sale and later repurchase, at a pre-determined price, of U.S. Treasury bills if required in support of a nation's currency.

49. The APEC Finance Ministers' meetings of 1996 and 1997 concluded that responsibility for maintaining currency stability lay with individual members. The meetings limited themselves to endorsing "sound macroeconomic policies" and supporting the IMF's efforts towards multilateral surveillance [*ST* 18 March 1996; APEC Finance Ministers' Joint Ministerial Statement 18 March 1996].

50. The contributors were as follows: the IMF and Japan each pledged $4 billion, Hong Kong, Australia, Malaysia, Singapore and China each pledged $1 billion, Korea and Indonesia pledged $500 million, and $1 billion was expected from the ADB and the World Bank. Japanese banks and private financiers were also expected to contribute $2 to $5 billion [*AWSJ* 12 August 1997].

51. The second line of support, to be used if necessary, was made up by commitments of $5 billion each from Japan and Singapore, $3 billion from the U.S., and $1 billion each from Australia, Malaysia and China [*AFR* 3 November 1997]. Only $3 billion of the entire package for Indonesia had been disbursed in the first six months of Indonesia's crisis.

52. Arase 1995; Doner 1997; Shiraishi 1997.

53. Ching and Hirono 1984; Ng et al. 1987; Yamazawa 1994; Thee 1994.

54. Ideas for an ASEAN financial institution date back to a UN study team proposal in the early 1970s [Skully 1985, 43].

55. The statement issued by the meeting is documented in *ASEAN Economic Bulletin* 14(1), July 1997, 91-92.

56. Singh 1984, 376. Interviews with former central bank governors Tun Ismail (Kuala Lumpur, October 1996), Rachmat Salleh (Jakarta, April 1997) and Wong Pakshong (Singapore, August 1997).

57. See the Joint Press Statement of the Meeting of the Heads of ASEAN Investment Agencies July 1996, in *ASEAN Economic Bulletin* 13(3), March 1997.

58. The statement of principles is documented in *ASEAN Economic Bulletin* 11(3), March 1995, 363-64.

59. Stubbs 1995; Fruin 1995; Pauly 1994.

60. On Japan as a model and source of influence on domestic institutions, see Jomo, ed. 1985; Johnson 1987; Cumings 1987; Arase 1995; Doner 1997, 216; and Katzenstein 1997a, 35-37. On Singapore, see Tan 1991; Margolin 1993; and *ST* 23 December 1993, 25 August 1997.

61. This has included training, staff exchanges and meetings of senior officials in regular conferences. The most recent major civil service conference, the ninth, was held in Singapore in 1997. Thailand in particular has played a role in this process, being responsible for coordinating and publishing studies on regional civil service systems. See OCSC 1985, 1986.

62. *FEER* 28 March 1991; *FEER* 18 June 1992; Abe 1993.

63. The inaugural ASEM meeting, at Heads of State level, was held in Bangkok in March 1996. The group agreed to hold an Economic Ministers' meeting in Japan in 1997. See the Chairman's statement in *ASEAN Economic Bulletin* 13(1), July 1996, 129-34. The meeting had been preceded by other Asia-Europe meetings such as the Europe/East Asia Economic Summit held in Singapore in October 1994.

64. Comments that ASEM is "de facto of EAEC" and provides Japan with a diplomatic way of dealing with U.S. opposition to EAEC were made by Stephen Leong of Malaysia and Ito Kenichi of Japan respectively at a non-official Asian colloquium on security in Kuala Lumpur in August 1997 [*NST* 15 August 1997].

65. The text of the agreement is documented in *ASEAN Economic Bulletin* 17(3), March 1996, 415-19.

66. See, for example, *Malaysian Digest* May 1993; APEC EPG 1993; Aggarwal 1993; and Sopiee 1996.

67. Katzenstein 1997a, 28-31; Stubbs 1995; Pauly 1994; Fruin 1995.

68. This notion of regularized or institutionalized state systems builds on Huntington's concept of institutionalization [1968, 8-32] and Weber's discussion of rational bureaucratic systems [1947, 329-36].

69. The continuity of the informal and personalized nature of interaction among power-brokers and investors on both sides is evident from a number of accounts. See Dauvergne 1997, 68; Kuntjoro-Jakti 1988, 66-81; Malley 1989; and Nishihara 1975.

70. On Japan, see van den Berg 1995; Doner 1997; Huber 1994; Pempel 1993; Katzenstein 1997a; and Katzenstein and Shiraishi 1997. On Singapore, see Rodan 1993; Smith 1997; and Hamilton-Hart 1999, 250-57.

71. Bernard and Ravenhill 1995; Bernard 1996; Hatch and Yamamura 1996; Dauvergne 1997.

72. Haggard 1989, 8-11; Kahler 1994, 20; Cumings 1997, 155; Katzenstein 1997a, 23-27.

73. American efforts have been aided by being able to draw on support from some groups in target countries, where interests are clearly not static [Haggard and Cheng 1989; Bello and Cunningham 1994; Ito 1993; Rosenbluth 1996; Woo 1991, 187-94].

74. As well as the account in the preceding section, see a strongly-worded article by Anthony Rowley in the *Business Times* 27 February 1998, which characterizes Japan as having its hands tied by the U.S. determination to maintain a leading role.

75. The ultimately unsuccessful American attempt to secure the figleaf of a multilateral regional security structure in the early years of the cold war in Asia is described by Buszynski 1983. On American policy on regional organization see Rostow 1986. Clearly, the U.S. did not pursue regional organization that would have constrained its freedom of action but it did at times see advantage in region-wide structures which, had they been successful, would have mitigated the extreme under-institutionalization of the region in formal terms.

76. With regard to Asia and the Pacific see Higgott et al. 1990; Crone 1993; Rix 1993. It is telling that hegemonic stability theory is rarely advanced in relation to cooperation in Europe, where various strands of constructivist, neo-functionalist and inter-governmental bargaining theory have the field virtually to themselves [Katzenstein 1997b].

77. A telling example of ASEAN's regulatory weakness is the transboundary haze problem due to uncontrolled forest burning experienced—though not for the first or last time—in 1997. On the domestic obstacles facing ASEAN attempts to deal with the haze issue, see Dauvergne 1998.

REFERENCES

Abe, S. 1993. "Contributing to Development in South Asia," *Japan Echo* 20 (special issue): 64-71.

Acharya, A. 1997. "Ideas, Identity, and Institution-building: From the 'ASEAN Way' to the 'Asia-Pacific Way'?" *Pacific Review* 10(3): 319-346.

AFR. *Australian Financial Review* (Sydney).

Aggarwal, V. 1993. "Building International Institutions in the Asia-Pacific," *Asian Survey* 33(1)1: 1029-42.

Allen, G. and A. Donnithorne. 1957. *Western Enterprise in Indonesia and Malaya: A Study in Economic Development*. London: Allen and Unwin.

Aoki, T. 1992. "Integration in the Asia Pacific Rim—Formation of Networks by Japanese Foreign Direct Investment as the Driving Force to Integrate," presentation at FAIR Conference, 5-7 July, Kuala Lumpur.

APEC EPG (Asia Pacific Economic Cooperation Eminent Persons Group). 1993. *A Vision for APEC*. Singapore: APEC Secretariat.

Arase, D. 1995. *Buying Power: The Political Economy of Japan's Foreign Aid.* Boulder, CO: Lynne Reiner.

AWSJ. *Asian Wall Street Journal.*

Barnhart, M. 1987. *Japan Prepares for Total War: The Search for Economic Security, 1919-1941.* Ithaca, NY: Cornell University Press.

Beeson, M. and K. Jayasuriya. 1998. "The Political Rationalities of Regionalism: APEC and the EU in Comparative Perspective," *The Pacific Review* 11(3): 311-36.

Bello, W. and S. Cunningham. 1994. "Trade Warfare and Regional Integration in the Pacific: the USA, Japan and the Asian NICs," *Third World Quarterly* 15(3): 445-58.

Berg, M. van den. 1995. "Culture as Ideology in the Conquest of Modernity: The Historical Roots of Japan's Regional Regulation Strategies," *Review of International Political Economy* 2(3): 371-93.

Berg, N.P. van den. 1996 [1895]. *Currency and the Economy of Netherlands India, 1870-95.* (ed. P. van der Eng). Singapore: ISEAS.

Bergsten, C.F. and M. Noland, eds. 1993. *Pacific Dynamism and the International Economic System.* Washington, DC: Institute for International Economics.

Bernard, M. 1996. "States, Social Forces, and Regions in Historical Time: Toward a Critical Political Economy of Eastern Asia," *Third World Quarterly* 17(4): 649-65.

Bernard, M. and J. Ravenhill. 1995. "Beyond Product Cycles and Flying Geese: Regionalization, Hierarchy, and the Industrialization of East Asia," *World Politics* 47: 171-209.

Betts, R. 1993/94. "Wealth, Power, and Instability: East Asia and the United States After the Cold War," *International Security* 18(3): 34-77.

Bhagwati, J. 1998. 'The Capital Myth: The Difference Between Trade in Widgets and Dollars," *Foreign Affairs* 77(3): 7-12.

BIS (Bank for International Settlements). 1997. *67th Annual Report.* Basle: BIS.

BNM (Bank Negara Malaysia). *Annual Report, Quarterly Economic Bulletin* (Kuala Lumpur).

Bonin, H. 1994. "The French Banks' Activity in the Pacific Area of Asia," in O. Checkland, et al., eds. *Pacific Banking, 1859-1959: East Meets West.* New York: St. Martin's Press, pp. 61-74.

Bowie, A. and D. Unger. 1997. *The Politics of Open Economies: Indonesia, Malaysia, the Philippines, and Thailand.* Cambridge: Cambridge University Press.

Brouwer, G. de. 1997. "Interest Parity Conditions as Indicators of Financial Integration in East Asia," Canberra: Pacific Economic Papers No. 268, Australia-Japan Research Centre, Australian National University.

BT. *Business Times* (Singapore).

Buszynski, L. 1983. *SEATO: The Failure of an Alliance Strategy.* Singapore: Singapore University Press.

Buzan, B. 1994. "The Post-Cold War Asia-Pacific Security Order: Conflict or Cooperation?" in A. Mack and J. Ravenhill, eds. *Pacific Cooperation: Building Economic and Security Regimes in the Asia-Pacific Region.* St. Leonards, NSW: Allen and Unwin, pp. 130-51.

Checkland, O., S. Nishimura, and N. Tamaki, eds. 1994. *Pacific Banking, 1859-1959: East Meets West.* New York: St. Martin's Press.

Chen, X. 1996. "Taiwan Investments in China and Southeast Asia," *Asian Survey* 36(5): 447-67.

Chinn, M.D. and J. Frankel. 1995. "Who Drives Real Interest Rates Around the Pacific Rim: The USA or Japan?" *Journal of International Money and Finance* 14(6): 801-21.

Ching, M.K. and Hirono, R. 1984. *ASEAN-Japan Industrial Cooperation: An Overview.* Singapore: ISEAS.

Cohen, B. 1993. "The Triad and the Unholy Trinity: Lessons for the Pacific Region," in R. Higgott et al., eds. *Pacific Economic Relations in the 1990s: Cooperation or Conflict?* Boulder, CO: Lynne Reiner, pp. 133-58.

———. 1998. *The Geography of Money.* Ithaca, NY: Cornell University Press.

Crone, D. 1993. "Does Hegemony Matter? The Reorganization of the Pacific Political Economy," *World Politics* 45: 501-25.

Crouch, H. 1984. *Domestic Political Structures and Regional Economic Cooperation.* Singapore: ISEAS.

Cumings, B. 1987. "The Origins and Development of the Northeast Asian Political Economy: Industrial Sectors, Product Cycles and Political Consequences," in F.C. Deyo, ed. *The Political Economy of the New Asian Industrialism.* Ithaca, NY: Cornell University Press, pp. 44-83.

———. 1997. "Japan and Northeast Asia into the Twenty-first Century," in P. Katzenstein and T. Shiraishi, eds. *Network Power: Japan and Asia.* Ithaca, NY: Cornell University Press, pp. 136-68.

Dauvergne, P. 1997. *Shadows in the Forest: Japan and the Politics of Timber in Southeast Asia.* Cambridge, MA: MIT Press.

———. 1998. "The Political Economy of Indonesia's 1997 Forest Fires," *Australian Journal of International Affairs* 52(1): 13-17.

DBS (Development Bank of Singapore). 1986. "China and Singapore: Problems and Prospects of Expanding Business Ties," Singapore: DBS, Occasional Papers Series, No. 5.

Dean, W.J. 1996. "Recent Capital Flows to Asia Pacific Countries: Trade-offs and Dilemmas," *Journal of the Asia Pacific Economy* 1(3): 287-317.

Department of Statistics (Singapore). 1995. "The Extent and Pattern of Foreign Investment Activities in Singapore," Singapore: Occasional Paper Series, Department of Statistics.

———. 1997. "Foreign Direct Investment Activities of Singapore Companies 1995," Singapore: Occasional Paper Series, Department of Statistics.

———. (various years). *Yearbook of Statistics,* Singapore.

DFAT (Department of Foreign Affairs and Trade). 1995. *Overseas Chinese Business Networks in Asia*. East Asia Analytical Unit, Commonwealth of Australia, Canberra.

Doner, R. 1993. "Japanese Foreign Investment and the Creation of a Pacific Asian Region," in J. Frankel and M. Kahler, eds. *Regionalism and Rivalry: Japan and the United States in Pacific Asia*. Chicago: NBER and University of Chicago Press, pp. 159-214.

————. 1997. "Japan in East Asia: Institutions and Regional Leadership," in P. Katzenstein and T. Shiraishi, eds. *Network Power: Japan and Asia*. Ithaca, NY: Cornell University Press, pp. 197-233.

Drysdale, P. and R. Garnaut. 1993. "The Pacific: An Application of a General Theory of Economic Integration," in C.F. Bergsten and M. Noland, eds. *Pacific Dynamism and the International Economic System*. Washington, DC: Institute for International Economics, pp. 183-224.

EDB. Economic Development Board, *Yearbook* (Singapore).

Eichengreen, B., J. Tobin, and C. Wyplosz. 1995. "Two Cases for Sand in the Wheels of International Finance," *The Economic Journal* 105 (January): 162-72.

Emmott, B. 1989. *The Sun Also Sets: Why Japan Will Not be Number One*. London: Simon and Schuster.

FEER. *Far Eastern Economic Review* (Hong Kong).

Frankel, J. 1993. "Is Japan Creating a Yen Bloc in East Asia and the Pacific?" in J. Frankel and M. Kahler, eds. *Regionalism and Rivalry: Japan and the United States in Pacific Asia*. Chicago: NBER and University of Chicago Press, pp. 53-85.

Frankel, J. and M. Kahler, eds. 1993. *Regionalism and Rivalry: Japan and the United States in Pacific Asia*. Chicago: NBER and University of Chicago Press.

Friedberg, A.L. 1993/94. "Ripe for Rivalry: Prospects for Peace in a Multipolar Asia," *International Security* 18(3): 5-33.

Frieden, J. 1993. "Domestic Politics and Regional Cooperation: The United States, Japan and Pacific Money and Finance," in J. Frankel and M. Kahler, eds. *Regionalism and Rivalry: Japan and the United States in Pacific Asia*. Chicago: NBER and University of Chicago Press, pp. 423-44.

Fruin, W.M. 1995. "Prospects for Economic Cooperation in the Asia-Pacific Region," *Asian Survey* 35(9): 798-811.

Fujii, M. 1992. "The Role of the Yen in the Pacific and World Economies," in C. McKenzie and M. Stutchbury, eds. *Japanese Financial Markets and the Role of the Yen*. Sydney: Allen and Unwin, pp. 87-96.

Funabashi, Y. 1993. "The Asianization of Asia," *Foreign Affairs* 72(5): 75-84.

Garnaut, R. 1996. *Open Regionalism and Trade Liberalization: an Asia-Pacific Contribution to the World Trade System*. Singapore: ISEAS and Sydney: Allen and Unwin.

Gerlach, M. 1992. *Alliance Capitalism: The Social Organization of Japanese Business*. Berkeley, CA: University of California Press.

Gilpin, R. 1987. *The Political Economy of International Relations*. Princeton: Princeton University Press.

Gomez, E. and Jomo K.S. 1997. *Malaysia's Political Economy: Politics, Patronage and Profits*. Cambridge: Cambridge University Press.

Haggard, S. 1989. "Introduction: the International Politics of Industrial Change," in S. Haggard and C. Moon, eds. *Pacific Dynamics: The International Politics of Industrial Change*. Inchon, Korea: CIS-Inha and Boulder, CO, Westview, pp. 1-21.

————. 1997. "Regionalism in Asia and the Americas," in E. Mansfield and H. Milner, eds. *The Political Economy of Regionalism*. New York: Columbia University Press, pp. 20-49.

Haggard, S. and T. Cheng. 1989. "The New Bilateralism: The East Asian NICs in American Foreign Economic Policy," in S. Haggard and C. Moon, eds. *Pacific Dynamics: The International Politics of Industrial Change*. Inchon, Korea: CIS-Inha and Boulder, CO: Westview, pp. 305-29.

Hamashita, T. 1991. "The Asian Network and Silver Circulation," in E.H.G. van Cauwenberghe, ed. *Money, Coins, and Commerce: Essays in the Monetary History of Asia and Europe (From Antiquity to Modern Times)*. Leuven: Leuven University Press, pp. 47-54.

————. 1994. "Overseas Chinese Remittance and Asian Banking History," in O. Checkland et al., eds. *Pacific Banking, 1859-1959: East Meets West*. New York: St. Martin's Press, pp. 52-60.

Hamilton, G., ed. 1996. *Asian Business Networks*. Berlin and New York: Walter de Gruyter.

Hamilton-Hart, N. 1999. *States and Capital Mobility: Indonesia, Malaysia and Singapore in the Asian Region*. PhD dissertation, Cornell University.

Hatch, W. and K. Yamamura. 1996. *Asia in Japan's Embrace: Building a Regional Production Alliance*. Melbourne: Cambridge University Press.

Helleiner, E. 1994a. *States and the Reemergence of Global Finance*. Ithaca, NY: Cornell University Press.

————. 1994b. "Freeing Money: Why Have States Been More Willing to Liberalize Capital Controls than Trade Barriers?" *Policy Sciences* 27(4): 299-318.

Henning, C.R. 1994. *Currencies and Politics in the United States, Germany, and Japan*. Washington, DC: Institute for International Economics.

Herring, R. and R. Litan. 1995. *Financial Regulation in the Global Economy*. Washington, DC: Brookings Institution.

Hewison, K. 1989. *Bankers and Bureaucrats: Capital and the Role of the State in Thailand*. New Haven: Yale University Southeast Asia Studies.

Hicks, G., ed. 1993. *Overseas Chinese Remittances from Southeast Asia, 1910-1940*. Singapore: Select Books.

Higgott, R., R. Leaver, and J. Ravenhill, eds. 1993. *Pacific Economic Relations in the 1990s: Cooperation or Conflict?* Boulder, CO: Lynne Reiner Publishers.

Higgott, R., A.F. Cooper, and J. Bonnor. 1990. "Asia-Pacific Economic Cooperation: An Evolving Case-study in Leadership and Cooperation-building," *International Journal* (Autumn): 823-66.

Higgott, R. and R. Stubbs. 1995. "Competing Conceptions of Economic Regionalism: APEC versus EAEC," *Review of International Political Economy* 2(3): 516-35.

Huber, T. 1994. *Strategic Economy in Japan.* Boulder, CO: Westview Press.

Huff, W.G. 1994. *The Economic Growth of Singapore: Trade and Development in the Twentieth Century.* Cambridge: Cambridge University Press.

Huntington, S. 1968. *Political Order in Changing Societies.* New Haven: Yale University Press.

IFS. *Indonesian Financial Statistics*, Bank Indonesia (Jakarta).

IO. *Indonesian Observer* (Jakarta).

Ishii, K. 1994. "Japanese Foreign Trade and the Yokohama Specie Bank," in O. Checkland et al., eds. *Pacific Banking, 1859-1959: East Meets West.* New York: St. Martin's Press, pp. 1-23.

Ito, T. 1993. "U.S. Political Pressure and Economic Liberalization in East Asia," in J. Frankel and M. Kahler, eds. *Regionalism and Rivalry: Japan and the United States in Pacific Asia.* Chicago: NBER and University of Chicago Press, pp. 391-420.

———. 1994. "On the Possibility of a Yen Bloc," in R. Glick and M. Hutchison, eds. *Exchange Rate Policy and Interdependence: Perspectives from the Pacific Basin.* Cambridge: Cambridge University Press, pp. 317-43.

Johnson, C. 1987. "Political Institutions and Economic Performance: The Government-Business Relationship in Japan, South Korea and Taiwan," in F.C. Deyo, ed. *The Political Economy of the New Asian Industrialism.* Ithaca, NY: Cornell University Press, pp. 136-64.

———. 1993. "History Restarted: Japanese-American Relations at the End of the Century," in R. Higgott et al., eds. *Pacific Economic Relations in the 1990s: Cooperation or Conflict?* Boulder, CO: Lynne Reiner, pp. 39-61.

———. 1998. "Economic Crisis in East Asia: The Clash of Capitalisms," *Cambridge Journal of Economics* 22(6): 653-61.

Jomo, K.S., ed. 1985. *The Sun Also Sets: Lessons in 'Looking East'* (2nd ed.). Kuala Lumpur: INSAN.

JP. *Jakarta Post* (Jakarta).

Kahler, M. 1988. "Organizing the Pacific," in R. Scalapino, S. Sato, J. Wanandi, and S.J. Han, eds. *Pacific-Asian Economic Policies and Regional Interdependence.* Berkeley: Institute of East Asian Studies, University of California, pp. 329-50.

———. 1994. "Institution-building in the Pacific," in A. Mack and J. Ravenhill, eds. *Pacific Cooperation: Building Economic and Security Regimes in the Asia-Pacific Region*. St. Leonards, NSW: Allen and Unwin, pp. 16-39.

Kao, J. 1993. "The Worldwide Web of Chinese Business," *Harvard Business Review* (March-April): 24-36.

Kapstein, E. 1994. *Governing the Global Economy: International Finance and the State*. Cambridge: Harvard University Press.

Katzenstein, P. 1997a. "Introduction: Asian Regionalism in Comparative Perspective," in P. Katzenstein and T. Shiraishi, eds. *Network Power: Japan and Asia*. Ithaca, NY: Cornell University Press, pp. 1-44.

———. 1997b. "United Germany in an Integrating Europe," in P. Katzenstein, ed. *Tamed Power: Germany in Europe*. Ithaca, NY: Cornell University Press, pp. 1-48.

Katzenstein, P. and T. Shiraishi. 1997. "Conclusion: Regions in World Politics, Japan in Asia—Germany in Europe," in P. Katzenstein and T. Shiraishi, eds. *Network Power: Japan and Asia*. Ithaca, NY: Cornell University Press, pp. 341-81.

Katzenstein, P. and T. Shiraishi, eds. 1997. *Network Power: Japan and Asia*. Ithaca, NY: Cornell University Press.

Khan, M.S. and C.M. Reinhart, eds. 1995. "Capital Flows in the Apec Region," Washington, DC: IMF, Occasional Paper 122.

King, F. 1979. *Asian Policy, History and Development: Collected Essays*. Hong Kong: Centre of Asian Studies, University of Hong Kong.

———. 1987-1991. *The History of the Hongkong and Shanghai Banking Corporation* (4 vols.). Cambridge: Cambridge University Press.

KLSE. Kuala Lumpur Stock Exchange, *Companies Handbook*.

Kohsaka, A. 1996. "Interdependence Rhrough Capital Flows in Pacific Asia and the Role of Japan," in T. Ito and A. Krueger, eds. *Financial Deregulation and Integration in East Asia*. Chicago: University of Chicago Press, pp. 107-42.

Konan, D.E. 1996. "The Need for Common Investment Measures Within ASEAN," *ASEAN Economic Bulletin* 12(3): 339-50.

Krause, L., Koh A.T., and Lee T.Y. 1987. *The Singapore Economy Reconsidered*. Singapore: ISEAS.

Kuntjoro-Jakti, H.U. 1988. *External and Domestic Coalitions of the Bureaucratic Authoritarian State in Indonesia*. PhD dissertation, University of Washington.

Kwan, C.H. 1994. *Economic Interdependence in the Asia-Pacific Region - Towards a Yen Bloc*. London: Routledge.

———. 1996. "A Yen Bloc in Asia," *Journal of the Asia Pacific Economy* 1(1): 1-21.

———. 1997. "Towards a Borderless Economy in Asia," in E.K.Y. Chen and C.H. Kwan, eds. *Asia's Borderless Economy: The Emergence of Subregional Economic Zones*. St. Leonards, NSW: Allen and Unwin, pp. 152-77.

Laanen, J.T.M. van. 1990. "Between the Java Bank and the Chinese Money-lender: Banking and Credit in Colonial Indonesia," in A. Booth, W.J. O'Malley and A. Weidemann, eds. *Indonesian Economic History in the Dutch Colonial Era*. New Haven: Monograph Series 35, Yale University Southeast Asia Studies, pp. 244-66.

Leaver, R. 1993. "Running on Empty? Complex Interdependence and the Future of Japanese-American Monetary Coordination," in R. Higgott et al., eds. *Pacific Economic Relations in the 1990s: Cooperation or Conflict?* Boulder, CO: Lynne Reiner Publishers, pp. 159-83.

Lee, S.Y. 1990. *The Monetary and Banking Development of Singapore and Malaysia* (3rd ed.). Singapore: Singapore University Press.

Lien, Y.C. 1992. *From Chinese Villager to Singapore Tycoon: My Life Story*. Singapore and Kuala Lumpur: Times Books International.

Lim, M.H. 1981. *Ownership and Control of the One Hundred Largest Corporations in Malaysia*. Singapore: Oxford University Press.

Low, L. and Toh M.H. 1993. *Regional Cooperation and Growth Triangles in ASEAN*. Singapore: Times Academic Press.

MacIntyre, A. 1994. "Business, Government and Development: Northeast and Southeast Asian Comparisons," in A. MacIntyre, ed. *Business and Government in Industrialising Asia*. Ithaca, NY: Cornell University Press, pp. 1-28.

Mack, A. and J. Ravenhill, eds. 1994. *Pacific Cooperation: Building Economic and Security Regimes in the Asia-Pacific Region*. St. Leonards, NSW: Allen and Unwin.

MacKenzie, C. 1954. *Realms of Silver: One Hundred Years of Banking in the East*. London: Routledge and Kegan Paul.

Mackie, J. 1991. "Towkays and Tycoons: The Chinese in Indonesian Economic Life in the 1920s and 1980s," in *The Role of the Indonesian Chinese in Shaping Modern Indonesian Life*. (special issue) *Indonesia*, pp. 83-96.

―――. 1992. "Overseas Chinese Entrepreneurship," *Asian-Pacific Economic Literature* 6(1): 41-64.

Malley, M. 1989. "Soedjono Hoemardani and Indonesian-Japanese relations 1966-1974," *Indonesia* 48: 47-64.

Margolin, J.-L. 1993. "Foreign Models in Singapore's Development and Theories of a Singaporean Model," in G. Rodan, ed. *Singapore Changes Guard: Social, Political and Economic Directions in the 1990s*. New York: St. Martin's Press and Melbourne: Longman Cheshire, pp. 84-98.

MAS. Monetary Authority of Singapore, *Annual Report* (Singapore).

Meuleau, M. 1990. *Des Pionniers en Extreme-Orient: Histoire de la Banque de l'Indochine (1875-1975)*. Paris: Fayard.

Menkhoff, T. and C. Labig. 1996. "Trading Networks of Chinese Entrepreneurs in Singapore," *Sojourn* 11(1): 128-51.

Ministry of Finance (Singapore). 1961. *Annual Report of the Division of Commerce and Industry 1959*. Singapore: Government Printers.

Morris-Suzuki, T. 1992. "Technology and the Division of Knowledge in Asia," in S. Tokunaga, ed. *Japan's Foreign Investment and Asian Economic Interdependence: Production, Trade and Financial Systems*. Tokyo: University of Tokyo Press, pp. 135-52.

Nakamura, T. 1996. "The Yen Bloc, 1931-1941," in P. Duus, R. Myers, and M. Peattie, eds. *The Japanese Wartime Empire, 1931-1945*. Princeton: Princeton University Press, pp. 171-86.

Nakao, S. 1995. *The Political Economy of Japan Money*. Tokyo: University of Tokyo Press.

Ng, C.Y., R. Hirono, and N. Akrasanee, eds. 1987. *Industrial Restructuring and Adjustment for ASEAN-Japan Investment and Trade Expansion: An Overview*. Singapore: ISEAS.

Nishihara, M. 1975. *The Japanese and Sukarno's Indonesia: Tokyo-Jakarta Relations 1951-1966*. Honolulu: University Press of Hawaii.

NST. *New Straits Times* (Kuala Lumpur).

Oatley, T. and R. Nabors. 1998. "Redistributive Cooperation: Market Failure, Wealth Transfers, and the Basle Accord," *International Organization* 52(1): 35-54.

OCSC (Office of the Civil Service Commission). 1985. *Trends in Civil Service Reforms in ASEAN Countries*. Bangkok: OCSC, Royal Government of Thailand.

————. 1986. *Comparative Studies of ASEAN Civil Services for Joint Efforts*. Bangkok: OCSC, Royal Government of Thailand.

OECD. 1996. *International Capital Market Statistics 1950-1995*. Paris: OECD.

OUB (Overseas Union Bank). 1974. *25th Anniversary, 1949-1974*. Singapore: OUB.

Owyang, H. 1996. *The Barefoot Boy from Songwad: the Life of Chi Owyang*. Singapore and Kuala Lumpur: Times Books International.

Pangestu, M. 1994. "Investment and the Asia Pacific Region," *Indonesian Quarterly* 12(4): 333-40.

Panglaykim, J. and I. Palmer. 1970. "Study of Entrepreneurialship in Developing Countries: The Development of One Chinese Concern in Indonesia," *Journal of Southeast Asian Studies* 1(1): 85-95.

Pauly, L. 1994. "National Financial Structures, Capital Mobility, and International Economic Rules: The Normative Consequences of East Asian, European, and American Distinctiveness," *Policy Sciences* 27(4): 343-63.

Peattie, M. 1996. "*Nanshin:* The 'Southward Advance,' 1931-1941, as a Prelude to the Japanese Occupation of Southeast Asia," in P. Duus, R. Myers and M. Peattie, eds. *The Japanese Wartime Empire, 1931-1945*. Princeton: Princeton University Press, pp. 189-242.

Pempel, T.J. 1993. "From Exporter to Investor: Japanese Foreign Economic Policy," in G. Curtis, ed. *Japan's Foreign Policy After the Cold War: Coping with Change*. Armonk, NY: M.E. Sharpe, pp. 105-36.

————. 1997. "Transpacific Torii: Japan and the Emerging Asian Regionalism," in P. Katzenstein and T. Shiraishi, eds. *Network Power: Japan and Asia.* Ithaca, NY: Cornell University Press, pp. 47-82.

PEO (Pacific Economic Outlook). 1995. *Capital Flows in the Pacific Region: Past Trends and Future Prospects.* Osaka: Japan Committee for Pacific Economic Outlook and Singapore: PECC.

Ramu, S.S. 1995. *The Dragons of Asia: Asia-Pacific Rim Countries and Their Multinationals.* New Delhi: Wheeler Publishing.

Ravenhill, J. 1995. "Economic Cooperation in Southeast Asia: Changing Incentives," *Asian Survey* 35(9): 850-66.

Rix, A. 1993. "Japan and the Region: Leading from Behind," in R. Higgott et al., eds. *Pacific Economic Relations in the 1990s: Cooperation or Conflict?* Boulder, CO: Lynne Reiner, pp. 62-82.

Robison, R. 1986. *Indonesia: The Rise of Capital.* Sydney: Allen and Unwin.

Rodan, G. 1993. "Reconstructing Divisions of Labour: Singapore's New Regional Emphasis," in R. Higgott et al., eds. *Pacific Economic Relations in the 1990s: Cooperation or Conflict?* Boulder, CO: Lynne Reiner, pp. 223-49.

Rosenbluth, F. 1993. "Japan's Response to the Strong Yen: Party Leadership and the Market for Political Favors," in G. Curtis, ed. *Japan's Foreign Policy After the Cold War: Coping with Change.* Armonk, NY: M.E. Sharpe, pp. 137-59.

————. 1996. "Internationalization and Electoral Politics in Japan," in R. Keohane and H. Milner, eds. Internationalization and Domestic Politics. Cambridge: Cambridge University Press, pp. 137-56.

Rostow, W.W. 1986. *The United States and the Regional Organization of Asia and the Pacific, 1965-1985.* Austin: University of Texas Press.

Ruggie, J. 1995. "At Home Abroad, Abroad at Home: International Liberalization and Domestic Stability in the New World Economy," *Millennium* 24(3): 507-26.

Sato, Y. 1993. "The Salim Group in Indonesia: The Development and Behaviour of the Largest Conglomerate in Southeast Asia," *The Developing Economies* 31(4): 408-441.

Schubert, J. 1978. "Toward a 'Working Peace System' in Asia: Organizational Growth and State Participation in Asian Regionalism," *International Organization* 32(2): 425-62.

Schwarz, A. 1994. *A Nation in Waiting: Indonesia in the 1990s.* Sydney: Allen and Unwin.

Seki, M. 1994. *Beyond the Full Set Industrial Structure.* Tokyo: LTCB International Library Foundation.

SEMS. Stock Exchange of Malaysia and Singapore (Singapore).

SES. Stock Exchange of Singapore, *Companies Handbook* (Singapore).

Shiraishi, S. and T. Shiraishi. 1993. "The Japanese in Colonial Southeast Asia: An Overview," in T. Shiraishi and S. Shiraishi, eds. *The Japanese in Colo-*

nial Southeast Asia. Ithaca, NY: Southeast Asia Program, Cornell University, pp. 5-20.

Shiraishi, T. 1997. "Japan and Southeast Asia," in P. Katzenstein and T. Shiraishi, eds. *Network Power: Japan and Asia*. Ithaca, NY: Cornell University Press, pp. 169-94.

Shulze, D. 1988. "The ASEAN Finance Corporation," *ASEAN Economic Bulletin* 5(1): 71-80.

Singh, S. 1984. *Bank Negara Malaysia: The First 25 Years, 1959-1984*. Kuala Lumpur: Bank Negara Malaysia.

Skully, M. 1985. *ASEAN Regional Financial Cooperation: Developments in Banking and Finance*. London: Macmillan Press.

Smith, S. 1997. "The Indonesia-Malaysia-Singapore Growth Triangle: A Political and Economic Equation," *Australian Journal of International Affairs* 51(3): 369-82.

Soedradjad Djiwandono and Hendra Esmara, eds. 1985. *International Financial Instability and Asean Financial Cooperation*. Singapore: Chopmen.

Soesastro, H. 1983. "ASEAN and the Political Economy of Pacific Cooperation," *Asian Survey* 23(12): 1255-70.

———. 1995. "ASEAN and APEC: Do Concentric Circles Work?" *Pacific Review* 8(3): 475-93.

Sopiee, N. 1996. *EAEC: Fact and Fiction*. Kuala Lumpur: ISIS.

SRMS. Systems and Resources Management Series, *Comparative Survey of Commercial Banks in Singapore* (Singapore).

ST. *Straits Times* (Singapore).

STI. *Singapore Trade and Industry* (Singapore).

Stubbs, R. 1995. "Asia-Pacific Regionalization and the Global Economy: A Third Form of Capitalism?" *Asian Survey* 35(9): 785-97.

Sudo, S. 1992. *The Fukuda Doctrine and ASEAN*. Singapore: ISEAS.

Suryadinata, L, ed. 1995. *Southeast Asian Chinese and China: The Politico-Economic Dimension*. Singapore: Times Academic Press.

Tamaki, N. 1995. *Japanese Banking: A History, 1859-1959*. Cambridge: Cambridge University Press.

Tan, E.L. 1961. "The Chinese Banks Incorporated in Singapore and the Federation of Malaya," in T.H. Silcock, ed. *Readings in Malayan Economics*. Singapore: Eastern Universities Press, pp. 454-79.

Tan, K.Y. 1991. "Singapore's Role in the Economic Development of China,"*The Singapore Economic Review* 36(2): 27-42.

Tan, K.Y. and E. Ng. 1997. "ASEAN Beyond AFTA: Initiatives in Financial Co-Operation and Integration," paper presented at the ASEAN Roundtable 1997, 4-5 August, Singapore.

Tantramongkol, N. 1995. *Baht Currency in Indochina*. MA thesis, Thammasat University, Bangkok.

Thee, K.W. 1994. "Interaction of Japanese Aid and Direct Investment in Indonesia," *ASEAN Economic Bulletin* 11(1): 25-35.

Tokunaga, S. 1992. "Japan's FDI Promotion and Intra-Asian Networks," in S. Tokunaga, ed. *Japan's Foreign Investment and Asian Economic Interdependence: Production, Trade and Financial Systems*. Tokyo: University of Tokyo Press, pp. 5-47.

Underhill, G. 1991. "Markets Beyond Politics? The State and the Internationalisation of Financial Markets," *European Journal of Political Research* 19(2): 197-225.

———. 1993. "Negotiating Financial Openness: The Uruguay Round and Trade in Financial Services," in P. Cerny, ed. *Finance and World Politics: Markets, Regimes and States in the Post-Hegemonic Era*. Aldershot: Edward Elgar, pp. 114-51.

UOB (United Overseas Bank). 1985. *Growing with Singapore: United Overseas Bank 1935-1985*. Singapore: UOB.

Vorachattarn, Y. 1977. *Financial Cooperation Among ASEAN Countries: Gains from Establishing an ASEAN Clearing House*. MA thesis, Thammasat University, Bangkok.

Wade, R. and F. Veneroso. 1998. "The Asian Crisis: The High Debt Model vs. the Wall Street-Treasury-IMF Complex," Russell Sage Foundation. [http://epn.org/sage/imf24.html]

Weber, M. 1947. *The Theory of Social and Economic Organization* (ed. T. Parsons). New York: The Free Press.

Wilson, D. 1972. *Solid as a Rock: the First Forty Years of the Oversea-Chinese Banking Corporation*. Singapore: Oversea-Chinese Banking Corporation.

Winters, J. 1996. *Power in Motion: Capital Mobility and the Indonesian State*. Ithaca, NY: Cornell University Press.

Woo, J.E. 1991. *Race to the Swift: State and Finance in Korean Industrialization*. New York: Columbia University Press.

World Bank. 1996. *Managing Capital Flows in East Asia*. Washington, DC: World Bank.

Yamazawa, I. 1994. "Promotion of SMEs for Industrial Upgrading in ASEAN: A Japanese Proposal for Industrial Cooperation," *ASEAN Economic Bulletin* 11(1): 16-24.

Yasutomo, D. 1983. *Japan and the Asian Development Bank*. New York: Praeger.

Yoshihara, K. 1978. *Japanese Investment in Southeast Asia*. Honolulu: University Press of Hawaii.

———. 1982. *Sogo Shosha: the Vanguard of the Japanese Economy*. Tokyo: Oxford University Press.

———. 1988. *The Rise of Ersatz Capitalism in South-East Asia*. Singapore: Oxford University Press.

Yoshihara, K., ed. 1989. *The Oei Tiong Ham Concern: the First Business Empire in Southeast Asia*. Kyoto: Center for Southeast Asian Studies, Kyoto University.

Yuen, C.L. 1978. "The Japanese Community in Malaya Before the Pacific War: Its Genesis and Growth," *Journal of Southeast Asian Studies* 9(2): 163-77.

CORNELL EAST ASIA SERIES

FORTHCOMING

To order, please contact the Cornell East Asia Series, East Asia Program, Cornell University, 140 Uris Hall, Ithaca, NY 14853-7601, USA; phone (607) 255-6222, fax (607) 255-1388, ceas@cornell.edu, http://www.einaudi.cornell.edu/eastasia/EastAsiaSeries.html.

2-00/.7 M pb